Japan Journal

HENRY HEUSKEN

Japan Journal

1855-1861

Translated and edited by

JEANNETTE C. VAN DER CORPUT

and

ROBERT A. WILSON

RUTGERS UNIVERSITY PRESS

New Brunswick   *New Jersey*

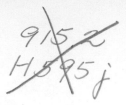

Manufactured in the United States of America
by Quinn & Boden Company, Inc., Rahway, New Jersey

This book was manufactured with the assistance of a grant from
the Ford Foundation.

Preface

When Professor Mario Cosenza published *The Complete Journal of Townsend Harris* in 1930, he remarked in a footnote that "it would be a great good fortune and a distinct boon to students of the early diplomatic days in Japan to find and publish the entire Diary of the martyred Heusken, the first secretary of the American Legation in Japan." Professor Cosenza's footnotes contain frequent references to the French manuscript of the Heusken Journal, excerpts from which had been published in 1883 by Dr. G. Wagener, a German scholar, under the title, *Aus dem Tagebuche Hendrik Heusken,* in the Tokyo *Deutsche Gesellschaft für Natür-und Völkerkunde Ostasiens, Mittheilungen.* However, the Heusken Journal did not receive further scholarly attention until 1951, when Dr. Lawrence C. Powell, Librarian of the University of California at Los Angeles, discovered the French manuscript of the "Mémoires de Voyage" by Henri Heusken in the Netherlands and immediately began negotiations for its purchase.

Shortly after this discovery Dr. Jeannette C. van der Corput, a Dutch attorney and novelist, purchased a Dutch manuscript of the Heusken Journal at an auction in the Netherlands. She thereafter devoted her spare time from her professional activities as an attorney to translating the manuscript into English and to examining other material relating to the Heusken story. This was undertaken in Berkeley, California, where her husband became Professor of Mathematics and Research Mathematician on the Berkeley campus of the University of California. Meanwhile, on the Los Angeles campus of the same university, Professor Robert A. Wilson, the specialist in Japanese history, was preparing the French manuscript for publication. Ultimately the fact of parallel effort became known to the two principals, and they agreed to collaborate. The pages that follow are a product of that collaboration.

There is no doubt that the French manuscript is the original journal and the Dutch manuscript a translation of it. It is believed that Heusken elected to write his journal in French in order to maintain his facility in that language since it was presumed that he would be employing primarily English and Dutch in his professional endeavors.

Heusken's journal is, in some ways, a curious document. During the long voyage of the *San Jacinto* to Japan he made occasional entries describing his adventures and personal reactions. While at sea and for a time after his arrival in Japan, he enriched his narrative with pen and ink sketches, many of which were very well done. He occasionally gave free reign to his poetic fancy. From time to time he vented his prejudice against the English and Chinese. Frequently the dates mean little since he often wrote under a given date about events that took place over a period of days or even weeks before or after that date. There are long intervals of silence, and as Heusken approached the time when he ceased keeping his record, the style and penmanship deteriorate badly. It is doubtful that his duties were so onerous that he lacked the time and energy to continue writing. A more probable explanation is that he simply became bored with his journal and finally abandoned it.

The care that Heusken employed throughout a considerable part of the journal suggests that he began with the hope of publishing it one day. It is not known whether he was aware that William Maxwell Wood, the surgeon on Commodore Armstrong's staff and author of several travel accounts, was preparing the story of the voyage of the *San Jacinto*. Heusken makes no mention of Wood in his journal and Wood's book contains only very infrequent references to Heusken. Wood was an old Navy man beginning his thirtieth year of service when the *San Jacinto* sailed from New York. It seems unlikely that he and Heusken would have had much in common, since the latter was only twenty-three.

Heusken's journal is written in an entertaining style until the period of deterioration noted above. Occasionally he complicates the translators' task by giving free reign to his thoughts and indeed his emotions without much concern for grammatical rules. However, such lapses are infrequent, and in preparing this manuscript we have tried to convey some of the flavor of his style.

In common with all others who lived and traveled in Japan in these early years, Heusken was faced with the problem of reproducing Oriental personal and place names in the "roman" alphabet. We have taken the liberty of altering such names to the accepted English "romanization" found in most scholarly works.

Occasionally we have interrupted Heusken's narrative in order to acquaint the reader with various aspects of the political climate of Japan upon which the ensuing endeavors of Townsend Harris and Henry Heusken were to exert a very signal influence. We must also note here that minor deletions, comprising a few poems and occasional flights of fancy, have been made in the first quarter of the manuscript.

JEANNETTE C. VAN DER CÓRPUT
Berkeley, California

ROBERT A. WILSON
Los Angeles, California

Contents

Contents

Introduction

Little is known concerning the life of Henry Heusken in the years before his path crossed that of Townsend Harris. He was born in Amsterdam on January 20, 1832. From his death certificate we learn that his full name was Henricus Conradus Joannes Heusken. His father was an Amsterdam merchant named Joannes Franciscus Heusken, and his mother is mentioned in the records only as Mrs. Smit-Heusken.

Henry Heusken was sent to a boarding school in the province of Brabant, in the southern part of the Netherlands, where many Dutchmen sent their sons to be educated. In his fifteenth year young Heusken returned to Amsterdam with the intention of beginning a business career under the guidance of his father. However, his father died shortly thereafter, and during the ensuing six years young Henry was unable to cope with the problems of a gradually failing family business. It was urgent that he assume the responsibility of providing for his mother, who was frequently in poor health. Something was apparently salvaged from the family business to provide for her minimum needs.

In 1853, when he was twenty-one, he decided to emigrate to America, the land of opportunity, where youth was more of an asset than it was at that time in the Netherlands, and

where he might also be able to see and do things more congenial to a spirited nature. It is entirely probable that he
abandoned a business career without regret and departed
for New York with great expectations.

His first years in New York, however, were disappointing.
His income was meager. He moved from job to job and was
without employment during some intervals. His clothing
and shoes soon became worn, and there was little money for
repairs or replacements. A warm meal was a luxury in which
he could not indulge frequently. Then came a turn for the
better, although it again meant a career in business. From
then on, everything might have proceeded smoothly. He
could have succeeded or failed in life without anyone in our
time having been at all interested in what befell him. His
career would not have been different from that of many
others, who, coming from all parts of Europe, tried to build
new lives in the strange, vast land of the United States.

However, something else was in store for him. Heusken
heard that a secretary who knew Dutch was being sought
for the first American Consul-General to Japan, Townsend
Harris. For the nations of the Western world, Dutch was the
only possible language of diplomacy in Japan. In trading
with the Dutch, Japanese interpreters had learned a peculiar
Dutch patois with which even Heusken was to have some
difficulties. The Dutch language was also the medium
through which a group of Japanese scholars had learned
something of Western science and technology. The fact that
some scholarly Japanese were proficient in Chinese was not
of much help to the Americans as they now approached the
task of beginning diplomatic relations with Japan on a
formal and enduring basis. To these facts Heusken owed his
appointment as secretary and interpreter for Townsend
Harris and, later on, as first secretary of the American Legation in Japan when Harris was promoted to Minister Resi-

dent. His salary at the beginning was $1500 per annum and, in addition, free passage to Japan. Unhappily for Heusken, though, his salary did not begin until March 1, 1856, although he departed from New York aboard the *San Jacinto* on October 25, 1855.

Townsend Harris was, however, charged with a second mission. In addition to his appointment as Consul-General to Japan, he was designated special envoy to Siam to negotiate a new treaty to replace the Roberts Treaty of 1833. Heusken was of little assistance to Harris in these labors, which were discharged with complete success during an interruption of the voyage of the *San Jacinto* to Japan. Then ensued the greater achievements upon which the enduring stature of Townsend Harris in history rests.

Since the Japan into which Harris and Heusken were about to venture was in the throes of ferment, some explanation of the setting for their adventures is required. During the century from 1542 to 1638, Japan had enjoyed considerable intercourse with the Western world. For many years this Western intercourse was a Portuguese monopoly, involving both trading and missionary activity. Ultimately the Spanish, English, and Dutch intruded upon this monopoly, but only the Dutch brought much energy and determination to the new competition. The Spanish were little interested in commercial activity and devoted their energies primarily to missionary endeavors. The English showed little interest in missionary activity but soon became discouraged with the commercial opportunities offered by Japan and withdrew from their factory at Hirado in 1623.

In the following year, 1624, the Spanish were ejected from Japan, leaving the Portuguese and the Dutch as competitors for the trade. However, the Portuguese were to enjoy a tenure of only another fifteen years before they, too, were ejected, and the Dutch remained as the only representatives of the Western world with any privileges in Japan. Significantly, the Dutch had shown no interest in missionary activity in Japan and had, thereby, avoided the rocks upon which Spanish and Portuguese enterprises had foundered. It must be made clear that it was not religious bigotry that led the Japanese to become suspicious and then hostile to Catholic missionary activity in Japan, but rather the fear of having a section of the native population give its ecclesiastical and possibly political allegiance to an alien religious leader. The introduction of Buddhism into Japan many centuries earlier had produced no such political implications. However, in time, even Buddhist monastic institutions had produced problems for Japan's political leaders. It is sometimes argued that the favors shown to early Jesuit missionaries in Japan resulted, in part, from the fact that Japan's feudal masters and the missionaries had a common foe in the turbulent Buddhist sects of Japan.

It is perhaps significant that it was only after the Buddhists were reduced to a proper obedience to political authority that the behavior of the Jesuit and Franciscan missionaries came under close scrutiny. Such scrutiny finally convinced Japan's authorities that missionary enterprise was but a prelude to political action by the foreigners in support of Japanese Christians, having as its ultimate goal the subjugation of Japan.

The fact that the Dutch undertook no missionary activity in Japan won them some favor in Japanese eyes, but why the Dutch should have been made exceptions to the general exclusion policy after 1639 is not entirely clear. Aid given by the Dutch in putting down the rebellion of Japanese Christians at Shimabara in 1637 did not hurt the Dutch cause. Nevertheless there were important Japanese leaders in the Tokugawa government who favored the complete closure of the country after 1639. The limited position of the Dutch at Deshima after 1641 seems to have been the result of a compromise in the government between leaders who favored open trade limited to the Dutch and those of extreme exclusionist views.

Until the exclusionist acts, the Dutch had conducted their trading activity from their factory on the island of Hirado off the western coast of Kyushu. In 1641 they were compelled to abandon their properties at Hirado and to take up a new station on a spit of sand called Deshima in Nagasaki harbor. For more than two centuries thereafter Japanese contacts with the outside world were limited to the Dutch and the Chinese, who were permitted to engage in a certain amount of closely supervised and heavily regulated trading activity. The new conditions at Deshima were so onerous that in 1652 the Dutch authorities at Batavia raised the question with the governing body of the Dutch East India Company in Amsterdam as to whether further trading activity at Deshima should not be abandoned to save the national honor. However, although the volume of trade conducted by the Dutch at Deshima varied throughout the ensuing two centuries and more, the profits to be made were important enough to cause the Dutch to endure these degrading conditions. Perhaps the fact that the Dutch at Deshima were permitted to engage in some private as well as company trading consoled them during their periods of service in this outpost of the Empire. During the Napoleonic Era, when the Netherlands disappeared for a time as an independent nation in Europe, and when the British took control of the Dutch East Indies, Deshima was for five years the only place in the world where the Dutch flag still flew.

Under these conditions it was difficult for the Dutch to exert much political influence on the Japanese government, though they kept the Tokugawa authorities informed of important developments in the outside world. The cultural influence of the Dutch was destined to be important in Japan. During her long period of seclusion, Japan saw the outside world through the eyes of only the Dutch and the Chinese. In time there developed in Japan a small group of scholars, who, working through the Dutch language, kept abreast of many of the scientific and technological developments in the Western world. Members of Perry's expedition in 1853 and 1854 noted with surprise that some Japanese were quite well informed on many aspects of Western civilization.

The regime under which the Japanese lived and worked during these centuries defies easy description. A great feudal family, the Tokugawa, had seized political power in 1600, destroyed their only remaining antagonists in 1615, and thereafter created a new political and governmental system designed to freeze society in a fixed and unchanging mold. Order and stability were their primary goals, and in the main they were successful, since their regime endured for more than two and a half centuries. Although the Tokugawa Age witnessed occasional outbursts of man and nature, the term "Pax Tokugawa," which is sometimes employed to describe it, is no great exaggeration, because Japan during this period was spared anything resembling the dynastic and religious wars that then plagued the Western world.

The peculiar feudal order over which the Tokugawa presided was one in which no real reconciliation was ever achieved between the Tokugawa and their supporters on the one hand and, on the other, the sections of the feudal order that had been compelled by force of arms to accept the Tokugawa supremacy. Throughout the period, the latter were denied any role in the central government and thus remained a group apart, having in common their tradition of hostility to the Tokugawa and their supporters. However, a system of controls had been worked out during the administrations

of the first three Tokugawa Shoguns in the seventeenth
century that precluded any effective expression of this hostility as long as the power position of the Tokugawa remained unimpaired. No nationwide system of taxation had
ever been established by the Tokugawa who elected, instead,
to take for themselves a large section of the best agricultural
lands in Japan and to defray the costs of the government
from the wealth produced on these lands.

The attempt to freeze society was, of course, destined to
failure from the start. It has frequently been observed that
the birth pangs of modern capitalism were observable in
Japan prior to the Tokugawa Age and that the Tokugawa
policy was a reactionary and, in the long run, futile attempt
to halt the normal processes of change and growth. A money
economy, already nascent, developed fairly rapidly in Tokugawa times and eroded not only feudal moral and ethical
values but also the power relationships of feudal society,
because the merchants who stood at the bottom of the social
scale, in accordance with the Confucian system of values,
came to enjoy great power and influence in a society not of
their own making nor entirely to their liking.

By the middle of the nineteenth century the Tokugawa
authorities were the heirs of generations of incompetent
financial administrations and deplorable fiscal policy. When
Perry arrived off Japanese shores in 1853, the authorities
were deeply troubled by a problem that they dared not reveal
to the nation at large. The treasury was empty. Though still
secure in their control of Japan itself, they were in no position to lead the nation in any real resistance to determined
foreign pressure.

This was the Japan to which Perry and later Harris and
Heusken came. It was on the surface fairly serene when
Perry arrived to set in motion new developments destined
to have the most profound consequences. The fact that

within a decade and a half after the coming of Perry the old order fell suggests that the serene surface hid a seething discontent with the status quo.

Important as the Perry expedition was in the history of modern Japan, its practical results were rather disappointing from the Western point of view. The Treaty of Kanagawa of 1854 was little more than a shipwreck convention and was, therefore, wholly unsatisfactory except as an opening wedge. It was the mission of Townsend Harris to improve upon it, and, if possible, to procure a full commercial treaty.

Perry had left Japan in 1854 with no appreciation of the new currents in domestic politics he had set in motion. Harris and Heusken were to approach the same shores equally ignorant of the fact that a crisis faced the old order, a crisis in no way lessened by the demands that Harris was to make.

Japan Journal

The Journal of Henry Heusken

Steam Frigate San Jacinto   *New York, October 25, 1855*

May God protect the *San Jacinto!* May he lead it safely to its destination. The rains have ceased; the sky is free of clouds; the pale dawn has just painted the eastern horizon the color of a rose; the steeple of Trinity Church is silvered by the first rays of the sun; Jersey and Hoboken are freeing themselves from their veils formed by the vapors of the night; the waters of the Hudson follow their accustomed course along the Palisades, regretfully leaving the charming shores of the Highlands and the Catskill Mountains whose venerable summits lose themselves in the clouds.

The anchor has just been raised.[1] Once again, farewell to New York where most of my friends are still deep in slumber. Farewell to Staten Island where, after having discharged my weekly duty I have spent so many sweet moments; it seems to me that its hills still resound with "Wien Neerlands Bloed" [2] and with the "Marseillaise" sung by voices I know so well and the memory of which will never disappear from my heart; Fort Hamilton which our imagination compares to Sebastopol; and finally the Ocean, in turn gentle, foamy, impetuous and sleepy, which has tumbled its bluish waves ever since the beginning of time.

These same waves carried me far from my homeland to these places which I can still faintly see in the distance. I have spent almost three years in New York, this forest of masts, these clouds of steam and smoke pouring out of its giant smokestacks. These signs of its universal trade, of its peerless industry, disappear behind the horizon. And these same waves have just now received me again on their bosom. Already they are accompanying this humble adventurer to the enchanted palaces of the East, to the treasures of Lahore, and enabling him to penetrate the mysteries of Japan.

All changes upon the Earth. The ardent youth turns into a weakened old man; the young maiden exchanges the lilies and the roses of her diaphanous complexion for livid and yellowish features, furrowed by wrinkles; the eloquent orator and the poet, beloved children of the Muses, when bent by the years are deserted by their eloquence and their wit. Their genius disappears and even little children mock their childish babbling produced by the same organs which used to bring forth masterpieces of poetry and intelligence; fortresses hewn out of rock crumble, but your waves, Oh! Ocean, roll and foam and crash with the same force upon the shore as they did thousands of years ago; they raise heavenwards the greatest ships and cast them down into the abyss; they swallow up the most powerful fleets.

October 27, 1855

This morning we came upon an abandoned ship. It was moving towards us with the planking removed from its sides, like a skeleton. No man walked its deck; no sound was heard except the wind whistling through the rigging and the waves breaking on the abandoned bridge and falling back into the sea in salty cataracts. They were like the tears of orphans, of mothers, and of wives seeking again from the ship the hope of their old age, the love of their youthful years.

A young man, a good fellow but exceedingly stupid, is entirely absorbed in writing his diary. He has already been writing for a full hour without stopping and as fast as a school-boy who conjugates "I must be obedient and docile" for the hundredth time. I compliment him on his adeptness which flatters him to such a point that he begins with a smile of pride and self-complacency to read to me the product of his burning imagination. But soon I understand. The phenomenon is explained. The first page contains a mathematical description of our frigate; the second, the names of all the officers; the third, the crew members and the naval infantry. I believe that the first half of the book will give a faithful account of the number of flying fish and of waves which throw themselves upon the deck, and the other half will end with a magnificent description of the quantity of rations which the crew receives daily and with an apotheosis of our Commodore between two stewards, sons of Africa, with New York in the background.

"How could you ever write all that?" said I, carried away by admiration. "Oh," he answered, "I write only what I *feel.*" Sometime later our young man comes towards me looking as though he had just conquered the world. He had been talking with the Commodore. "A darned fine and clever old fellow that Commodore is," he said to me. "Why? What did he tell you?" "Ah, my dear fellow, he has asked me if I don't suffer from seasickness."

And that is how judgments are formed in the world! Because a commodore enquires about the state of your health, that makes him a pleasant and intelligent man, but if a sailor or some simple member of the naval infantry had delivered a speech like Cicero or Demosthenes, he would certainly have seemed a fool.

November 1, 1855

The sun rose in a cloudless sky and running its immaculate course is going down again, dipping its purple globe into an azure sea. What man wouldn't wish to give up the pleasures and the luxury that a town like New York offers in order to contemplate nature where it appears in all its splendor? Where is there a base soul who prefers to breathe an atmosphere polluted by seven hundred thousand mouths rather than the pure and free air of the ocean, to look at the golden rays of the rising sun through the fissures of an old wall rather than to admire Phoebus leaving, resplendent with light, his humid place of rest, who can give his preference to an old writing desk and books covered with dust, to nourishing his mind with addition of legions of figures, to comparing the terrible "debit" and "credit," rather than to let his gaze wander into infinite reaches? Who does not prefer to hear the waves breaking or to contemplate the elegant dorado rather than to argue about the value of merchandise, and sharpen one's mind in order to fill our coffers while emptying those of others; to sing of the magnificence and the peerless beauty of the ocean rather than to patronize every night the same cafes, drinking the same beer out of the same glasses served by the same waiter; to hear with a forced admiration the divine Casta Diva or Grace Grace, which are being murdered in fashionable gatherings, rather than to contemplate the clouds, gilded by the setting sun which disappears into the sea? Its rays become fainter bit by bit and cast only an uncertain light upon the top of our masts, but night is going to spread her veil strewn with stars. Turn your head to the place where the sun has disappeared and you will see pale Diana rising in the Orient, silvering the waves until it seems that our frigate is sailing into a silver sea. I find myself alone on the bridge.

Carried away by admiration for nature, I haven't noticed that everyone has retired. One hears only the ringing of the bell and the measured tread of the officer on duty; the helm turning on its bearings, and the smoke pouring from the smokestack are the only signs that nearly three hundred men are lulled here upon the deep and have entrusted their lives to the faithfulness of the *San Jacinto*. I go below and, throwing myself upon my lonely bunk, I soon forget that each moment removes me further from New York and brings me closer to Madeira, that I am upon the great route to Japan.

November 11, 1855

Land Ho! We are at Madeira.[3]

Various skiffs soon approach our frigate, but of all those that surrounded us I was not about to forget one. An old lady occupied its stern, continuously smiling and making deep bows in our direction, holding in her right hand some obviously ancient documents, while she had on her left arm a huge basket which disappeared under an immense umbrella, large enough to protect the whole bay of Funchal from a shower. For an hour this lady had been greeting us, while showing us her precious documents with gracious smiles which succeeded one another on her weathered complexion, tanned by a sun which shows as little kindness for the sweet little face that it visits for the fifteenth season as it does for the changed features of an old matron who sees again its light for the ninetieth season. She managed to climb on board. She was the laundress who had come to pay her respects to the American flag, and place at the feet of our staff her services, her basket, and her umbrella. With a triumphant smile she displayed before the eyes of the surprised assembly her letters of recommendation, attesting that the aforementioned lady Juanita was an exceedingly honest woman, of high morals and, what matters much more for a laundress, that she washed the linen one would entrust to her motherly care in such an exquisite manner that one would not recognize it, repairing at the same time both the damages inflicted to it by time and by the lack of patience of its lords and masters. All this for five sous apiece. And then came the signatures of an infinite number of commodores, captains, etc., etc.

The sun had just set and, the Junior Lieutenant having placed one of the launches of the ship at our disposal, we set foot again on the ground after an absence of seventeen days.

Since the beach at Madeira slopes gently towards the level of the sea, it is impossible to reach it in our launch unless one gets wet from head to foot. We are therefore obliged to jump into small skiffs and they drag us, skiffs and passengers, upon the sand. What a delicious sensation to find oneself on Terra Firma especially for people like myself who do not boast at all that the sea is their element. With what pleasure one inhales the pure air of the mountains, what joy to breathe the sweet fragrance of the flowers, to be able to walk and continue to walk without having to turn around every twenty paces, as on the deck of the *San Jacinto*. We are not masters of our impatience until we have swallowed a glass of very fresh water.

You laugh, reader, or you, charming lady. A glass of water! Ah! You have never made a sea voyage! We go to the English Hotel. Coming out of the hotel where, I assure you, we did not limit ourselves to a glass of water, a crowd of beggars besieges us.[4] It seems that in all the countries favored by nature, where the delightful climate and the enchanting surroundings attract strangers from every part of the world, beggars gather in crowds, especially those who have some kind of monstrosity to offer you. Here are two on my right who have no arms and a third one lacks a nose. I turn away quite disgusted, but now my left is besieged by a monster whose maimed face has nothing left that is human about it, and by a woman whose mouth is joined to her throat. I can't stand it any longer. The more you give them, the greedier they get. Should you chase one away, two replace him. It's exactly like the Hydra of Lerna.

Here are the little beggars again, but I owe these something. They amply recompense me for the monsters. Imagine angel faces, framed with curly hair in the most graceful disarray such as only nature can achieve, eyes black and very dark, a complexion tanned by the sun and voices so sweet, so wistful that it seems as though I still hear these sounds so tuneful, so sweet, so beseeching, slurring each syllable. These are not rude beggars demanding alms. This is suffering humanity, bewailing its miseries and rendered eloquent by suffering. *Senhores Ingleises! Senhores Ingleises!,* and these beseeching eyes, these expressive gestures, these belong to the child Jesus of Murillo,[5] which I find again in Madeira.

November 12, 1855

The desire to return to Madeira prompts me to leave my lonesome bunk early, and the launch brings us back to the shore.[6] I have put on civilian clothes with a few military touches, in order to look like an admiral incognito who does not want to expose his dignity to the eyes of the populace. My companions are already in the saddle. I mount and we leave at a slow trot which does not satisfy my worthy steed, and he breaks into a gallop. We pass like the wind through the little town of Funchal. By clinging vigorously to the pommel and consigning to the devil all the rules of Baptiste and Franconi,[7] I remain firmly in the saddle despite the fear of losing my cap now and then, for the Gods who protect unskilled horsemen have taught the people of Madeira to fasten to the tail of each horse a guardian angel; I say "fasten" because these good people, not wishing to follow us without some sort of support, hang onto the tail of the horse and refuse to let go of it no matter what you may tell them.

The path gets more and more difficult, rising rapidly. The never changing climate allows the inhabitants of this blessed country to grow all kinds of plants and fruit. The path is lined with tall walls which form the enclosure of the Quintas, inhabited mostly by the English, who seek here a refuge from the fogs and the extremes of their own climate. Banana trees with their lush foliage, chestnut trees heavy with fruit, orange trees on which one glimpses the plump fruit, brilliant with color alongside groves of fig trees which, although humble in appearance and less gaudy than the superb orange, refreshed us nevertheless; how many delights fill my adoring soul; how I admire in everything the Supreme Being, creator of this garden of delights, heaping everywhere his gifts, the beauty of which attests to their heavenly origin, favoring with an impartial hand even the least of his creatures.

An hour's walk leads us to Nossa Senhora del Monte, a church located about three thousand feet above sea level. The church itself has nothing noteworthy outside of its isolated and picturesque site. From its towers one discovers the Ocean, the town of Funchal. The *San Jacinto* in the bay seems devoid of life, for distance makes it impossible for us to see her crew on the deck. Her black hull seems smaller than the fly buzzing around me; and yet that is the same ship which carried me across the Ocean, which, sailing upon the depths of the sea, defying the tempests and the fury of the waves, brought almost three hundred men safely to the beach of Madeira.

We return by way of the Little Coral, an extinct crater. Our horses, accustomed to precipices, carry us with a steady pace up some paths so narrow that two men can hardly walk them abreast, and we look down into precipices in which the

arid rock outcroppings and the deeply cut river bed bear witness to their volcanic origin. The incline of the path winding
around the crater becomes steeper and steeper. Brooks, whose
quiet murmurs lull us to sweet reveries, small freestone
bridges thrown across the precipices, contemplation of nature
in all her splendor more than make up for the hardships at
sea.

The Great Coral offers the same perspectives as the little
one, except that it is still more impressive. It rises about six
thousand feet above sea level. The nuns took refuge there
during the British invasion. Poor nuns!

Funchal is a true Portuguese town. One finds there winding
and narrow streets, houses with balconies and blinds from
which the dark-eyed senhoritas await the serenades of their
lovers. Oil lanterns shed just enough light to make us realize
how dark it is. Once in a while you see a palanquin, carried
by two men and preceded by lighted torches, bringing a lady
back home. Although the flames cast a red and mysterious
glow on the carefully drawn curtains of the palanquin, these
curtains prevent us from admiring the charms of the oc-
cupant, and an inclination seizes me to tear them up. I resent
just as much the veils in New York as I do these curtains
of Portugal. It is with them as with those people who own
magnificent furniture and keep it hidden under covers of
calico. Mercy! Mercy! Miladies; for having compared you to
furniture I am ready as a second Mucius Scaevola [8] to burn
the hand guilty of writing these blasphemous lines. Poets say
that illusion is better than reality. Cautious people would
add that, tearing the curtains, you would be quite likely to
get stabbed with stilettos, or at least beaten with clubs, and
cynics that, after all your trouble, you would be rewarded by
bringing to light the respectable charms of an old dowager
who has passed her seventy-fifth spring.

We meet a few cavalcades. They are English people. The

amazons with their long, flowing skirts show at least their faces to whomever might care to admire them, and they cast languishing glances all around.

The kind hostess of the English Hotel gives me a very comfortable room for which, including breakfast, I am charged one dollar. We are also served there a good dinner for a dollar per person. A Portuguese soup of broth, bread, cheese, and vegetables—in short, a blend of the animal and vegetable world—enlivens my palate. The herbs of the mountains where the cattle graze give the meat a certain aromatic fragrance. The potatoes are very mealy and the fruits!—the memory of these, at once lovely and delicious, tempting taste, smell and sight at the same time, the yellowish bananas melting in the mouth, more flavorful than any I have seen in the West Indies; the oranges—well, it is just useless to talk about them; their universal renown speaks for itself.

"But," you will say, "you mention everything except that which makes the glory of Madeira. I mean its grapes!" Poor grapes! Poor vineyards! Source of that delicious nectar which bears, as a grateful son should, the name of the land that gave birth to it. Even as cruel epidemics, like the plague or cholera, take their toll of the poor humans and count among their victims young people full of life and vigor as well as old people nearing the grave, so a destructive disease has made its way into your vineyards, O! Madeira! [9] Your leaves had unfolded, your fruit full of the bloom of life held promise of countless delights to the gourmet and of a noble and refreshing drink to the whole world. But your vineyards have suddenly withered and their dried fruit droops to the earth. Instead of heavenly juice, it holds only maggots that consume the remains. The desiccated root has lost its strength to nourish, and, instead of channeling the essentials of life to the branches that stem from its heart, now lies rotting away in the soil and will be just good enough to heat up the peasant's soup. They are trying to replace the vineyards with cochineal and sugar. This seems to promise satisfactory results.

The memory of a visit to Santa Clara's Convent will never leave me. I was allowed to talk to the nuns through a double gate. A charming Sister answered in a melodious Spanish accent the questions I asked her, accompanying each answer with a soft smile. The emotion I felt at the sight of these grim walls, the antechamber separated from the convent by a double row of iron bars, the poor sisters sentenced to life-long imprisonment, whom one could see walking beyond the iron-barred gate, the Chapel, the house of the Lord, where again a grated door separated the poor girls like ferocious beasts from the rest of the faithful, prompted in me the most melancholy reflections.

Saturday, November 17, 1855

The order is given to set sail. We are leaving. Farewell, enchanted island, delightful climate, favorite abode of fruits and flowers. The high mountains disappear beyond the horizon. Aided by the dim twilight, I still distinguish a bluish mass rising from the sea. Soon, complete darkness will hide from us all that is left of Madeira.

November 18, 1855

This morning I received from the Commodore an invitation to dinner. I was at the table at the appointed hour. All the formalities of etiquette that one has to observe during such a dinner are not of a nature to stimulate gaiety; but a good old Madeira, which had just been brought forth from the cellars of that island after a beneficial rest of twenty-five years, soon dissipated restraint, and helped by an array of bottles of champagne, we were soon having as much fun as can be had aboard a warship.

December 9, 1855

Instead of touching at St. Helena, the Commodore deems it appropriate to go to Ascension,[10] to our great disappointment, losing thereby the unique opportunity, an opportunity which will never reoccur, to visit the tomb of the Emperor, the place of exile of the great Napoleon! How many souls, burning with enthusiasm for the first man of his century, have longed for the places made forever sacred by the presence of the great General. How anxious I was to see the weeping willows and the clear water spring where the Emperor liked to sit and meditate upon his past grandeur, these trees which have been witnesses of his brooding reveries. God only knows what immense plans his mind still shaped for the future upon this arid and lonely rock where, instead of a triumphant army and floating banners, he saw only desolation and cruel jailers; instead of clarions sounding conquest, the hurried gallop of the noble steeds ridden by his French Cuirassiers; instead of the roar of cannons throwing panic among the square battalions of the enemy, nothing but the monotonous sound of the waves breaking against the rock of St. Helena. St. Helena, I said to myself, St. Helena alone is enough of a reward for my voyage, to see Longwood, to devote one hour to contemplating the room where he breathed his last and gave back his soul and his genius to the Creator, to shed a tear upon his deserted grave which he has left to rest among his heroes, and to tremble with indignation when walking past the lair of Sir Hudson Lowe, the executioner, the willful murderer of the Emperor.[11]

Like a new Tantalus who sees fresh water flow near his burning lips and feels the most exquisite fruit brush past his mouth and sees the water and the fruit withdraw as, dying with thirst and hunger, he draws near them, I was going to pass near St. Helena without being able even to see it in the distance. And look, instead, the most arid, the most desolate place now appears to our eyes. The island of Ascension, an extinct volcano, a deserted island ever since the first moments of its existence until the time when the presence of Napoleon at St. Helena induced the British to deem it necessary to station a garrison there.

> Barren spot
> I wish'd to God
> I never trod
> Thy soil.
> Lava banks
> Watertanks
> Robbers' spoil.
> Dirty rags
> Wrinkled flags
> Rotten eggs
> Are thine.
>
> Salted meat
> Scorching heat
> Place for swine
> And to crown
> With a frown
> Thy renown
> Poor slave.
> Preventedst me
> By Jove! to see
> Napoleon's grave.

Here are the lines which expressed my indignation at the sight of that island where there is now a coal and supply dump, a fact which spared us the TROUBLE to go and get them at St. Helena. There is nothing but cone-shaped hills bearing on them the marks of frightful eruptions. A warship is always stationed there. A part of its crew lives on the island where John Bull, always faithful to his principles, has had some very comfortable barracks built, as well as a little Episcopalian church.

As in all British possessions, ale and porter constitute the main beverages. These two beers are there in such abundance that, in spite of the mountains and the barren fields, I expected to come upon a brewery in some isolated cavern. Instead of vegetation the island is, so to speak, covered with broken bottles, where the peering eye of the antiquarian can still trace the words "East India Pale Ale."

A path, four or five miles long, took us through the lava, to a small valley called Wide Awake's Fair. Terns, a kind of sea swallow, gather there in flocks to lay their eggs which are so plentiful that the whole valley seems covered with snow formed by the white throats of the birds and the aforementioned eggs. While we were crossing the valley, the birds remained quietly sitting on the eggs until we came close to stepping on them. Then they would rise, flying around my head. One of them was bold enough to peck at my hat! They can easily be seized by hand. The eggs are very good to eat. These poor little birds, discovering this refuge in the midst of the sea, immediately took possession of the best spot in order to lay their eggs. With what tenacity they would stay in their places! With what maternal care they watched every one of our movements! There were men who, taking unfair advantage of their trust, threw stones at these little winged creatures. What wretched courage and wonderful skill it indeed takes to throw a stone in the midst of a hundred little birds who, trusting and happy, fly about you! Man shudders with indignation when reading stories of hungry wolves devouring a herd of sheep, of a bloodthirsty tiger stealing out of his den at night and pouncing upon the fleet, sleeping buck, of snakes which, endowed with supernatural powers, attract the turtledove towards their gaping mouths. And yet man, man himself, isn't he more of a ferocious beast than all the others? He who, endowed with a sensitive soul, can appreciate the advantages of life and freedom, while the others are only mechanisms of their instincts. The intelligent man, masterpiece of nature, praised to heaven by some, identified with the Gods by others, this man makes it a sport of killing with stones graceful and fleet creatures, for the sole pleasure of watching them fall and of enjoying their agony.

December 11, 1855

This morning one of the officers on board the English steamer *Antelope,* Mr. Goldsmith, was kind enough to call for me to go on an excursion to the Green Mountain. After a two and one-half hour's trip through arid plains covered with lava and through conical hills, we reached the summit of the mountain, three thousand feet above sea level. Strange thing, in the midst of so much desolation, the summit alone of that mountain is covered with green. What a refreshing sight these blades of grass are, these dwarfed trees, to which man in a happier climate would not grant a single glance! To pick a leaf, to discover a thousand unknown beauties in a plain blade of grass, that was for us more enjoyment than it was formerly to wander under venerable oaks raising their thick branches heavenwards, and to enjoy the perfume of a thousand flowers adorning the surrounding fields with myriad colors. How little we need to be happy! But what am I saying? Doesn't a blade of grass alone hold in itself a world of beauties, the least of which reveals the handiwork of the Almighty?

We entered a lovely little vegetable garden, near which a soldier's wife who supplied us with lunch lives in a cottage.

Imagine our surprise upon seeing a table set with fresh eggs, lamb chops, and milk on an island where, an hour before, we had not glimpsed the slightest sign of vegetation, no animal except the birds of the valley and those who were making sport of killing them. I could see two handsome cows peacefully grazing in front of the cottage, and honest-to-goodness chickens, apparently as comfortable there as in their native land.

Sitting on top of the mountains we enjoyed a unique vantage point. Around us a few acres (arpents) of cultivated land, while all the rest formed a picture of perfect desolation: extinct craters, red hills, a few wild goats frisking in the arid plain, the little white valley of the terns, and the bluish waves which surround the little island of Ascension. At great expense they have succeeded in building an aqueduct which brings water from the mountain to the city, if you can call it a city. It has been observed that since the summit has been under cultivation the rains have increased in frequency.

I must still tell of a visit that I paid King Pepple of Grand Bonny.[12] The English government keeps him a prisoner at Ascension. He is a handsome African Negro. Mr. Goldsmith told us that he lives here at the expense of the government. The indignation of his African Majesty was something to see. "Me," he cried, "great kingdom, no need of the English. Oh, those English." And his scowls betrayed his deep-seated hatred. One of my companions, noticing an earthenware plate bearing the inscription "His Majesty King Pepple," expressed the desire to buy it. "I give it to you," said the King with a truly regal air drawing himself up to his full height. "Me no accept money."

December 12, 1855

We set sail for the Cape of Good Hope.

December 24, 1855

Christmas Eve passed peacefully and warmly, if I can use this last word. A tropical temperature, no snow or ice, no joyful sound of sleds sliding over the New York streets strikes my ears. We are not consoled by the vain hope of enjoying tomorrow a well-truffled turkey, a huge plum pudding, and that famous eggnog. Oh, no! Our food supplies are beginning to run short. A somewhat spoiled ham, a few old potatoes, and the shadow of a plum pudding—that's our festive fare for tomorrow.

My goodness, but it feels good to lie down! How hot it is here. It is stifling. I cast off my sheet and finally close my eyes. My wandering thoughts turn themselves to remote places, towards a bygone time; a great fire burns in the fireplace; the room is filled with familiar faces, shining with happiness. I see again the loved ones of my childhood. A gentleman and a lady have just walked in. To judge by the fuss that is being made over them they must be dearly loved. An old man, sitting by the fire, looks at them happily—and why shouldn't he be happy, thus surrounded by his children? How many Christmas days have passed since he saw them grow up! A little boy mingles with the family group; he seems to be the object of all their endearments. Everything for him looks rosy and he thinks that all of his Christmas days will pass this way, that these beloved people will always be around him. Ah! How mistaken, how cruelly mistaken he is! How fortunate is man not to be able to read into the future; he does not know when his friends, his parents will leave him. He does not know that each new Christmas day will show him an empty place in this family group, that this happy couple who loved each other as dearly as they did on their wedding day will soon be separated by the grave. And he lives, and he plays in that happy carelessness of youth. He has no memories yet; he lives only in the present; and as for the future—but the future will come.

The dim sound of a drum call wakes me. Everybody gets up. In order to train the crew and familiarize it with the duties that pertain to service on a warship, the Captain had an alarm sounded and called everybody to their battle stations to fight an imaginary enemy and a simulated night attack.

The bell rings midnight. Merry Christmas! I was not mistaken. My dream comes true and this is Christmas day indeed; but of those that I saw in my dream, of those beloved faces of parents and friends, none is here except the child; that child, however, does not play any more; many a Christmas day has seen him grow; he has become a man now; he had no past then, no memories, but today, Heavens! He has too many.[18] Alone among a crowd of strangers, he belongs only to his memories. Withdraw, grim reality, and let us go and seek in slumber the beloved pictures that have embellished our childhood.

Saturday, January 12, 1856

Finally we sight the Cape. A desolate beach backed by mountains of uniform characteristics enables me to recognize the southernmost part of Africa. We enter False Bay and after a two-hour crossing we anchor at Simons Bay. Eager to become acquainted with the African soil, I take advantage of the first launch to leave the ship, after having seen and, what is much more impressive, heard, the shooting of a twenty-one gun salute in honor of the British flag, and a thirteen-gun salute in honor of Commodore Trotter who commands here the fleet of Her British Majesty. The gun salutes echoing from the mountains; the British frigate *Castor* which, in sounding her answer to our salute, gets shrouded in clouds of smoke; the gunpowder which blowing around us blackens instantly the clean linen and the last pair of white trousers which we had put on to honor old Africa; the waves splashing into the frail skiff carrying me ashore, soaking all that the gunpowder had spared—none of this is of a nature to put me in high spirits. But as soon as my feet touch the ground, after a thirty-one day absence, I feel like a new man; my dark mood clears up. But what are these familiar sounds that so pleasantly strike my ears? And yet the sound of these words and the manner in which these two Negroes next to me are speaking is by no means harmonious. On the contrary, they are insults, barbarous words: [14]

"Why don't you do what I told you, you damned son of a bitch?"

"Because I don't want to, you sheep's head."

However barbarous they may be, these words that reflect a loathsome dialectical form are spoken in a language which is the first in which I have ever expressed my thoughts, a language my mother has taught me through zealous and affectionate efforts, a language so aptly called the mother tongue.

Simons Bay has about fifteen hundred inhabitants and has nothing noteworthy to offer. The British maintain a naval ammunition depot there as well as the base of their fleet for this part of the world. I go to Green's Hotel where for three shillings sterling I am served a substantial lunch. In the afternoon we climb the highest mountain which rises to about two thousand feet, but we discover nothing of interest and the surroundings remain stubbornly desolate. The rock is granite, covered with a thin layer of top soil where an infinity of curious plants grow. One especially, called Hottentot's-fig, attracts our attention. It is planted along the public roads to keep away the sand which is plentiful in these parts. The chain of mountains that line the opposite shore of False Bay is dimly visible in the distance. They are the mountains of Stellenbosch, Hottentot's Holland, and Cape Hanglip. The idea the traveler forms of the Cape of Good Hope upon arriving at Simons Bay must be very unfavorable.

January 13, 1856 [15]

Thanks to the kindness of Messieurs Harrington and Gary, who offer me a place in their coach, I am able to leave towards evening for Capetown, approximately twenty-one miles from Simons Bay. The road, as is usual in the British possessions, is excellent, except that you have to cross the beach four times, which is very difficult when the tide is in because sand always constitutes a very difficult passage.

If a visit to the Cape of Good Hope is interesting, it is doubly so for a Dutchman who finds everywhere memories of his forebears. We pass Fishhook Bay and Kalk Bay and the famous Muysenberg. The tops of the mountains, where the granite is bared, assume the most fantastic forms. The summit of one of them looks like an old Roman fortress. Near the Muysenberg one sees the ruins of the Dutch barracks and the dismal remains of the ancient fortress of Muysenberg. Old cannons are half buried in the sand and a few caissons protrude here and there, as though begging the passer-by to have mercy and to end for them an existence, formerly glorious, but now only burdensome. Many times I went and sat on the old guns near the ruins of the ancient fortress; it seemed as though I could recognize them, and didn't they have a right to my sympathy? How many glorious days were thus brought back to my mind of the times when Holland, triumphant on land and sea, was the forerunner of civilization in the Indies, when her ships carried a broom atop their mainmast to mean that they had swept the sea free of all their enemies? How many times, I said to myself, did these cannons bring terror and destruction in the midst of the British fleet? Perhaps they accompanied de Ruyter in his victorious advance upon Chatham and their distant roar brought fear to the heart of London, and now they lie on vanquished soil; the banners of proud Albion wave in the winds instead of our tricolor. If guns could blush, if the crumbling walls of the old fortress could speak, wouldn't they find an echo in poor Holland herself, this fallen country, shadow of the past where degenerate sons watch with an indifferent eye the gigantic work of their fathers decay and tumble down?

Beyond the Muysenberg, the countryside, arid and flat up to now, changes suddenly as though touched by a magic wand. A mountain appears, rising in steep, vertical lines, to a flat, level summit. It fully deserves its name of Table Mountain. The celebrated vineyards of Constantia are on the lower slopes.

We arrive at Mr. Rathfalder's Halfway House and, since all the Halfway Houses of the world are inns, we stop there to rest our horses and to get ourselves some refreshment. Horses would really have a difficult time if horsemen were never thirsty! The countryside becomes more and more picturesque: beautiful Scottish pines planted on both sides of the road, lovely groves, vine-planted fields, and the pale Diana who so faithfully has led us to the Cape of Good Hope, silvering the waves of the ocean, now appears through the thick foliage of a proud oak tree, true king of these countrysides, and presently she casts her rays upon the Eden around us. We pass through Claremont and Rondbosch, two lovely villages, and arrive at Capetown, where the good Captain Harrington leaves us safe and sound at the Masonic Hotel.

Capetown, a city of about twenty-eight thousand people, was built by the Dutch on the plain which separates Table

Bay from Table Mountain. The promenade, a square surrounded by trees, has lost a great deal since it no longer belongs to the Dutch East India Company. The botanical garden is full of promise and very carefully tended. We were
shown two beautiful church owls, if church owls can be
beautiful, which were, as one of the guardians said in a true
English, "the howling Hafrican heagle howl."

I believe that every religion of the world owns a temple
at Capetown; one finds there the synagogues of the Jews and
the mosques of the Moslems. The Table Mountain is flanked
by two other mountains, one called Devil's Head, and the
other Lion's Head. If you look at them long and carefully
you may recognize a faint resemblance to these two creatures.
And people still say the Dutch have no imagination! A white
cloud sometimes comes to rest upon the Table Mountain and
then proceeds to majestically descend to its foot. The cloud
is called the Tablespread. Then, look out! Close the doors
and windows, for the good inhabitants will tell you, "If the
Tablespread is placed on the Table, the wind that we know
so well around here, the southeaster, can't be far away." Good
Heavens! How well I know what it is like! Whirlwinds of
sand picked up by the wind enter everywhere, through your
nostrils, your mouth, and into your eyes; careful housewives
close doors and windows in vain, for the sand knows no
obstacles and penetrates everything. However, instead of
loathing that wind, the people love it, and they call it the
"Doctor," for in its absence all kinds of diseases appear,
whereas everyone is well when it blows.

Mr. Pieter van der Byl, to whom I carried a letter of introduction, was kind enough to invite me to his country
house near Claremont. I enjoyed the hospitality of Mr. and
Mrs. van der Byl until the next day. Mr. Pieter Schulz, who
came to see me at the Masonic Hotel, did everything he
could to make my stay at the Cape pleasant. Since he had

been my neighbor in Amsterdam, we were immediately on the best of terms. I shall always remember the warm welcome which he and his family gave me, inviting me to stay at their home for the rest of my visit, and introducing me to Messieurs P. J. de Goor, van Koetsveld, van der Vliet, de Vos et Halbersma, and to Captain Tromp. Since Mr. O. T. Truter informed me that the steam corvette, the *Monterado* under Captain André, was leaving for Batavia, I hurried to go aboard and had the pleasure, after three years, to set foot again on Dutch territory and to salute the tricolor of my native country.

The officers of the English frigate, *Castor,* gave a ball for the ladies of the neighboring towns and we attended it. That day I was introduced to Mr. Cloete, the owner of Constantia.[16] Since he was paying a visit to our Commodore, the latter called me in and introduced me to Mr. Cloete as to a countryman. Unaware yet of who he was, I greeted him in English, but he interrupted me quickly and said: "We should speak Dutch, Sir!"

Honor those whom you should honor, and honor is due to the officers of the *Castor.* At first glance one would never recognize in this ballroom the deck of a war frigate. All the cannons have been removed; the masts are wrapped in flags and garlands; a beautifully arranged tent is set up.

The beauties of Capetown and its vicinity are here with languishing eyes and long, dark tresses which caress alabaster throats, white dresses of the finest material which reveal the graceful forms of these ladies of Africa, small Cinderella feet tripping about in time with the music. The fragrance of flowers and of scented waters fill the air, as do the gay tunes of Strauss, the newest polkas, the most ancient schottisches, and quadrilles in which every lady endeavors to display her best manners, to make inimitable curtsies, to extend her hand with expressions which emphasize the beauty of some

and the ugliness of others. There, ladies of mature years try
to act naïve, whereas mere children who have spent the night
in curlers in the most frightful tortures try to pose as inveter-
ate coquettes, casting scornful glances at the young midship-
men. For these young ladies nothing but commissioned officers will do.

After the magnificent repast where wine flowed freely,
when burning words of love poured from heaving bosoms and
languishing glances penetrated the depths of souls, when the
most sullen personalities were becoming pleasant and old
sea wolves were beginning to smile, when felicity seemed
to reign as a supreme goddess—who could have told that this
smooth dance floor, barely touched by the small satin-shod
feet of the dancers turning always faster to the strains of the
orchestra in an ecstasy of love and pleasure, who could have
told that this same polished floor had been the scene of
bloody battles, battles in which projectiles of destruction were
shot by heavy masses of metal into enemy ranks, where the
cries of the wounded and the shouts of triumph of the
victors vied with the elements, where blood flowed in streams,
where so many brave men heaved their last sighs? Who could
have recognized in this temple dedicated to Venus and Love
the deck of the old *Castor,* frigate of the British Navy?

Near us floated the hull of the old navy brig, the *Badger,*
which one could not contemplate without a feeling of veneration. It was the first command of that hero of so many naval
battles, the immortal Nelson.

I had the pleasure to meet at the ball Mr. and Mrs. Dirk
Cloete, who invited me to visit with them. I could not resist
the open manner in which the invitation was expressed and
on Sunday, January 27, 1856, I set off at six o'clock in the
morning for Wynberg. That is a good three-hour march, and,
having exhausted the contents of my purse, I was forced to
entrust to my feet what it did not allow me to entrust to a

good carriage and four frisky horses. But one has to be philo-
sophical about those things, and having arrived at Alphen, I
pretended (for appearances' sake) to have preferred crossing
the wood on foot, being one of nature's most devoted admirers, and to have left my carriage, *my coachman,* and my
horses on the main road two miles distant from Alphen.

Just a few steps away from their house I meet Mr. and
Mrs. Cloete in their carriage on their way to church. I am
greeted like an old family friend and immediately settle quite
comfortably in the carriage (a real carriage, this time) and
have the pleasure to hear, so great a distance away from my
homeland, a sermon in the purest Dutch. On the way back
from the church, Mr. Cloete shows me his lands. They take
me to a grove of oranges, not one with those dwarf shrubs
which you find in the north, but one of real trees more than
a hundred feet tall, of gigantic peach trees bearing more
fruit than leaves, whose branches bend so much under their
burden of juicy fruit that they have to be supported by
poles. The ground under those trees is littered with peaches
whose stems could not sustain their weight. To my horror
they tell me: "That's nothing. The chickens will eat them."
To give peaches to chickens! What a sacrilege for a Dutchman! I pick some nectarines, fully worthy of their name, and
I wander through thickets whose silvery leaves shine in the
sunlight like the metal of that name. They call them *Poten-
tille anserine* [wild tansy].

For the first time in my life I admire that tree, king of the
firs, called Norfolk fir or Australia fir, the needles of which
are fine and slender. Then there are the vineyards, growing
here only one or two feet above ground, whose grapes ripen
not from the direct rays of the sun (which would burn them)
but from their reflection by the ground. It seems to me that
I can still taste them, those peerless grapes called Hane-
pooten. At dinner I am so moved by the attentions of which

I, a stranger, an unknown man, am the object, so appreciative of the open and friendly welcome, that, proposing a toast, I elaborate on and praise to the skies the truly patriarchal hospitality of the Cape; and what is very rare in today's toasts, mere formalities dictated by hypocrisy or convention, I do really mean what I say and the words that my mouth utters are directly dictated by my heart.

Why did hospitality, this lovely virtue, disappear from the Earth, and why can it only be found in the most remote regions? Why doesn't everyone see in the stranger a friend, a brother? Oh! Civilization, when will you cease making barbarians of us, making us more and more suspicious of one another? A time will come when each man will think of himself alone in the world and the world for him alone, and the world will perish because its inhabitants have lost the art of sustaining one another.

After dessert the horses are harnessed and we ride to Constantia. Constantia and its magnificent vineyards, named after the wife of one of the early Dutch governors, is located on an isolated mountain called Constantiaberg. Mr. Cloete and his lovely family receive me as it is the custom to receive strangers at the Cape, and that means everything. Miss Cloete, a lovely young lady, is kind enough to show me around the gardens and the neighboring parts of the property. I see nice little groves of myrtle, symbol of love, where narrow paths wind just wide enough for two to walk side by side. God only knows how many sighs, how many tender promises of love these places have witnessed! We climb on a high plateau and from there we enjoy a superb view. Below us, the great house of Constantia, with its small-paned windows shaded by gigantic oak trees; the vine-covered fields; in the distance a white line—the road from Capetown to Simonstown. All of it is surrounded by mountains and the Muysenberg, beyond which you can glimpse the bluish waves of the Ocean, giving an added charm to the scenery. And then, to complete the picture of happiness, a lovely girl by your side who, while pointing out the surrounding points of interest, reveals with her silver-toned voice, her witty remarks, and artless simplicity the riches of her womanly heart and the treasures of her cultured mind, so sensitive to the beauties of nature. Ah! How monotonous life at sea seems to me, how devoid of any charm a life that forces you to live exiled from the society of these beneficial beings called women. Only they know how to scatter roses on the path that man is fated to follow. Only they know how to cultivate his mind. Only they know how to dominate his evil inclinations and direct his qualities towards good. The man who hates women thereby hates God in the most perfect of his creatures.

In the cellars of Constantia, where the huge barrels remind me of Heidelberg, I taste the wine of Constantia, favorite of Louis Philippe. The wine is very sweet and almost as thick as Genoa oil. In no wine of the world does the fruity taste dominate so much as in that nectar of the Cape of Good Hope. Thanks to the superiority of the soil of Constantia-berg, no vineyard of the vicinity can produce a wine comparable to that one. We return to Alphen, and after having seen the moon add new charms to the landscape, Mr. Dirk Cloete shows me to my room. Walking through the wide corridors, the spacious rooms with ceilings so high that they form two stories of today, I recognize the good, solid architecture of the Holland of a century ago. Mrs. Cloete was born in Holland of the Oosterzee family.

The next day I rise early and, saying farewell to Alphen, I feel sadness at the parting. It seems that, instead of twenty-four hours, I have spent entire years here, so dear has that lovely family become to me, and it costs me a great deal to leave them.

I note January 27, 1856, in the calendar of my life as one

of those blessed days, those brilliant meteors which do not often occur, and once gone leave tender memories which follow us whenever we think about them as a blessed shadow of things once loved. The day spent at Alphen and Constantia is like an oasis in the desert; that day, witness of a bliss at once peaceful and rapturous, stands out in my restless life.

Mr. Hugo of Simonstad, who contributed so much to making my stay in that town pleasant, asked me to write a few lines in his album. Being on the point of departure, I wrote hurriedly:

> Although on my way to Japan, to undiscovered country
> Wherever fortune leads me in the course of life
> I'll always remember with the keenest of pleasures
> The hospitality of the most hospitable people on earth.
> The Cape of Good Hope

The race of Hottentots, formerly lords and masters of this country, is almost extinct, or rather quite interbred with other races. It has suffered so much humiliation and servitude that a Hottentot of three centuries ago would not recognize his grandnephews.

The Kaffirs, that bellicose nation which gave so much trouble to the colonists, are giving way more and more before the giant strides of civilization. They are handsome men of a coppery color, of slender build, and have the fleetness of the desert antelope. They do not deserve at all the name of Negroes. Then you see at Capetown the Malays (Mohammedan), heads wrapped in a handkerchief which serves as a turban, and whose priests, dragging their long robes, walk around majestically and seem to have admiration only for their luxuriant beards. Then, there are the Bushmen, short and stocky Negroes, and the Mozambique Negro.

Since the emancipation of the slaves in 1836, the Dutch

landowners have suffered a great deal and the slaves are not faring any better.

A number of Boers have migrated towards the north and established two republics over which the tricolor flag of Holland reigns with uncontested supremacy. The British government has been forced to recognize their independence. These Boers are robust men, familiar from childhood with danger, tireless hunters whose rifles never miss their aim. They are the terror of the Kaffirs.

Even though among the lower classes of the Cape the language has degenerated a great deal, Dutch is spoken everywhere. Even the English living here are forced to learn it. Though Capetown is more Anglicized, a marked sympathy for the homeland is still maintained here. A Dutchman is sure to be welcomed with open arms. If he travels through the rural districts, the Boers regard him as a member of their own family and they would feel insulted if he took a notion to give them the title of *Mynheer*. One must say to the older men: *"Oom"* (uncle), and to the younger ones: *"Neef"* (cousin or nephew). I would not mind residing for some time in that country of kinsmen and getting better acquainted with my charming feminine "cousins."

The main religion being the reformed Protestant faith, all those who want to become members of the church must know by heart their catechism in Dutch, which contributes more than a little to preserving the language.

Except for a few winter frosts there is no real winter in this colony. Many people have been ruined by a widespread folly for speculation on the mines, though the copper mines of Numa Qua Land could be very promising under good management. The sheep have exceedingly thick tails which they can hardly drag. People melt the grease from it, which makes a delicious butter-like spread on bread. Antelopes are very numerous. The Cape tiger, which is really a leopard, still lives in the caves of Table Mountain, but he would never attack a man, except in self-defense. Mr. Cloete has a handsome specimen of it mounted in his entrance hall which he had killed very near his home one fine morning while taking a walk to breathe the fresh air of the fields. The country carts are usually drawn by nine teams of oxen whose gigantic horns have a six foot span from tip to tip.

Monday, January 28, 1856

We say farewell to the Cape, with Cape Hanglip on our left and Cape Dias on our right. I shall always think with the greatest pleasure of my stay at the Cape. Its history and its people had already given it claims to my affection, even before I ever dreamed of setting foot on African soil. The marks of friendship I received from all those with whom I became acquainted and the thousand kind attentions directed towards me have filled my heart with the deepest feeling of friendship and caused me to form the most ardent wishes for the welfare of its people.

The lust for conquest and territorial expansion must be forgotten in this present century. I don't wish that the Cape change masters and return to Dutch domination. It is my wish that it join its two sisters and form an independent republic, thus becoming in these remote regions, a beacon from which the light of true civilization, of fine arts and letters, once so brilliant in the north of Africa, would shine again in the South. What Egypt has been, the Cape can become.

And thus, here we are back at sea. My stay at the Cape seems like an illusion, a dream. The sea with all its realities is here.

February 15, 1856 [17]

Unable to enter yesterday on account of bad weather, we cruised all night before the promised land of the Île de

France (Mauritius), and, as soon as the sun had turned the mountain tops to gold and made visible the narrow passage to Port St. Louis between the many reefs which guard its entrance, we resume our course. The pilot comes aboard and we anchor. I have cast aside my sea garb and am walking all dressed up on the deck, watchful of a chance to go ashore as soon as possible.

Ah! Here are two men with very British features under exceedingly large-brimmed hats coming to visit us. They look like people of ill omen. A long consultation takes place in the Captain's cabin; they turn out to be doctors, come to tell us that there is an epidemic of smallpox at Port St. Louis which takes a daily toll among the Mauritian population.[18] Rumors begin to spread that no one will be allowed to go ashore. I look mournfully upon my snow-white linen, my patent leather shoes and my sword cane. "Dear objects," I said to them, "you will not be allowed to go ashore. The people of the Île de France, stunned by so many dazzling wonders, have called smallpox to their aid, in order to bar you from their island." Fortunately, the Commodore and the Captain have decided in their infinite wisdom to allow the Staff to go ashore: it is only the members of the crew and the soldiers who must stay on board, because smallpox may attack the rabble but would never dare raise a sacrilegious hand against officers.

"Our poets have often enough shown their lovers reclining on the banks of brooks, among meadows and under the shade of the beech tree. I have wished for mine to sit on the shore of the Sea, at the foot of rocks, under the shade of coconut trees, of banana trees, or of lemon trees in bloom."

Thus, Bernardin de St. Pierre, poet of nature, began his wonderful story of Paul and Virginia; and here I am, on that same island, witness of the love and the unfortunate end of this appealing young couple.[19]

I recognize these places already so vividly described by the

pen of the great master of St. Pierre. This range of high
mountains surrounding Port St. Louis with their sharp and
steep profile, these summits which seem to pierce the clouds,
and the Pouce [the Thumb], upon which my imagination
placed Paul, with his long hair floating in the wind, his hag-
gard eye fixed on a dark spot disappearing in the distance:
the *St. Geran,* carrying away towards a distant shore the one
whom he loved, his life, his only happiness in the world, his
Virginia. Behind this mountain range rises the Pieter Both
[Pieter Botte], whose sharp summit is topped by a globe
which makes it look like a champagne bottle, almost inaccessible to those who would like to reach its summit. There are
only two or three fearless travelers who have succeeded in
resting on that huge ball of stone which tops the steep rock,
at the foot of which is buried one of the first governor-gen-
erals of the Dutch East Indies, named Pieter Both.

The Île de France, although for forty-six years under English domination, is more French than ever before. Don't get
a notion to speak English there—you won't be understood;
the creoles even forbid their children to learn it. We enter
the Bazaar, a huge market place, where all the treasures of the
Tropics are displayed to the eyes of the pale sons of the
north—pineapples, mangoes, bananas, the most succulent
products of nature, here fill the atmosphere with their fra-
grances. The smallest coin available is enough to buy fruit
worth its weight in gold in Europe. What a new spectacle is
offered here to the traveler! Creole ladies, with their dark eyes
and passionate faces, copper-skinned Indians, whose women
are scantily clad in a piece of knee-length calico that leaves
half their bosom bare, children as naked as the day they were
born, then the grave Moslems, the Parsees, and the ugly
Chinese slinking through the crowd like rattlesnakes.
Thieves! Be thrifty, make money, ruin these Christian dogs,
and may Confucius bless you!

The great square is filled with carts, whose coachmen force
the sullen old nags to prance about, and who cry to each
passer-by: "Two dollars, Monsieur le Capitaine, to go to the
Pamplemousses." One of my friends makes the reassuring
observation that, after careful examination, he finds that all
these coachmen bear on their faces the fresh marks of smallpox. Let's take a bath for two shillings to refresh ourselves.

Ah! here is a café! But it seems that the ice cream parlor
over there attracts us even more. "Garçon!" Ah! this word, indispensable in a French café, strikes my ears so pleasantly.
"Garçon!" And I start calling out "garçon" at the top of
my lungs, to the admiration of the whole assembly who can't
quite understand how an American officer could so well call
out: "Garçon, garçon! Some ice cream." "How many, Monsieur?" "For a hundred people, if you like, so long as I get
one myself." "Garçon!" "Monsieur?" "Some water." "Garçon!" "Monsieur?" "A light." "Garçon!" "Monsieur?" "That
is all, go away." If I hadn't been afraid of losing my voice I
would have continued calling "garçon" for the rest of the
day, such was my pleasure in pronouncing and hearing that
magical word. I arrive at the Hôtel d'Europe, the best hotel
in town, but that goes without saying, since I honor it with
my distinguished patronage. The waiters there usually speak
only French. However, they can also speak Hindu and Arabic.
That's a consolation for the British! Tonight at six, table
d'hôte. Ah! That's what I like, and what I like even more is
that I'm invited to it. Obviously the British have not yet
spoiled the ways of life of the Île de France.

At the table we laugh, we sing; we are served some soup,
genuine Julienne. Wine is plentiful and water scarce, thank
God! Champagne is now beginning to pop, to foam, and
make the rounds. We discuss theater, parties, women, and
beautiful France, so far away, and little France where we are
here all together. A gentleman from Marseilles joins us and

we discuss the Canebièrre,[20] the beautiful ladies of Arles,[21] and spend a delightful evening together.

The next day, a party is organized to go to the Pample-mousses, seven miles away from St. Louis. All along the way we see a teeming crowd composed mostly of Hindus whom the British government sends here, instead of the emancipated slaves, to work the fields. The road is lined with magnificent trees, mostly tamarisks. Their leaves are very fine and deli-cate; by their quantity they form a delightful shade which protects the pilgrim from the rays of the tropical sun.

Immense fields, covered with sugar cane, bear witness to the fact that there is no country in the world that produces as much per acre of that honeyed substance which sweetens all that nature has made too acid or too bitter, so indispensable in tea and coffee and without which confectioners might as well bury themselves alive. In the distance high mountains loom, above which rises the Pieter Both, bearing like another Atlas a globe on his head.

Never say upon leaving a botanical garden: "I have seen palm trees and coconut trees." Instead, go to the Indies. There you will see the palm tree, that graceful column hold-ing aloft its swaying plume of foliage high in the air. There you will see the coconuts smile at you from atop their slender trunk, so tall and slim that reaching them seems impossible. You need but extend your hand in order to pick the pine-apple, that ornament of our tables. In foliage so brilliantly green that your eyes can hardly rest on it, you will see the mango and banana. It is in the garden of Pamplemousse that I picked, for the first time in my life, the nutmeg coated with mace. Here in the tropics what an infinite field is offered by Nature for man's contemplation! What force, what vigor in vegetation! You see the trees grow, the plants unfold their leaves, grass grow under your very steps, and the millions of shades of that endless number of variegated colors, each more brilliant than the next, and the vertical sun which lends life, so it seems, even to the stony matter of rocks. No doubt that Italian, whose name escapes me, was quite right when he told an Englishman: "How I pity you, for you have no sun in your country!" Then, there are the Philoas, replacing here our weeping willows, which make a wailing sound when the wind agitates their foliage, the bamboos which, once deprived of their leaves, will be used as canes by the pale inhabitants of the north, and the Pandanus whose bark is used to make sugar sacks.

At the Hôtel d'Europe, I became acquainted with Captain Ben Hamet, a frigate captain of His Highness, the Sultan of Muscat, a charming fellow who, in spite of Mohammed, drank wine like a Knight Templar, spoke French and English beautifully, and squandered his money like any true Christian. Mr. J. Tennant, to whom I had a letter of introduction, welcomed me most cordially. I shall never forget a certain gentleman I met, whose name I have forgotten. I saw him almost every day during my stay in St. Louis. As I was about to leave St. Louis, I went to say farewell, when that model of hospitality told me: "My dear Sir, if you ever return here, you must allow me to have you at my home and introduce you to my wife and my children." Good Heavens! Wouldn't it be worthwhile returning to the Île de France just to meet Madame and the family?

Tonight I had the pleasure of seeing a Hindu procession. There was a huge crowd. The Hindus carried their idols preceded by lighted torches and followed by a band of musicians making a frightful noise with their drums and their cymbals. These dark and coppery figures—half nude, screaming and singing, the eerie light of the torches, the white robes—created a most picturesque scene.

Vermouth wine is drunk a lot on the Île de France. That's a wine which you couldn't value enough in the Indies and it is sold here quite cheaply, five dollars a dozen [bottles]. You can buy a dozen bottles of red wine for three dollars. At the Hôtel d'Europe they charge three dollars a day. Business places open at seven in the morning and close at four in the afternoon. The officers of the English garrison don't like it too much here, because the Creoles, considering them usurpers, are completely indifferent towards them and almost never invite them into their homes.

Thursday, February 21, 1856

After having received aboard the mail for Point de Galle which we had agreed to carry, we left at six in the evening. It was a magnificent evening. The sky, which until now had been overcast, was now of that brilliant blue one sees only in the tropical regions. The island unfolds before our eyes with the peaks of its mountains. The first rays of the moon silver the last summits of the Île de France which soon disappear in the horizon, leaving us with the slumbering waves of the Indian Ocean.

March 6, 1856

This morning we cast our anchor before Point de Galle.[22] As I enter the city I can't help but admire the still-solid walls that surround it and I regret for a moment the fickleness of things human. Three and one-half centuries have gone by during which the island of Ceylon has three times changed masters. About three hundred and sixty years ago, the intrepid Vasco da Gama, with a handful of men, went ashore in the long boat when he saw the smooth beach of the Spice Island. Setting foot aground, he heard the familiar crowing of a great many roosters and for that reason he called it Punto di Galle, Rooster's Point. This handful of heroes immediately started working and built a fortress whose solid walls have resisted so far the ravages of time. For one hundred and fifty years the glorious descendants of Albuquerque and Vasco da Gama knew how to maintain their position on the "Pearl of the Indies," but another sun was rising on the seas of the Indies before which all others were going to wane. A small nation of merchants, occupying a territory no larger than that of Ceylon, having shaken off the yoke of the most powerful monarch of the Earth, was now sending her tricolor flag sailing to all the known places of the new El Dorado. The Portuguese, weary of exploits and triumphs, degenerated by luxury, were no longer those brave companions of Albuquerque, full of energy and courage, and they surrendered, almost without resistance, the fruits of their ancestors' efforts and perseverance. The gate and the walls of the old fortress has remained the same, to this day bearing witness to the rights of the original masters. But the coat of arms of Portugal was replaced by the Lion of Holland, and it, in turn, gave way to another one, flanked by a unicorn and the melodious harp of the Emerald Isle.

Point de Galle has a lovely little bay surrounded by coconut groves, and in the distance high mountains appear with the famous Adam's peak from which, according to tradition, that venerable father—others say it was the god Buddha—betook himself in one single stride into the Kingdom of Siam. The inhabitants will still show you his footprint, five times longer than that of an ordinary foot.

I went to the Lighthouse Hotel. Its worthy owner, Monsieur André, greeted us like old friends. He belonged to an old Dutch family, and, although he had never left the island where he was born, had never known any other dominion than that of the British, old Dutch blood bubbled in his veins. He took me aside and treated me to a genuine gin and bitters. "Ah! the Dutch!" he said. "They knew how to treat the natives. Even today, the Hindus will address the descendants of the Dutch families with the deepest respect, and they will never dare step ahead of them in the street—but the English! Bah—!" "But which one of the three nations," I interrupted, "that ever held dominion over Ceylon was the best liked?" "Well," he answered, "that's certainly the British. They were the ones that abolished slavery and they gave equitable laws. But the Dutch," he sighed again, "they knew how to govern with an iron hand, and how to keep the natives within the limits of respect and obedience. May it please God that, before I close my eyes, I would have the pleasure to see the Dutch flag raised over the battlements of Point de Galle." And the old Dutchman blew billows of smoke and drank his genuine gin and bitters, alone faithful to his ancestors.

The Dutch language is not spoken any more at Point de Galle. Mr. André is the only one who speaks it well. At Colombo it is better preserved, but here they speak only Singhalese [the vernacular of the native], a degenerated Portuguese, and English. Great pictures on the walls of the church indicate that here rest the remains of Hoog Wel Edelgeboren Heeren Governors of Galle, overleden 16 . . . , "the noble and well-born Governors of Galle who died in the 16 . . . [seventeenth century]." [23]

Once out of the city you see nothing but a multitude of coconut groves, the tree par excellence of the Indies. A man who owns even only five such trees is a man of independent means. They supply him with enough food for the year, oil, milk, wood to build a hut with palm fronds for the roof. Ships are sometimes made entirely of that tree. The ship itself is built of coconut wood, the masts are coconut tree trunks, the rigging is made of coco fiber, and even the cargo is coconuts and coconut trees.

On the main road to Colombo, I saw a genuine elephant

doing the work of sixty men. When we arrived, that well-trained animal fell on his knees, walked on three legs and performed a thousand other such tricks, all at the command of his master. Snakes are plentiful here. There are thirty-three species, all venomous, especially the frightful *cobra de capello* (hooded cobra).

It was in Ceylon that, for the first time in my life, I saw a Buddhist temple. It was located a few steps away from the road on a small hillock and surrounded by groves. The priests, clad in yellow robes, their heads completely shaven, let us inside. There one sees the great god Buddha in all possible postures, standing, sitting, and lying. The largest statue measures about twenty feet in height, is yellow and made of clay. The walls are covered with figures depicting the different noteworthy episodes of the great God's life. Incense always burns before the statue. There, for the first time in my life, I saw these fervent disciples of Reincarnation bowing before their God. Poor Buddhists, whose greatest desire is, after purification by several reincarnations, to re-enter nothingness, or, as they naïvely explain it, to be absorbed by the rays of the divine essence. Not to exist anymore, to be completely extinct—that is the utmost bliss for them.

The Singhalese are a mild and shy people by nature, and chaste of morals. When you represent to them the "truths of the Gospel," they answer: "We do not see that you Christian people live better than we do. Before judging of a faith, we judge of its works, and we fail to see how you carry out these holy doctrines of your great prophet, Jesus."

Mr. Austin, a merchant of Galle, was kind enough to take me to visit his plantation at Wackwalla, where he grows citronella, from which he extracts the aromatic oil known the world over under the name *oleum citronellum*. I shall never forget the pleasant surprise Mr. Austin had in store for me. After having passed in his carriage through coconut tree plantations on a land which, only twenty years before, was nothing but an impenetrable jungle infested with ferocious animals, we arrived at his bungalow built on a hilltop. There I found myself carried back instantly into the civilized world, that of elegant apartments and magnificent furniture, and I allowed myself to recline casually in a great Chinese easy chair. A Hindu was ordered to prepare dinner, and, within half an hour, we were served a meal worthy of "Very" or one of the "Provençal Brothers," [24] with even a genuine steak. After having passed the Cape of Good Hope, one abandons all hope of eating any beef or veal, for the wretched Brahma oxen, about as large as our house cats, certainly do not deserve that name.

Strolling in the vicinity of Galle, I chanced to pass a very lovely country house. I was invited to enter and the owner, a native, showed me about his house with the courtesy of a perfect English gentleman. His name was Don Nicholas Dias. He showed me the ornaments that Singhalese chiefs wear on festive days. Men and women both wear their hair pulled back and tied in a knot at the nape of the neck and in that knot they place combs of tortoise shell, golden arrows encrusted with diamonds, and other precious stones; a dagger whose sheath and handle are strewn with diamonds is worn hanging from a gold-embroidered belt.

"Ah!" said my host, "you American officers behave much better than the English. You are gay, and you do not treat us in that condescending manner that they have." Wasn't that good man entitled to our consideration, entertaining us as he did in his own home, making it his duty to instruct us in the customs and ancestral traditions of his people? Oh, you civilized nations, fair-skinned people, how many lessons of true barbarism you give those aborigines of the two Indies, whom you call savages! You use the term as a sort of excuse for the outrageous thefts you have committed and will commit against them.

When I left the home of our worthy Singhalese friend, it was dark. I saw, rising from the tall grasses, an infinite number of fireflies, which lit our path with their phosphorescent glow.

These thousands of lights flying about us, the somber depths of the coconut palm forest, the flickering of a torch carried by a small Hindu boy, the calm sea, now silent, now breaking suddenly against the reefs with a dull sound, covering them with sprays of luminous foam, the towering walls of the old Portuguese fortress outlined in a darker shade against the bluish waves of the Ocean—all these impressed me so deeply that I began to think that *The Thousand and One Nights* tales were coming true.

March 11, 1856

We weigh anchor, and, as this fertile island disappears from view, I want to caution those who may visit these parts against the merchants of precious stones who will try to sell you their wares. These stones are of no value, sometimes even being pieces of cut glass imported from Marseilles. There are some most elegant, fancy boxes, wonderfully made. For those you will be asked three pounds sterling. Offer ten shillings and they will be glad to give them to you at that price.

March 21, 1856

There are places which, through the serenity of their climate, the fertility of their soil, the freshness of their vegetation, and the beauty of their landscapes, have acquired the name of pearl, of queen, etc.[25] Thus, the island of Cuba is the pearl of the West Indies, Provence is the garden of France, and by the same token I do not hesitate to name the island of Penang, the "Pearl of the Indies," a real little jewel, where the nabobs of Calcutta, exhausted and debilitated by the burning sun of India, come to recover their health and the strength of their youth in the cool and aromatic air of its mountains. Pulo Penang is not large. It is but a pygmy compared to its neighbors, Java, Borneo, Sumatra. It was given as a dowry to an Englishman who married the daughter of the King of Queda,[26] himself a vassal of his Magnificent Majesty, the King of Siam. In turn, our Englishman sold the island to the honorable company of the East Indies.

Mr. Currier, the American Consul, was really most hospitable to our staff. His house was always open to us. His table, always covered with everything that the Indies produces or that Europe sends, was subjected during two weeks to the lusty attacks of our appetites, rendered voracious by the restrictions at sea.

I had the pleasure to meet, at Mr. Currier's, my Chief, Mr. Townsend Harris, Plenipotentiary of the United States to the Court of Siam and Consul-General of Japan.[27]

The city of Penang is built on a plain; a five-mile road leads from the wharf to the foot of the moutain. I went there every day by palanquin in order to avail myself of a magnificent bath which nature has been kind enough to place there. I refer to a brook which, having its source on top of the mountains, flows here into a lovely cascade. The water leaps and foams from stone to stone and when it reaches the bottom is clearer and purer than it could be made by all the filtering systems of the Earth, patented by all the governments of the world. Then it falls into a pool whose depth is not in excess of five feet. This pool is set in a grove of nutmeg trees. What a pleasure, when you are hot and tired from the trip, to divest yourself of your clothes, those encumbrances of civilization, and to dive into the pool. The water pours upon you in torrents and the current is so strong that if you did not huddle by a granite rock, you would soon be carried away in the swift rapids. You leave the bath another man; you feel yourself electrified; every pore of your skin is breathing; not a speck of dirt remains on you. Then, you take a freshly picked coconut, cut a hole in it, and drink the milk in a single draught. This is living! "Living as a savage," you will perhaps tell me, but the savages are not as deprived of common sense as they may seem to be.

I spent a few days at Mr. Currier's bungalow, located on the top of a mountain. Riding ponies, we slowly climbed the steep slope of the mountain. The foliage alongside the road is so thick that we could not glimpse any of the surroundings. At a point rather high up, a clearing in the forest allows us a lovely view of the valley. Once at the bungalow, built atop a huge block of granite, the most magnificent landscape I have ever seen unfolds before my enchanted eyes. The setting sun was painting with gold the summits of the mountains, while the uncertain glow of twilight had replaced in the valley the brilliant light of day. From where I sat on the front steps of the bungalow, the steep slope of the mountain led my gaze into a magnificent valley, covered with trees, bestrewn with gigantic rocks of granite weathered into a black hue. On the opposite side of that valley I could see another mountain, and behind that one, the triangular-shaped plain on which we could make out the buildings of the city, then the Strait of Malacca, as peaceful there under our eyes as a silver lake spreading its limpid waters between the island of Penang and the peninsula of Malacca. Night had already spread out her dark veil, but the crystal-clear air of the Indies allowed us to distinguish the mountains of Quetta and the southernmost range of The Himalayas, ramifications of the Asiatic giant. All living things in the forest were singing their evensongs, the crickets beating their fast rhythms, the mon-

keys chattering high in the trees. But what use is there in trying to describe a scene which the pen of the greatest poet
would be incapable of transcribing on paper? I stop, for I
feel that it is a sacrilege against nature to go on with my description. Her charms must strike the senses directly, and not
through the inadequate medium of description. Let me take a
brush and trace a sketch of the beauties which surround me.
Once the sketch is finished, I raise my eyes and gaze upon the
original. Heavens! Just as the hideous old Malayan woman
who chews her betel nut and tints her toothless gums with its
red juice little resembles the Venus de Medici, so my miserable sketch scarcely resembles that Eden which I, wretched
mortal, have attempted to duplicate! Would that I were
endowed with the talent of a Ruysdael or of a Koekkoek,[28] or
that of so many other geniuses who have added a ray of light
to the halo of our schools of painting; then I would be able
to give life to the inanimate canvas. Genius, however, is not
something one can give oneself, and what we cannot re-
produce we can at least enjoy by feasting our eyes upon it.

I visited the establishment of the good priests of the French
Mission. There young savages learn all that is necessary in
order to practice the ministry of a Catholic priest, and once
ordained, they are sent back to their native countries. There
were Chinese, Cochin Chinese, Siamese, etc., each dressed in
the native costume of his own country. Father Martin showed
us his museum of natural science, in which he has collected a
sample of every kind of animal life on Penang. It is the only
relaxation he allows himself in a life devoid of all that could
make it pleasant, for he lives only for God and the good of the
Church, at a salary of twenty dollars a year!

April 2, 1856

We leave the island of Penang. Our voyage through the
Strait of Malacca is most peaceful. I feel as if I were sailing

on one of those great rivers that flow across the immense territory of the United States. We sail past Tanjong Boelus, the southernmost point of Asia, and arrive at Singapore on April 4, 1856.

Singapore and its harbor are filled with ships from all parts of the world; there are Chinese junks and ships owned by his Magnificent Majesty of Siam whose red ensign, with the famous white elephant in its center, waves in the breeze.

The London Hotel, the best of the place, is not renowned for its good food, but the prices there are quite reasonable, and that is a consolation.

The French squadron was anchored at Singapore—two corvettes and a steam corvette.

The esplanade of Singapore, a sea-front promenade, is very beautiful. We visit the famous Chinese Pagoda and the store of the illustrious Whampoa.[29] The latter gave us a letter of introduction to visit his house, a few miles from town. That house blends the European and the Chinese tastes. About forty years ago Singapore did not even exist, and now it is one of the busiest ports of the Indies, because Singapore is a free port, whereas the Dutch, in spite of so many examples, pursue their ill-advised system of exclusive trade.

April 7, 1856

We leave Singapore and after a seven-day sail we arrive on April 14 at the roadstead of Siam, at the mouth of the Menam River [Mother of Waters].[30] Eight days later a small steamboat called the *Royal Seat Siamese Steam Force* comes to pick us up. We get aboard and the little steamer sets its course for Bangkok, capital of Siam, sixty miles from our ship. We were accompanied by a band and a detachment of marines carried by two huge Cochin Chinese boats of one hundred forty oars each. A seventeen-gun salute, sounded in honor of the Ambassador, enveloped the *San Jacinto* in a cloud of smoke. Upon

arriving at Paknam, at the mouth of the Menam, we step
ashore. A dinner, arranged as much as possible in the European manner, is awaiting us in a Pondoppo with three
levels.[31] A Christian mandarin of Portuguese origin, Don
Gabriel Fereira de Valverde, served us as an interpreter. He
claimed to be an artillery officer and had on his head an old
round hat with a gold braid. He wore an old jacket embroidered in gold, Chinese style trousers of white silk with red
stripes, and his shoulders supported the burden of colonel's
epaulettes, most likely owned formerly by an officer of
Napoleon.[32]

After dinner we started again up river for Bangkok. The
river is rather wide. Its banks do not, anywhere, show any
sign of cultivation. The trees grow as God willed. The palm
trees and the graceful, slender arecas sway gracefully above
the jungle. Some bamboo huts built on stilts three or four
feet above the ground can be glimpsed through the foliage.

The king had had built for us a large bamboo house with a
huge dining hall and seven bedrooms with two beds each.
In adjacent houses were barracks for our soldiers and our
musicians, supply houses, etc.

The Siamese government did all in its power to treat us
well. We had three boats and seventy oarsmen as well as the
Portuguese interpreter at our disposal. The way of life here
being so different from that of civilized nations, it is not the
Siamese who are at fault if all food served to us was not always to our liking. Chickens, ducks, sweet potatoes, rice cur-
ries, birds'-nest soup, beef infrequently, and a few suckling
pigs—these were our fare. All that would certainly have been
quite satisfactory to our tastes if everything that was set before us had not been smothered in garlic! Even a Provençal
would have said, "That's too much!"

As for fruit, we received some continually from the two
kings and the nobles, all beautifully arranged on copper

dishes and carried by slaves. One night our great dining room was really filled with it. It was the present of the Second King—pyramids of mangoes, of litchi nuts, of mangosteens, of rambutans, of pineapples and a thousand other fruits were blending their fragrance under the roof of our embassy. I cherish a fond memory of the mangosteen, which I will never see again, these small, snow-white balls within a pink-hued shell. They have been compared to the lips of the young Malayan girls, these balls which when pressed gently between the tongue and palate melt like real country cream. The mangosteen is definitely the most exquisite fruit, the noblest, the most delightful one of the tropics. Its worthless counterpart, the durian, of which the natives are inordinately fond, spreads such a stench that I consider it very discourteous to even place it on the table. And yet, the Europeans, by trying over and over again, have convinced themselves that the durian is a delicious fruit. And why not? A prison's lonely cell becomes, through force of habit, dear to the prisoner; harlots are loved by their husbands. Why shouldn't a durian, though it be an essence of all the refuse of the world, seem like roses and hyacinths to its admirers? I wanted to do as the others and taste it. Holding my nose, I managed to eat a small piece. It tastes precisely like garlic and sugar in a state of putrefaction, and never again in my life will I defile my lips with this aggregate of all foul smells, although I have been told the Malayans may sell their wives' virtue for a durian.

On the day when His Magnificent Majesty made it his pleasure to grant us audience, richly decorated boats came for us.[33] In the first one, a sort of throne had been set up, intended for the letter from the President of the United States to His Majesty of Siam. I had the *honor* to place said letter on the throne, after having walked between a double row of soldiers. When I arrived they played drums and I was rendered all the military honors due to the Chief of State. I was very much like that donkey in the fable who walked down the street bearing a box of relics. Everyone knelt in the dust when he passed by, not on account of the donkey, but because of the relics he bore. Thus these honors were not for me, but for the letter of the President, of which I was the *lowly bearer*.

The second boat carried the presents from the President, the third, the Ambassador, his interpreter and myself in my capacity as secretary, while the Commodore and his staff followed in other boats.

Upon arrival at the royal palace, the American flag was saluted with twenty-one guns. Our musicians replied by playing "God Save the King." Waiting for us at the palace landing were litters upon which we were carried to the reception hall where we were served some refreshments. All along the way within the walls of the palace, we were carried between two rows of soldiers armed with different kinds of weapons and dressed in various costumes of the world. Two or three companies had uniforms similar to that of European soldiers, except that their feet were bare and their faces copper-colored. Others carried long knives fastened to sticks; still others, armed with crossbows, were clad only in long petticoats which made them look like old women. Some, again, had shields and halberds; to sum up, the army of His Magnificent Majesty was garbed so as to look like a troupe of extras belonging to some third-rate theater who, having shopped at all the used-clothes dealers in town, were now ready to stand indifferently as an army of five centuries ago, or a group of Swiss mountain folk. Thirty elephants, more or less, carrying on their enormous backs a kind of culverin, completed the scene. At last we arrived at the door of the reception hall.

The Ambassador took the letter of the President of the United States and carried it on a golden plate between the Commodore and the interpreter, then myself and the officers of the *San Jacinto*. The Siamese officers who accompanied us knelt down before the door. At a given signal, the doors swung open. The Siamese dignitaries salaamed three times (they first brought their joined hands to their foreheads, and then forehead and hands would be lowered to the ground, as though kissing the dust). Once that ceremony was over our escort of Siamese dignitaries proceeded on their knees towards the throne. We followed them, walking as free men do, as free men ought to do, with a firm stance and a steady gaze, in the midst of that *herd of slaves*.

What a sight that was for civilized men! The hall was filled with a thousand, more or less, of the most illustrious representatives of Siam's blue blood all lying on the floor and none daring to raise a sacrilegious glance toward the man—a man just as they were—for fear that his royal thunderbolt might strike them dead right then and there.

We walked about thirty paces and ascended a platform slightly raised above the rest of the room on which were dignitaries of a higher rank, and, taking another step up, we arrived at the highest level of the hall where the greatest dignitaries of the Kingdom, the ministers of state, the princes of royal blood, the brothers and sons of the King were all, to the last man, prostrate in the dust, in spite of their rich robes of silk encrusted with gold and gems, and in spite of their high rank and family ties which united them to the person of the King. Royalty eclipses all. Royalty can annihilate, erase with one stroke of the pen, rank, power, and high office because royalty and it alone is their source.

The audience hall has very high ceilings and is built in the shape of a cross. Outside, a pagoda towers over the center of the roof. This pagoda is supported by four immense Egyptian-style pillars, which, in spite of their gigantic size, seem very thin and slender because of their soaring height. Between these pillars stands the great white nine-storied umbrella, almost as high as the pillars. At the far end of the room stands

the throne, rising six feet above the level of the highest platform. There sits the King. You can't see the steps because the
throne is built right into the wall and the King ascends it
from the other side. His Majesty was not wearing a crown.
Instead, he wore a toque of velvet surrounded with diamonds
and topped by a yellow plume. At the foot of the throne
four dignitaries were each holding a saber of gold; two others
were holding muskets. We bowed deeply and sat on the floor
because the etiquette of the court of Siam does not permit
chairs.

The Ambassador first presented the letter to the King and
then addressed him upon a given signal. When the speech was
over we stood up, made another bow and then sat down again.
His Majesty, after having asked a few questions and having
read aloud the Presidential letter in English as well as in
Siamese, then gave a signal; immediately two immense curtains, hanging from the ceiling on either side of the room,
were drawn by an invisible hand slowly and with a thrice-
stopped motion, hiding in the final movement the sacred
person of His Magnificent Majesty behind their folds. At
each of the three pauses of the curtains the dignitaries brought
their fingers to their foreheads and prostrated themselves in
the dust. The audience being over, terminated by that bizarre
drawing of the two curtains, everyone rose and, after having
dined in an adjacent pavilion, we departed. I must not forget
to mention that wine and other refreshments were served
during the audience, as well as cigars, for where smoking is
concerned the etiquette of the Court of Siam is most liberal,
and all the dignitaries, although practically flat on their
stomachs, were smoking like chimneys.

The next day we had an audience with His Majesty, the
Second King,[34] who also had a court and state ministers of
his own, although the real power is in the hands of his
brother, the First King. The Second King is the heir-apparent

to the throne. Somdetch Phra Bard Pawarendr Phra Chau Yu Hua, Second King of Siam, bore the title of Prince Chou Fa [Lord of Heaven] before his accession to the throne. He is a very cultured man who speaks English fluently, is informed concerning all recent inventions and enjoys the conversation of those who come from Europe or America, as is quite understandable for a man whose intelligence and education are so immensely superior to that of his subjects. Let a stranger be announced; he will always find the palace door open and can be assured of spending a few hours in the most pleasant manner. The Second King has had a European-style house built within the enclosure of his palace, and has decorated it most tastefully. There you will find a library containing a nice assortment of classical and practical books, a laboratory filled with machines, electrical instruments, etc., a study where you will usually find him writing—and the Second King writes a beautiful hand. The drawing room is wonderfully well decorated; you will find there European chairs, sofas, and tables, some paintings and a magnificent mirror. There, the Second King, after he has performed the daily farce in the audience hall with everyone prostrated before him, will greet a stranger like a true gentleman and entertain him in the most gracious manner. He will invite him to sit down, will offer him cigars, and, performing the honors of the table himself, will pour tea or coffee for him, not even neglecting to ask whether he likes cream or sugar. Meanwhile, his own son, Prince George Washington—perhaps the future King of Siam—is kneeling behind him together with the King's wives.

The Second King has artillery which is admirably well served; his soldiers are dressed in the European manner and maneuver extremely well. Some élite companies drill as well as any of the best soldiers of the world. I saw in his barracks the carbine with bayonet of the Zouaves. He has, in his study, samples of the most recent models of guns and pistols.

The city of Bangkok is but one street of houses built along the river. The river, too, forms a street in itself, a street of floating houses moored in rows along either bank. The houses are wooden, of a very simple exterior, and they float on bamboos. Those that are built on firm ground rest on a stilt-like understructure, raised about eight feet above ground to protect the dwellers from miasma, animals, snakes, etc.

The Menam offers a very animated and quite unexpected scene, for it is the main street of Bangkok because of the floating houses. One very seldom goes on foot, most of the time by boat. Now and then you glimpse a young Siamese girl paddling her fragile canoe loaded with fruit and vegetables which she is bringing to market. Now you see a boat filled with merchandise of which the Chinese, always the same industrious and cunning scoundrels of the Celestial Empire, are trying to rid themselves. A large gondola in which a great Lord of the Court, lazily reclining on a richly embroidered cushion, is just going for a morning ride passes you swiftly as an arrow. Who are those shaven-pated men, draped in folds of yellow robes, who casually paddle their gondola as though nothing mattered to them? They are Buddhist priests. This boat, with its load of young women all dressed in yellow, means that some Lord of the Court has graciously allowed his harem to come and breathe the pure morning air on the peaceful water of the Menam, Mother of Waters.

But what sudden change has occurred among the boats that fairly covered the river a moment ago? The Menam, which offered a most animated spectacle, has become deserted as though by magic! Barks, boats, canoes, skiffs, and gondolas have sought refuge on the other side of the river and they huddle against the floating houses. In spite of my orders I am taken there too. I fulminate against the oarsmen; I gesticulate but they do not take any notice of my very explicit gestures. I turn to my interpreter, but the poor devil is already on his knees and is hiding his head between his hands. All the other visible heads are prostrated on the floor of the crafts and all the houses and shops are closing. Ah! I am beginning to understand. This great procession of boats drawing near belongs to His Magnificent Majesty and his retinue. As a mark of honor, the King's oarsmen, while paddling, make the most awful noise. The first one gives a cry so shrill that my ears are still sore from it and all the others answer with "Ba, wa, wa, wa." The performance is repeated every minute. Others bang long sticks against the gunwales, and, as if that is not enough, a band of musicians with gongs, drums, and instruments—my meager talent is not up to describing the astonishing qualities of these, but they make a lot of noise—illustrate very well the proverb: "More noise, more honor." When I ask my still prostrate interpreter for an explanation of this unholy racket, he answers—as he does all other questions—by the refrain of that Spanish comedy: *"Costumbres del pais!"* Local customs.

A magnificent boat, with about one hundred oarsmen, makes its way among the others. Under a red canopy with golden curtains sits the King; three dignitaries of the highest rank are lying prone in front of him. Too bad the oarsmen cannot paddle in that position too, otherwise they would surely have to stay prostrate like everyone else. The man who could invent a method to paddle a boat while keeping one's hands joined and one's face to the ground would make a fortune in Siam!

When His Magnificent Majesty enjoys a bit of cool air is precisely when all his subjects must suffocate, because whenever he passes one must close doors and windows, and those who can't hurry back home in time must flatten themselves against the earth. All the bridges on the route of the Royal Gondola are removed because Royalty cannot bear to pass underneath a path where others place their feet. Also, for this reason one seldom sees two-story houses in Siam.

One day, I was watching His Majesty inspect a stronghold (if you can call it that. The name of "weakhold" would be more appropriate). The King was walking leisurely on the battlements. Before the fortress an immense plain stretched and every person on it was lying prone, with the exception of an old dog who was sensible enough to go on with his walk (but dogs always have privileges of the kind, witness our military parades). With all those prone and motionless people, I felt as though I were surveying a battlefield where, by some extraordinary chance, the dead all have fallen forward instead of backwards.

Except for the palaces of the two Kings and those of a few nobles of the highest rank, the dwellings of the Siamese are very poor. As we did during our own Middle Ages, so here all the money is consumed in building temples called Watts. These edifices are usually topped by three or four roofs, one above the other, with tiles of different colors. At the extremity of the roofs you see a huge golden dragontail.

It is especially the Watt Pho, within the palace's enclosure, that distinguishes itself from the others by the elegance of its court, of its pagodas, and especially by the enormous statue of my old friend, the god Buddha, which is one hundred and seventy-five feet long, no more, no less. The god is in a sleeping position, and is gilt from head to foot. If you stand near the head, the feet, although perfectly well proportioned, do not seem any larger than those of an ordinary man. In the enclosure of that same Watt, surrounded by artificial rocks, there is a man-made pond in which live the two sacred crocodiles.

The Bangkok pagodas (each King has one built to commemorate his reign) seen from a distance seem to offer the most elegant proportions. Seen at close range they lose a great deal and appear as nothing more than a bizarre mixture of pieces of ceramic tile of various colors. Their slim and well-proportioned outlines end in spirals. When you sail on the Menam, you see them as shafts piercing the dense foliage of the trees to join the clouds.

Siam is a kingdom where everything belongs to the King: what he is kind enough to scorn goes to the nobles and the rest to the people. But although they are all slaves, one to the other, there is a caste of pariahs that are slaves to the slaves! I mean the *women*. A father may sell his daughter, a brother his sister. In the presence of her husband the wife is on her knees. If he is bored with her, he may sell her again. The husband can sleep all the time; he makes his wife do the work. In Bangkok more than half of the people I saw working were women, especially on the river. It was almost always women I saw paddling the boats. Once I saw a big fat fellow stretched out on his matting, smoking his *bourri* (a Siamese cigar) while two young girls were struggling with all their might to paddle the boat against the current. I was seized with a desire to throw the miserable wretch into the Menam. I expressed my indignation to the interpreter; but he answered with a shrug: *"Costumbres del pais!"* The nobles have several wives. His late Majesty of Siam had the rare bliss of being the father of twenty-one children within one year. When the nobles are short of money, they place two or three of their wives in a house of prostitution and withdraw them when the wives have earned enough. The poor usually have only one wife. Although by her work a wife brings a good rate of interest on the price she costs her husband, a wife is always expensive. That is why the poor have to be content with one. You find here some young girls who are fairly pretty, or rather would be if they did not chew the betel nut which dyes their gums red and fills their mouths with a liquid of the same color so that they spit constantly. They also shave their heads completely like the men with the exception of one small tuft which they suffer to remain on the crown, and they blacken their teeth. Thus, you will easily understand that they would not look precisely like Venus. Their arms and legs are well rounded and they have beautifully shaped little feet which support calves that would be the envy of a *grisette*.[35] Furthermore, the *grisette* must always raise her dress to show hers, while the Siamese girl's are always exposed to public admiration, since her clothing consists solely of a sarong which she is adept at wrapping around her hips in a short pants effect which covers only the tops of her knees and leaves all the bust uncovered. However, she usually wears a shawl tied around her breasts. A fact that doesn't contribute at all to the beauty of the sex is that the women usually have surprisingly long and hanging breasts. The men wear only the sarong. I am still speaking of the common people, although the King and the nobles, once they have put aside their ceremonial dress, wear only the sarong.

Everywhere in the streets you will find altars on which are male genitals hewn from wood. Women go there to pray to have children; they go there also to obtain cures for venereal diseases.

In the midst of these altars where the shame of man is displayed, and in the midst of these temples whose dragontails shine in the sun atop the roofs covered with their bizarre tiles, beneath which the *talapoins* (Buddhist monks) in their yellow robes burn incense while muttering the esoteric words of Pali before the statues of Buddha, you see now and then a humble and modest cross, glimpsed through the foliage of a tamarisk. Perhaps a palm tree offering the shade of its graceful plume to a chapel in which the clear-toned singing and humble prayers, rising towards heaven above these monuments of paganism, above the Watts and pagodas, recalls to our minds faraway places and the religion into which a be-

loved father or sweet mother took care to guide our childhood.

The French priests of the Brotherhood of Foreign Missions
do all that is in their power to propagate the Catholic religion
and lead a life of complete abnegation. Once I visited a
worthy priest in his home, and what a home! Good Heavens!
For a civilized man who has seen the dawn in the charming
countryside of beautiful France! A rough wooden table, two
or three chairs and an old bench surrounded by a partition
filled with cracks, a few poles supporting a coconut palm roof:
that was the parsonage. The priest entered; he wasn't expecting a stranger and he tried, when he saw me, to hide with his
left hand the holes in his cassock, while extending his right
hand. Do not hide these holes, oh, you generous soul who
sacrifices all that is enjoyable in life to bring poor Indians
back to their Saviour and their God! Do not hide these holes
of your cassock for they shine before the eyes of God with
more brilliance than the tiaras that adorn the brows of
Princes!

He told me he was perfectly happy working for the glory of
the Church; but the memory of one's homeland must be dear
even to the least mundane man, and it seemed to me that the
sounds of his mother tongue, when I spoke it, I who had
only recently left the land where the Sun sets, comforted him.

As I was bidding farewell to the Bishop of Mellos, Apostolic
Vicar in Siam,[36] I told him "But, Monseigneur, surely you
will not spend the rest of your days in this savage land. You
will return to France?" "A year ago," he answered, "I was in
France and they wanted to keep me there, but I came back
here." And he added with a smile, "One must die on the field
of battle."

I wish to avoid as far as possible disputes over religious
matters. These only irritate and they never convince, but if
one is to judge impartially from the facts that are evident, I

do not see the same spirit of self-denial in the manner of living of the Protestant missionaries who are here. They live in good houses, well aired and comfortable, with their wives and their children. They have servants, boats, and oarsmen always ready to take them wherever they please to go. They have well-chosen libraries. In short, they are as comfortable as anyone could be in Siam. Far from wanting to condemn them for living well, I confess I would do the same if I were in their place. But, in spite of all people can say, I cannot call this "to sacrifice one's self" as the missionaries of the Catholic faith do. They say themselves that they do not proselytize. Only the few children whom they adopt and a few servants attend their sermons; but they claim that by making the Siamese witness their manner of living, by showing them charming family scenes, and by teaching the youth of the country in their schools they will bring the Siamese, little by little, to civilization. Personally, I think they serve religious ideas, rather than political. That's all for the better. They serve a good cause, and I cannot deny that in their schools where they teach to all those who wish to learn, they will contribute to the civilization of the Siamese.

They sacrifice themselves for the holy cause of temperance by a rigorous abstention from intoxicating beverages. They feel a holy revulsion to even a little glass of wine. If they manage to make the Siamese drink only tea, arak [37] will be very cheap in Europe. I was spending an evening at one missionary's home and we were discussing Ida Pfeiffer's [38] travels: "Ah! my dear Sir," the missionary's lady said to me, "she does have abominable principles! Do you know what she has dared to write in the book she has just published?" "Why, no, my dear lady." "Well, she said it would be much better for the missionaries and their cause if they had no wives." "That is certainly a most abominable thing," I answered, "to want to deprive a man of his better half. But I see with pleasure that Ida Pfeiffer's book made no impression on your husband."

In Siam they don't bury the dead. Those who are wealthy enough to afford the expenses of a funeral pyre are burned. During my stay in Siam a priest who had held high rank in the Buddhist clergy was to be burned. An immense pyre had been prepared. Four iron bars held a grate of the same metal upon which they placed the body of the deceased in a sitting position. As soon as a man of distinguished rank is dead, he is placed in a sitting position in a hermetically closed box. Through a hole in the bottom of the box they insert a bamboo tube that leads to the liquids that run from the body. Through another tube that goes through the top of the box the gases that escape from the body go to join the atmosphere. After three or four months the body is completely dried out and they burn it.

The King, wishing to honor the departed, was to light the pyre himself. He ascended a throne erected for him, and, by means of a fuse that went from the throne to the pyre, he set fire to the latter, and within a couple of seconds the pyre was aflame. The relatives and friends of the deceased then ascended a platform above the pyre and threw odiferous woods into the fire.

In the Watts where the dead are burned there are also enclosures for the poor who can't afford cremation. A great number of dogs and vultures are maintained there. Since I had seen the place for the pyres, I walked over to the aforementioned enclosure.

A body, that of a still rather young man, had just been thrown into it. Suddenly, a cloud seemed to darken the sun, and I saw flying in from all the neighboring trees a countless number of vultures which made straight for the corpse, while the dogs came running and seemed to rival in speed the wings of the vultures. In a moment the eyes of the corpse had disappeared, leaving in their place two lugubrious holes; the jaws, half severed from the head, opened and closed as the dogs and vultures tugged at the corpse. Soon, tearing a hole in the belly, they tugged out the entrails and fought among themselves for them. I had seen more than enough! I left this accursed place, but in spite of myself I retraced my steps and I made a sketch of the awful scene. I felt faint and nauseated, while a number of Siamese watched that horrible sight, their own fate to come, with the greatest equanimity and wonder that I should be upset. And my worthy interpreter answers me as usual: *"Costumbres del pais."* I was told that during the cholera epidemic, the vultures, satiated with human flesh, wouldn't touch it anymore and left it to the sun to finish their gloomy chore.

In Siam you do not prostrate yourself only before the King, but before anyone who occupies a higher rank. The priests who bow only to the God, Buddha, are exceptions. One evening when I was at the home of the King's brother, Prince Wongsa Krom Hluang,[39] I found in the antechamber of the palace a dignitary with a bunch of slaves prostrated around him. He was certainly enjoying watching all those people groveling, when another dignitary of a higher rank, a Minister of State, arrived. Thereupon our man was forced to leave his sofa and to bend his knees. The other, in turn, had not been standing there more than a moment when Prince Wongsa himself came in—which sent our minister to join his colleague under the table. Even at home the son is always kneeling before his father, the wife in the presence of her husband. What a delightful family scene!

We attended an open air party to which the King had invited us (it was the celebration of the opening of the harvest season).[40] They had erected a huge tent upon a large plain within the enclosure of the Royal Palace. The King occupied a sort of loge expressly built for him, at the foot of which a great many courtiers were moving about on their knees. Someone had been considerate enough to supply us with chairs. In the middle of the tent was the theater. I cannot tell whether the backdrop of the stage represented rocks or clouds; I believe that the artist had made it with the purpose of using it to represent either, according to the circumstances. Around the theater were several orchestras. On one side a group of about fifty girls dressed in yellow were rhythmically knocking two pieces of wood against each other, accompanying that music with a mournful song quite similar to the monotonous chant of those poor women who cry in the streets: "Fried potatoes! A nickel a dozen!"

Another orchestra was comprised of clarinets, gongs, bells, etc. Others banged with hammers on pieces of metal. The King had expressed the wish to hear our music, so our band started to play and the native bands, instead of stopping, were seized with a noble spirit of emulation and they doubled their efforts to see who could make more noise, thus producing a diabolical racket from which my ears are still aching.

Upon the stage a group of about fifty girls were acting a sort of pantomime ballet. These girls are expressly reared within the palace and trained in the art of the dance in order to enchant His Magnificent Majesty in his leisure. The costumes were most lavish, consisting of gold lamé robes; on their heads they wore tiaras that sparkled with precious gems. I believe, however, that among these there were many pieces of crystal. Their arms, their feet, and their faces were painted yellow, and since their heads were shaved, as in the case of any self-respecting Siamese, they had provided themselves for the occasion with wigs, whose black curls framed their faces. Their nails, which they let grow as long as possible, were encased in sheaths of gold and silver. This is a most sophisticated feature in the East, for it proves that you cannot subject your hands to work.

Oh, Taglioni! Oh, Fanny Cerito! Oh, Carlotta Grisi! [41] I only wish that you could be here and could learn how one dances in Siam. No pirouettes, none of those swift figures in which the dancer, like a sylphid, seems endowed with real wings and seems to fly like the winged beings themselves. Here the movements—and I cannot deny that they are performed with a great deal of grace—are extremely slow, and dancing is done with the arms rather than with the feet.

The arms twist and turn in every direction and to outdo themselves the girls bend their arms, which are double-jointed, completely backwards. Instead of walking on their toes, they rest on their heels and elevate their toes. Now and then, the dancers approached the throne of the King, dancing on their knees, and made the customary curtsies. I frequently could see the pretty ballerina, without interrupting her most graceful figures, take a little vase of silver and gold and spit into it with infinite grace the reddish juice that fills her mouth because she does not stop chewing the indispensable betel. This last gesture is considered graceful in the extreme.

We had the pleasure of taking a ride on the back of the King's elephants and mine had no saddle. I can assure you that his back was hard as a rock. From the height of my mount, men, cows, gigantic bulls seemed to me like pygmies. Passing through a door of huge proportions I was afraid I might be crushed between the arch and the back of my mount and considered the roofs of the houses we passed as my ultimate recourse in case of an accident. Never have I been so rattled, shaken, moved, and jolted as on the back of my venerable mount, especially when he took up a slow trot. I was holding tight with both hands the cords that went around his belly and three days later my numbed legs were still feeling the effects of their acquaintance with the back of an elephant. We rode along a very narrow street, cluttered with displays of fruit and edible stuffs, the elephants walking with wonderful skillfulness without crushing anything under their feet. However, their trunks did not always spare the delicacies displayed before the shops, and while walking they pulled branches from the trees. But, as royal elephants go, these were really most decent. They will sometimes forget themselves so much as to kill their guardians, but these are mere trifles, youth's unimportant pranks. There are so many slaves in Siam that can take the place of a killed guardian, and anyway, what is the life of a Siamese in the eyes of His Magnificent Majesty? During the ride one of the beasts, on whose back rode a Christian general of Portuguese ancestry, may have felt religious scruples that he, a Buddhist elephant, should be carrying such a burden; anyway, he started shaking his back with all his might. The guardians and the driver were already biting the dust but the general was holding tightly a cord and crying out with the most awful faces: *"No estoy accostumbrado! No estoy accostumbrado, senores"* [42] [I am not used to this, gentlemen]. Poor general! I can easily believe that he wasn't accustomed to the jolting of an elephant's back. When a man does something extravagant there will always be another one to want to imitate him. The same thing is true of elephants. One of them, watching his companion doing such tricks, wanted to distinguish himself equally, and began to rub his sides against an old crumbling wall, at the risk of crushing the legs of his riders or elephant drivers. Soon, the wall gave way to his strength and tumbled down.

As in every part of the Indies, you find in Siam the ruins of Portuguese grandeur. Although the poor wretches still call themselves Portuguese, they are crossbred so much with the natives and have so thoroughly adopted their customs that they look like true Siamese. Their distinguishing mark is the

Catholic religion. You will see some of them who, half plunged into barbarism, still bear names illustrious in the annals of Portugal, such as Don Gabriel de Fereira de Valverde, Don Pascual de Albergaria, etc., etc. They, and the Cochin Chinese, have left their country because of persecution. Together with war prisoners from Cochin China, they comprise most of the Catholics here. The Christians do not shave their heads like the others, and wear their hair long.

After a great many delays, His Majesty condescended to appoint five plenipotentiaries to negotiate the treaty with the Ambassador:

His Royal Highness, Prince Krom Hluang Wongsa Dhiraj
  Snidh,
His Excellency, Somdetch Chau Phaya Param Maha Bijai
  Neate,
His Excellency, Chau Phaya Sri Suriwongse Samuha, Phra
  Kralahom (the Prime Minister),
His Excellency, Chau Phaya Rawe Wongee Maha Kosa
  Dhipade, the Phra Klang (Minister of Foreign Affairs),
His Excellency, Chau Phaya Yomray, the Lord Mayor.

Since they did not want to grant us more privileges than the British, we obtained a treaty similar to theirs and left Bangkok after an audience of dismissal with the two Kings on May 31, 1856.[43]

I shall always think with pleasure of the leisurely moments spent with Messrs. Moor, the worthy Consul of Portugal and son of an Amsterdam merchant who had settled in Macao, Mr. Parker, of an American establishment in Hong Kong, and Mr. Joaquin de Silva, secretary of the Consul-General of Portugal. Before leaving, Mr. Harris appointed the Reverend Stephen Mattoon, an American missionary, as Consul of the United States.[44]

June 12, 1856

After a pleasant crossing, we arrived on June 12 in Hong Kong.[45] The genie of the English, which seems to use a magic wand wherever the fertile lands of the two Indies are gathered together under the Crown of Her Britannic Majesty, has shown itself to advantage in Hong Kong also. The arid rocks of twelve years ago have been transformed into even streets; the pirate dens have given way to handsome, well-built and spacious houses; the bay, formerly of no use other than that of a shelter against the storm for a few wretched Chinese junks, is now covered with countless ships from every country of the world, and, unbelievable as it may seem, they even have succeeded in growing a few trees in the rocky soil of the island.

In spite of all these changes, Hong Kong is an abominable town. Talk there is only of business and the heat. If you don't want to risk your life, you must always go about in a palanquin because there is nothing to protect you from the heat of the sun. The vicinity of the town has nothing to offer except arid rock, with the exception of the Happy Valley, located two miles from the town, where you can enjoy a rather pretty view, comparatively speaking. The palace of the Governor, Sir John Bowring, is built on a hill and overlooks the town and the bay of Hong Kong.

It is a building with a colonnade and roomy apartments which are worthy of sheltering the representative in the China Seas of Her Majesty, Queen Victoria. The palace of the Bishop is very nice, as is the Episcopal church whose Gothic architecture reminds you of the landscapes of old England. In Hong Kong there are many American missionaries of the Presbyterian and Baptist religions as well as French missionaries.

Having heard that one of my countrymen worked in a commercial establishment and was Chancellor of the Dutch consulate of Canton, I went to his office. "Sir," I said to him, "I do not have the honor of being acquainted with you, but I heard that the same country has seen our birth. I am Mr. So and So and I would be delighted to become better acquainted with you."

That dear Keep! Without him I would have been bored to death in that stony Arabia. During the daytime we enjoyed ourselves as best we could, sitting in Chinese armchairs, feet up, smoking Manila cigars and drinking gin and bitters. When the sun descended upon the horizon and slanted a little more its rays on the poor Hong Kongese, we would take a walk towards the Champs Élysées of Hong Kong, namely the Happy Valley, where, sitting on a hillside we let the breezes of the bay fan us.

One day I told him: "My dear man, I came here to see China and it seems to me that being trapped within your room as I am by that Sun of Confucious cannot by any means be called seeing China. I have made a decision, if it is possible to make one in this frightful heat. I am going to Canton."

"Very well," he said. "I have already written to the Dutch Consul that a Dutchman would probably come to see him and he will be delighted to be your host during your stay in Canton."

The Commercial Hotel, the only establishment worthy of the name of a bad inn because all the others are thieves' dens, is managed by a Polish Jew who charges you heavily; there you will find only a diabolical room and an infernal meal. Consequently I was not sorry to leave this unhappy child of persecuted Poland and to sail one fine day on the lovely American steamship, the ———, for Canton.[46] Sailing up towards the mouth of the river, I failed to see anything interesting. We passed only arid islands, exact replicas of Hong Kong.

We arrived at Bocca Tigris where two enormous Chinese fortresses defend the entrance of the river. The Chinese believed them to be impregnable until the British during the Opium War overcame them with two or three cannon shots, and without losing a single man. Poor Chinese! How they must have suffered in their pride when they, inhabitants of the Celestial Empire, were overcome by a handful of Englishmen, and when those barbarians whom they had so long scorned became masters of their fortified castles, took Hong Kong, and dictated a treaty to the High Mandarins of the Court—all this because the Emperor of China had been careless enough to forbid his subjects to kill themselves with opium smoking.

The banks of the river gradually became more pleasant. What an immense picture of cultivation! As far as the eye can see there are fields covered with rice whose shade of green is so pleasant and so fresh as to defy description; the hills are topped with trees that take the most fanciful shapes. Pagodas, real Chinese pagodas, stand out in the landscape. The moment I discover the pagodas I begin to realize that I am in China. In Hong Kong, in Penang, in Siam, even in New York I had seen Chinese. I had walked through the Chinese quarters of Hong Kong, seen the fruit vendors, the barbers with their portable shops, merchants with their long robes of silk and their long queues, without paying any attention, without the least feeling in the world. But the pagodas, the real pagodas whose pictures I had admired so many times as a child, these pagodas remind me of the reality of my situation: I am like a man just fallen off the moon. I begin to understand that my dreams have come true, that I am really in China.

Three and a half years ago I said farewell to my parental

home. For the last time I had held in my arms the woman who had given life to me. With a violent effort I had torn myself out of my mother's arms. I found myself alone in the world. Poor adventurer that I was, I had set sail for the New World. That wasn't quite four years ago, but it seems to me like centuries ago. How many adverse conditions, how many obstacles I had to fight! Finally, a weak light begins to glimmer on the horizon of my life: I am established. I have no thought of leaving the United States when I hear that the Consul-General of the United States for Japan needs an interpreter-secretary. Pushed by that burning desire for travel that seems to grow with the years, I present myself. I am accepted by the American government. I sail out on a warship, and here I am now on the Chou-kieng River,[47] while the castles and pagodas of Canton are beginning to show their outline on the horizon. It is only through this reasoning, and by bringing back the past to mind that I can explain how I am really in China, that those people with the long queues and the slanted eyes are not theater Chinese, and that the pagodas gracefully soaring heavenwards are not figments of my imagination, but rather many realities.

After having stopped for a few minutes at Whampoa, where there were a great many merchant vessels waiting for the tenders from Canton to unload their cargo since the shallow river does not permit them to go further, we drop anchor before the foreign trading post after an eight-hour crossing. Arriving in Canton I found the whole garden and the adjoining streets [of the Dutch consulate] submerged by a high tide, and was forced to use the back of one of the Celestials in order to make a dry-footed entrance in the Dutch consulate. There my "horse" deposited me in the very middle of the stairs. I presented my letter of introduction to the Consul who received me in the most gracious manner imaginable, told me my room was ready and that he had been waiting for me for several days. We were going through the customary compliments when my Chinese "horse" climbed the stairs and burst into the Consul's office. There were at least a dozen of them who claimed the honor of having been my horse and they protested that the money I had given one of them was not enough for the others. Being aware that the best way in the world to present a letter of introduction is not in the company of a dozen howling ragamuffins, I gave the rascals what they wanted and had the pleasure of seeing my "horses" depart at a dogtrot.

Honor be rendered to those who deserve it, and honor goes to the Europeans of Canton, for they practice a kind of hospitality worthy of the good old times! Travelers would indeed have to be pitied if they were at the mercy of the old Chinaman who keeps in the suburbs an establishment of sorts where they find room and board. Thanks to my dear Van der Hoeven, I was able that night to slip between sheets of pristine freshness. I found at Mr. Van der Hoeven's two young men from Java, sent by their government to Canton so that they might study Chinese. After five years they are supposed to know how to read and speak Chinese sufficiently well to serve as interpreters in Java. When you have nothing else to do other than learn a language, five years seem like more than enough, but the Chinese language is so exceedingly difficult that even Chinese scholars, who have been studying it since their childhood, still don't understand every character.

Because of the high level of water in the river and the incessant rains that fell during my stay, I could almost never go out except in a palanquin.

Wanting to go around the city walls, I took a palanquin and a guide and we set forth, although I had been warned that the roads are none too safe and that the feelings of the Cantonese populace (the most unruly populace of the Empire) are not exactly favorable to Europeans. But fortunately I completed my trip without having received the slightest scratch. The only incident occurred when some children followed me shouting, *"Fan kwei!"* (foreign devil). A few projectiles made of mud glanced off my hat and I was insolently stared at by a few scamps. My only weapon was my sword cane. The streets called Old and New China Streets are most interesting. That is where Chinese merchants who deal with Europeans display their wares. I admired there the magnificent pieces of porcelain gathered from every part of that huge Empire, the silks and the crepes, the lacquered furniture covered with capricious and weird figures, the toys carved so beautifully from ivory and sandalwood, the painters who copy with amazing ease on paper or ivory the daguerreotypes you give them. I visited the Hongs, those immense stores where are collected thousands of chests containing the fragrant herb of China: tea. These are all ready to be shipped to delight with their aromatic flavors the palates of a whole world, especially those of the worthy members of temperance societies. The streets of Canton's suburbs are exceedingly narrow so that the roofs appear to touch. They are very dirty and thronged with passers-by. When a palanquin arrives, a runner goes ahead, calling out to the passers-by to step aside. The streets are so narrow that two palanquins can hardly pass. The signs, on which merchants advertise their wares and quote verses from Confucius, sometimes hang from the top of the roofs and almost touch the ground. The gold characters stand out on a red background, looking very effective and most Chinese indeed.

When I arrived at the city gates, Tartar soldiers who guard it prevented me from going any further, which I regret very much. But I have been told that the streets of the city and those of the suburbs are the same and that there is no difference except that they are perhaps dirtier and narrower than the others. We leave the suburbs and go along the walls, going up and down the hills on which they are built. These walls are very high and seem so noticeably ancient that, in spite of their great thickness, our guns would soon pierce a breach through them. The city encloses several hills and is divided by a second wall into two parts, one of which is occupied by Tartars, the other by Chinese.[48] From the top of a hill I enjoyed a lovely view. On one side are the walls wandering along the hills and the nine-storied pagoda that rose like a huge watchtower with its weird roofs and small bells; on the other side are the separate fortresses of the city, lost and regained many times when the rebel army was besieging Canton two years ago, and the heights which that army occupied, the river, the fertile rice fields which give a verdant look to the whole countryside, the pagodas, and pretty little bridges thrown across brooks—everything, in a word, looks as Chinese as could be. The factory located near the river is separated from the suburbs by another wall (I believe there are more walls than houses in Canton). In the enclosure there is a very pretty garden, the only place where residents of Canton can decently go for a walk. The garden is bordered on one side by the river, on the other by the houses of the Europeans. The houses present a very dignified facade. In the middle of the garden stands a small Episcopalian church. It is very interesting for a newcomer to walk through the garden of the trading post. He will see there Persians with their headdresses which date back to the days of Zoroaster, stern Moslems whose heads are swathed in huge turbans of white linen, Armenians and representatives of all the nations of the civilized world. It seems that one day the Consuls of Canton were seized with a commendable spirit of emulation and decided to see who could raise the highest staff so that they might hoist the flag of the nation they represented higher than any other. Among the four immense staffs erected in the garden—the French, English, Danish, and American—the last won. But the poor Consul who sent the bill to his government for the amount of fifteen hundred dollars was simply told that the American government did not authorize any such expense and that he would do well to pay it himself. One day I saw two Chinese swathed in long white robes with pointed shoes and the usual queues walking in the garden. I heard them talking in French, and they spoke the language as though they were born under the very sun of that great nation. Very surprised, I asked a friend about the cause of such a phenomenon. He soon dispelled my error when he told me that these two were Catholic priests, members of the Society of Foreign Missions, who had adopted the Chinese costume in order to introduce themselves into the city and into China proper in a manner calculated to gain the trust of the inhabitants. They can walk through the city without receiving any signs of hostility.

When I returned home, my friend Van der Hoeven, introduced me to a gentleman named Ali Ben Sou Ali, whose name and costume were most Turkish and whose green turban—which he kept on his head like a true Turk against all the rules of European courtesy—revealed he was a member of the Prophet's family. I was convinced that he was going to recite a verse from the Koran, such as "Allah is great and Mohammed is His prophet." Instead he said, in the purest Parisian accent you can imagine: "Sir, I am delighted to meet you." The gentleman was born in Paris. He played a new instrument called the turcophone and intended to give concerts in Canton. He had given concerts in Java and he had traveled all over India in Turkish costume, no doubt to play the turcophone better.

European households in China have in their employ a Chinese they call the comprador. He buys all that is needed and pays for everything and I suspect that he charges his master a liberal commission on all the articles he supplies. A comprador is an indispensable man in China and in Canton.

There is, in Canton, a large floating population; that is, people who live on the water, are born, grow up, get married, and die on the water and are probably buried in the water. They live in boats moored along the river and form an important part of Canton's population.

When a Chinese falls in the water no one will ever hurry to save him. He is abandoned to his fate because superstitious Chinese say that one should never interfere with the designs of Providence.

July, 1856

I take leave of my dear host Van der Hoeven and step aboard the steamer for Macao, where I arrive after an eight-hour trip.[49] When you arrive at Macao, the Catholic churches, the convents, the crosses in the street, the priests who walk in their sacerdotal clothes with banners and incense burners, the battlements of the fortresses—all make you believe you are carried away in a wink of the eye from the Celestial Empire to the very center of Portugal. Macao is nothing but a tomb; Macao, formerly jewel of the Portuguese crown; Macao, once the only port through which one could trade with China; Macao, unique point of departure in days gone by of the Portuguese caravels bound for the mysterious Empire, Japan; Macao, where these same caravels returned, having realized huge profits; Macao, where the Jesuits dispatched their missionaries to preach the gospel to the Japanese, and who barely missed converting this great empire to Christianity; Macao, advance post of the Portuguese; Macao is nothing but a tomb!

The houses still reveal the former wealth of their occupants, but they are [either] falling into ruin, or else they are occupied by the wealthy merchants of Canton and Hong Kong. The convents still present their thick walls and their iron bars to the traveler's eye, and bear witness to the past power and wealth of the Catholic clergy. The walls are still topped with ancient cannons, the same cannons that compelled the Dutch in 1622 to return to their ships. Everything in Macao speaks of the past, and the heart of the Portuguese must swell with pride when he sees what his forebears have done. However, when he considers the sadness of the present state of things—the harbor empty of ships; the degenerate inhabitants who, because of their alliance with the Indians and the Chinese, have fallen, if I may say so, lower than either of those two races; the handful of soldiers almost as dark as Negroes who form the garrison of the city; the palaces of their ancestors occupied by foreign merchants; young girls sold like cattle to serve as concubines to these same foreigners —how he must cry: "Oh, Portugal, thy glory is gone. Thou hast shone like a meteor in the firmament of the Indies. But thou hast disappeared to make room for others and all that is left to thee of thy possessions in the Indies bespeak only of wretchedness and destitution."

Forty years ago a fire destroyed the beautiful church of the Jesuits. The walls tumbled down, except the front one. Unbelievable as it may seem, although deprived of the support of the others, it withstands the fury of storms and the ravages of time and stands through its own strength, still holding high its noble and majestic brow topped with an iron cross towards heaven. I couldn't help but compare the noble ruin to its former masters who, even though tumbled from the summit of their grandeur, still maintain themselves with a spirit worthy of admiration.

One of the most interesting places in Macao is Camoens'

Cave. There the illustrious poet composed the verses of his *Lusiad*.[50]

I walked through a garden, and arrived at the cave which is formed by a granite block that projects out of the rock and is supported by another one. Instead of leaving the cave as it was when Camoens came there to meet his Muse, an indiscreet zealot, spurred on by bad taste, has built there an arch supported by two columns, and the bust of Camoens has been placed inside the grotto. In the visitors' book, where you sign your name and write the thoughts that the memories of the place suggest, I wrote the following verses:

> Hallow'd retreat of a poet,
> Humble stones of granite
> Where the divine anchorite
> Wept and sang for his country!
>
> Oh! Why should they profane
> The majesty of this holy place
> And erect memorials of stone
> Where nature alone ought to reign?
>
> Great Camoens, if thy shade
> Sometimes flutters down from Heaven,
> It shall curse the profane hands
> Which have defiled this hallowed place.

In the vestry of the Cathedral of Macao you are shown a painting representing the defeat of the Dutch who wanted to become masters of Macao.

The rules of perspective are very well respected. The Dutch fleet seems to float on clouds. Then comes the town and its walls. You see five figures armed with rifles fighting against five others similarly armed, and in the midst of all this shooting stands a saint, large out of all proportion. The sexton told me that the five figures were the Portuguese army, the five others the Dutch army, and that it was St. John the Baptist, who saved the city by his intervention, standing in the middle. You can see also another picture executed in the same manner representing the martyrdom of Christians in Japan.

The quay, located across the outer bay called the Praya Grande, is very beautiful. You can take some lovely walks there. You can see the Dutch cemetery where you find the graves of several high officials of the honorable East India Company and the now-deserted houses of the English and Dutch companies.

A wall that surrounds the city on the inland side was built by Dutch prisoners after the memorable victory won by the Portuguese over them and is so well described on the painting in the vestry of the Cathedral by the following lines: [51]

> A Glorious victory which, through the intercession of St. John the Baptist, the Portuguese inhabitants of the city won on June 24, 1622, over 800 soldiers of the Dutch nation who attempted to take the city in a landing which they made from 13 ships in the harbor.

Before the fall of Hong Kong, the Portuguese government had refused the most liberal offers of the British government that would have made Macao a free port. After the fall of Hong Kong, the port was opened without a cent in return. All commerce moved to Hong Kong and the city of Macao came close to an end. However, it revived somewhat during the siege of Canton by the rebels. The mandarins and rich Chinese sought refuge here. The present governor is taking the strongest possible measures to improve the wretched condition of finances. Employees have collected wages in arrears. He has established a bazaar and he does all he can to alleviate the infirmities of age of a city formerly so prosperous.

I paid a visit to Mr. le Comte de Courcy, Chargé d'Affaires of France in China, and to Mr. Cañeda y Moral, Consul-General of Spain.

July 10, 1856

Back in Hong Kong I meet again the *San Jacinto* ready to leave for Japan. The anchor is raised and we depart. After a mile's voyage, they discover that the propeller is damaged and we have to stop. I soon learn that the *San Jacinto* will have to go to Whampoa in order to repair the propeller and that we will stay a month in China. What am I to do? Shall I suffocate in the frigate where the breathing of four hundred men together forms a real carbon dioxide plant? Shall I entrust my person to the kindly care of my friend, the one from persecuted Poland? That's not much better. Let us return to my good friend Van der Hoeven in Canton.

He immediately offered me the room I had occupied two weeks earlier. In Canton I met Mr. Reynvaen of Leyden who arrived with the overland mail to work in the firm of Vaucher Brothers. Mr. and Mrs. Vaucher and Beauvais, the Vice-Consul of France, asked me to dinner several times, as did Mr. Perry, Consul of the United States.[52]

August, 1856

I leave my dear Van der Hoeven, and, while waiting for the arrival of the *San Jacinto*,[53] I accept the hospitality of Captain Buys,[54] who does everything in his power to make my stay on board comfortable, and who insists, in spite of my objections, that I have his own cabin.

A Dutch boat was burned by Chinese coolies who were to have been carried in it to Peru and who, seeking revenge against the captain, sacrificed both him and his crew as well as themselves to the flames. The ship was anchored three miles from the port of Macao. A few survivors were rescued by the steamship, the *Queen*.[55]

August 13, 1856

We leave for Shimoda.[56]

August 16, 1856

This morning, we see many chests of tea, pieces of masts, etc., afloat.[57] All indicates that there has been a typhoon in these waters and that it has destroyed many Chinese junks. We come upon a man adrift on a section of a mainmast and a few pieces of bamboo. A boat is sent to his rescue and soon the poor devil is carried on board, assisted by sailors since he is unable to walk. He is a Chinese and had spent forty-eight hours in this frightful predicament. Shortly after, we discover a mastless junk. As we draw near, the Chinese begin to beat their gongs and to call for help. The Commodore sends a Lieutenant to inquire about their condition. The Lieutenant returns, saying that the Captain refuses to abandon his ship and that, with the help of a compass, he intends to try and make for harbor. The crew, on the other hand, is clamoring to abandon ship. The Commodore, judging that he cannot interfere in the affairs of another ship's captain, and that he would aid and abet the mutiny of the crew if he were to receive them on board against their captain's will, leaves the Chinese junk, while the cries of sailors calling for help echo in our ears. They make signals of distress in our direction as long as we can see them.

We have just left this Chinese vessel when two other junks, also deprived of their masts, appear in the distance. To one we give a sail, a mast, and some rigging. The other, armed with ten cannon, is constantly shooting distress signals. The sun had already set in the Ocean when we approached this latter vessel. The Captain said his junk is taking water fast and asks to be accepted aboard with his crew. He is told that he may come aboard but under the conditions that his abandoned vessel will be set afire and all that anyone will be permitted to bring with him is a parcel of his own clothes.

The whole crew, consisting of a cat, a dog, and fifty-three Chinese sailors climbs aboard. One of the lieutenants is sent aboard the junk to set it afire. We depart upon his return. We keep our eyes on the dark shadow of the abandoned junk, but contrary to our expectations, we do not see the fire break out. At midnight, we assist a Siamese junk with some water.

It now becomes advisable to interrupt the Journal with a brief description of the political environment into which Harris and Heusken were soon to be plunged. More than three years had elapsed since Commodore Perry had first approached Japanese shores. On that occasion the American commander dealt with a people who, by and large, still held it as axiomatic that any real intercourse with the outside world was dangerous and undesirable. The Japanese authorities, however, were well informed of recent developments in China and had for some time felt grave apprehensions concerning the presence of the Russians on their northern frontier. It had been the responsibility of the Dutch and the Chinese to keep the authorities abreast of developments in the outside world and they were well informed concerning the growing power of Great Britain in Asia. Many Japanese leaders felt some anxiety concerning Japan's international position, but this anxiety led to no effective action within Japan prior to the coming of Perry.

When Perry's squadron entered Edo Bay in the summer of 1853, his arrival came as no surprise to the Edo authorities who had been informed some time before by the Dutch concerning the expedition and the purposes for which it was being sent. Nevertheless, the Japanese were completely unprepared to meet this development. They had no foreign policy worthy of the name, nor had they used the interval since the Dutch warnings to strengthen their defenses. Indeed, nothing had been done before the arrival of the Perry expedition at Naha on the island of Okinawa. Defensive efforts thereafter undertaken were entirely futile.

With the American squadron lying before them in Edo Bay, the Tokugawa authorities in their dilemma turned from their traditional practices and sought counsel from the nation at large. It had hitherto been their practice to take counsel among themselves and thereafter to announce decisions and policies to the Imperial Court and the nation. This traditional procedure was now abandoned in what must be regarded as a confession of weakness and indecision. Copies of the letters which had been received from Perry in 1853 were now circulated to all feudal lords, both those considered loyal and those excluded from any role in the government, and their views were invited on the procedures and policies to be followed when Perry returned for his reply in 1854.

By this single action the Tokugawa opened a floodgate which could not thereafter be closed. Many of the feudal lords were no longer effectively in control of their fiefs, either in actual administration or in formulation of policy. Some, indeed, spent most of their time in Edo, leaving the affairs of their estates to the control of subordinates. Consideration of the demands presented by Commodore Perry, therefore, went considerably beyond the narrow circle of feudal lords and included numbers of lesser men who, nevertheless, exercised real power on the estates. As the years passed, the numbers of those who held opinions on foreign policy and could safely express them grew, and this growth was in itself a measure of the decline of Tokugawa authority. Even so, these growing numbers represented no more than a tiny fragment of the numerous samurai (soldier) class.

When the memorials from the feudal lords came pouring in, the Tokugawa authorities found no comfort in their response. The nation was divided and confused, just as was the Tokugawa administration. All that the Tokugawa had achieved by this step was the initiation of a public debate on policy, sometimes foreign, sometimes domestic, which continued until the end of the Tokugawa regime in 1868.

Long before the coming of Perry many Japanese had begun to question privately the right of the Shogun to rule in Japan and to contend that the Emperor should be restored to his rightful position. Many who so argued came, as one might expect, from the fiefs long hostile to the Tokugawa monopoly of power. Their attitudes after 1853 often reflected a strange compounding of hostility to the Tokugawa with xenophobia. Some were more anti-Tokugawa than anti-foreign.

Under these circumstances the enemies of the Tokugawa had a golden opportunity. Nothing would serve their purposes better than to maneuver the Imperial Court into a position of opposition to the Tokugawa regime on matters of national policy. This soon came to pass and thereafter the regime fought for survival against its domestic enemies, a struggle seriously complicated by the demands which the foreigners now introduced.

When Perry returned to Japan in 1854 the authorities had little choice but to negotiate the limited concessions embodied in the Treaty of Kanagawa. These concessions could be defended on the grounds of simple humanity, and by and large the nation accepted them and the similar concessions made to other nations later as necessary under the circumstances. The arrival of Townsend Harris and his proposals were quite another matter, however, and the great national debate now began in earnest.

August 21, 1856

The day has finally arrived, the day that will see me at the place of my destination. We sight the mountains of Cape

Idzu and a few hours later we anchor in the Bay of Shimoda. The secretary of the Governor and two Dutch interpreters, Toko Juro and ——— [illegible],[58] come aboard to congratulate the Consul on his arrival at Shimoda. The Consul delivers to them a letter advising the Governor of his arrival. The Governors named the day they will receive the Consul-General at the government house called Goyosho. They also enquire whether the Commodore will or will not accompany the Consul, and which one of them has the highest rank.

They are told that the ranks of Consul-General and Commodore are completely different, that one is the diplomatic representative of his government while the other is the chief of the United States naval forces in the seas of China and Japan.

The audience takes place.[59] The Consul-General, accompanied by a dozen officers, leaves the frigate. Japanese officers with an escort of soldiers meet us at the landing. The two Governors of Shimoda, surrounded by their secretaries and officers, receive us at the entrance of the audience hall. We first go through the usual compliments: they are delighted to see the Consul; they hope that he is in good health, as well as all the officers of his escort; they announce that a dinner is prepared for us and servants bring us pipes with tobacco, different kinds of soups, of fish and chicken, ducks, eggs, etc., in lacquered wooden cups.

After all these nice compliments and these reiterations of friendship, they also say that they were not expecting the Consul quite so soon, that Shimoda has been hit by a flood and an earthquake,[60] that the Governors are busy having the damage repaired and that the whole country is, because of the disaster, in a state of disarray. In consequence, they would be delighted if His Excellency, the Consul-General, didn't mind leaving and coming back in a year or two.

The Consul answered that he could do nothing of the kind, that he had to obey the orders of his government.

Well, they did not see the necessity of having a Consul here and they would like to know the reason for his presence, since the Treaty said that a Consul would be appointed for Japan if either [61] [sic] of the two governments deemed it necessary.

The rights and privileges of a Consul and the fact that he was here to protect his countrymen and to assist those United States sailors who might be wrecked on the coast of Japan, etc., was explained to them.

The Governors answered that it was not at all necessary, that they would take care of all that. In brief, it seemed that the Japanese government felt the greatest aversion to receiving a Consul on its territory and that it intended to persevere in the system of isolation it had kept for two or three centuries. After many debates and arguments, they decided to offer the Consul one of the Temples of Shimoda or of Kakizaki because they had no house ready; they would send boats to bring ashore our belongings; they would make the alterations and repairs which the Consul would indicate to be necessary. All seemed settled and we were congratulating ourselves on the happy outcome of the conferences. But the poor Governors wanted to make a last attempt at ridding themselves of His Excellency—a title they never missed repeating at every moment—their dear, dear friend, the Consul-General whom they were so glad to see and whom they would be so glad to see returning to the United States.

The Commodore—for the first time—the Consul-General and an escort of officers went, at a set date, to pay a visit to the Governors.[62] The latter received us with great protestations of friendship. They then turned directly to the Commodore and asked him in the most naïve manner if he would not take the Consul-General with him and return to the

United States. The Commodore answered that he belonged to the military service, that there was nothing he could do but obey orders from his government, that he had received orders to leave the Consul-General at Shimoda, and that he had to act in compliance with his orders.

The poor Governors were at a loss. Their last attempt had failed! We were served a dinner equal to that of the first time. Every guest had, beside his plate, some kind of candy wrapped in paper, which it is customary to take home. The Japanese insisted that we should observe, at least, this one rule of Japanese etiquette. The Commodore, the Consul, and I received presents of Japanese curios of lacquer. The officers were told that the Governors would send each of them a present to the frigate and that the latter apologized for not being able to give them the presents here, but they did not know the number of their visitors today. Upon their return to the *San Jacinto,* the poor officers found half of a large fish for everyone of them. After the first visit the Governors had sent them each a pair of chickens.

It was finally agreed that we would be given as a residence the Jocsenti (Gyokusenji) Temple.[63] During the inspection of the temple we were informed that two or three rooms would be needed in the temple for Japanese officers who would be here as an honor guard, so to speak. They would protect us from the insults to which the populace might subject two foreigners, and if we needed anything we need only say the word to these officers and they would execute our orders with dispatch. It was easy to understand that the purpose of the whole thing was to treat us like the Dutch trading post of Deshima, that the temple was to be our prison and the helpful officers our wardens, placed here to observe our slightest move and to prevent any communication between us and the people. The Consul-General answered that he was deeply grateful for the attentions lavished upon him by the Governors of Shimoda, but that he did not want to cause them so much trouble, that he felt quite capable of protecting himself and that, in a word, he wanted in his house only those who were immediately employed by himself. The answer was that they had wanted to honor us, that they had not wanted to abandon us to our fate, that if the Consul wanted to accept in his house only those attached to the consulate and to his person, then there was in the temple court a small house perfectly suitable to shelter two Japanese officers who would be, day and night, at our disposal.

Since he did not want to appear too difficult from the outset, the Consul decided to submit for a while to that kind of spying.

After the crew of the frigate had erected a mast in the court of the consulate and hoisted the American flag without receiving the slightest opposition from the Japanese government which was so jealous of its power, the *San Jacinto* hoisted its anchor on September 3, 1856.[64]

From atop a hill I had seen disappear the last object that still linked me to the civilized world and I sang out with more reason to do so than Lusignan,[65] who at least was King of Cyprus, the famous lines:

> Wretched exile upon a foreign strand,
> How he mourns for his beloved land!

September 21, 1856

A frightful hurricane laid waste the coast of Japan.[66] All the junks in the Bay were cast against the shore. Almost a third of the town of Shimoda was destroyed. When, the next morning, I sighted the destruction of the night, the masts scattered on the beach, the debris of ships and houses, I was astonished at the behavior of the Japanese. Not a cry was heard. Despair? What! Not even sorrow was visible on their faces. On the contrary, they seemed quite indifferent to the typhoon and everyone was already busy repairing the damage caused by the tempest.

September 25, 1856

The Consul-General wrote a letter to the Minister of Foreign Affairs of Japan to inform him that he had, besides the powers of a Consul, the full powers of an Ambassador and that he was the bearer of a letter from the President of the United States to His Majesty the Emperor of Japan and that consequently he intended to go to Iedo [Edo].[67]

September 30, 1856

The steam corvette *Medusa* under Captain Fabius of the Dutch Navy, cast anchor in the Bay of Shimoda.[68] Having seen the destruction of the last hurricane, and that the harbor provided no sanctuary, Captain Fabius hurried to leave Shimoda, and so after a three-day visit, the flag of my native country disappeared.[69] The officers of the ship had received me most warmly; we had been able to speak of subjects dear to my memory, and the departure of the ship left a great void in my heart.

October 9, 1856

The monotonous life I lead here is relieved by the arrival of the American schooner *General Pierce* with a supercargo, Mr. Leidorff aboard.[70] The *General Pierce* had a cargo of rifles, but the Japanese said these were too old. The ship sold nothing at all and bought only a few lacquered cabinets.

November 12, 1856

The Russian corvette *Olivuzza* arrives here with Captain Korsakoff.[71] It has on board First Rank Captain Constantin Possiet, bearer of the ratified treaty between Russia and Japan. I shall always remember with pleasure the time the Russian corvette spent here. Her staff was comprised of charming, courteous, well-bred young men. Captain, or Commander Possiet was a very genial man, as was Captain Korsakoff.[72] I spent many a happy day with them in the cabin. They often came to see us at the consulate, which contributed a great deal to helping us spend the months of November and December pleasantly. But every pleasure has an end and on December 15 the corvette *Olivuzza* left us, taking with her my most sincere regrets.[73] The Russian officers had received a quantity of letters by way of Nagasaki and the Japanese government had not hesitated to open every one of them, which proved that European governments are not the only ones guilty of such an indignity.

February 22, 1857

At the Consul's request, the authorities of Shimoda fired a twenty-one gun salute in honor of Washington's birthday. The gunners served their artillery pieces in the most remarkable manner, and with utmost accuracy. There were two small canons, exact copies of a model given to them by Commodore Perry. One of the Governors who had gone to Edo returns with the communication that the Edo government does not want to enter into direct negotiations with the Consul-General because the Governors of Shimoda have full powers to act themselves. At the same time he hands to the Consul a letter from the Great Council of State of Japan in answer to two the former had addressed to the Ministry of Foreign Affairs, stating that dealings can be established only with the Governors of Shimoda, and—an unheard of thing certainly in order to mitigate this refusal—he invites us to visit him in his home, whereas up to now we have visited with the Governors only in the Goyosho because the laws of Japan forbade them to receive us at home.[74]

February 23, 1857

The two *norimons* [*norimono* or palanquin] of the Governors arrive to take us to the Governor's home.[75] These *norimons* are such exceedingly short litters that you don't know what to do with your legs. The Japanese will bend their own back under their bodies but we are prevented from emulating this wonderful custom by our pants which are tight fitting and our muscles which are not as supple. Therefore, I expressed thanks to Heaven when I was freed from my uncomfortable *norimon* and was able to restore my legs to their normal position. High government officials received us at the entrance of the house with every mark of deep respect. We were then led to an antechamber where the two Governors received us. We were asked to sit down, and, after having drunk a cup of excellent tea, we went together into another room. The Governors and the officers of their retinue are all wearing kamisimo [*kamishimo* or ceremonial dress]. We are seated at the Governor's table. The two Vice-Governors are sitting at another table. We are served dinner of more than twelve entrees, comprising soups, poultry, radishes, fish, raw and boiled, oysters, sausage, etc., etc., all served in cups of lacquered wood. At the same time we are served in small porcelain cups hot sake, a drink distilled from rice. They bring a huge dish on which stands a tree whose branches hold cranes carved from radishes. We are told that this is a compliment from the Governors to their guests, for the crane is the symbol of longevity. This dish soon gave way to another bearing a large boiled fish on whose back stood a mast and a sail.

The first Governor now explains through his interpreter, Moriyama Takitsiro [Takichiro],[76] that if persons of distinguished rank want to pay a great compliment to other persons equally distinguished who happen to be at their homes, they make them some tea with their own hands, and the first Governor wishes to pay that compliment to His Excellency and close friend, the Consul-General. A Japanese dignitary brings a box from which the noble Governor takes a small brazier, a cute little teapot, and other necessities. He explains, with all the pride of an amateur, the different phases of the process to which he submits the aromatic herb. He warms the tea and places it in the teapot. He boils the water, pours it over the tea and presents the tea to the Consul while making him a present of the box and all the objects he used to prepare the tea for him.

The first Governor wishes to drink to my health. He does that drinking sake, the Japanese wine, from a small porcelain cup. I do the same thing, keeping a pleasant countenance, although the drink is detestable. Then I am told that the porcelain cup is mine and I must take it along with me. I then go through the same ceremonies with the second Governor and the Vice-Governors which makes me the proud owner of a number of cups of the beautiful Japanese porcelain. But at the same time my palate suffers unbearable tortures in the transferring of the awful liquor from the cups to my stomach.

The two Governors, Inoue, Prince of Shinano, and Okada, Prince of Bingo, as well as the Imperial officers here, live all together in a compound a mile from Shimoda.[77] Each has a small house of his own where he lives with his servants. No woman is allowed to remain with them. High government officials are forced to leave their families as hostages in Edo. Although concubines are allowed in Japan, Imperial officers can't have them and as long as they are here, stern laws force them to lead the lives of bachelors.

The Japanese government has promulgated that law because women might betray state secrets. Poor enchanting sex! This absence of man's angel of mercy gives a sort of emptiness, a certain sadness to the Governors' dinner. Had some noble Japanese matron been hostess at the table, had we been able to dance a polka with the Governors' daughters, what a good time we would have had! What a dismal life the poor Japanese officers must lead, forced as they are by a suspicious and cruel law to forsake that which makes the charm of existence.

The austerity of the Japanese is truly worthy of the ancient Spartans. Here, in the palace (if I may call it that) of one of the first princes of the Empire, the rooms presented the same appearance as those of any shopkeeper of Shimoda.[78] The floor was covered with the same matting. There was paper instead of panes at the windows, a total lack of ostentation or luxury, not a single piece of furniture except the two benches and the table expressly built for our use, because the Japanese, bending their legs under their bodies, sit on their matting, eat on it, and at night stretch out on it to sleep.

All the nobles wear the same costume. The only distinguishing mark between the Governors and the common Imperial soldiers is a sort of shirt bosom of white crepe which they wear over their *kabaya*[79] or dressing gown. Also, the nobles may wear a sort of pantaloon with deep folds which others may not. Each has his family's coat of arms painted on each arm and on the chest of his dress. It usually consists of a flower in a white circle. The great ambition of Japanese nobles is to wear the coat of arms of the Shogun, that is, the mulberry leaf. The two Governors and a few other high-ranking officers of their suite had received that distinction. Sometimes the Governors give nobles of their suite permission to wear their arms on their clothes. The Governors, officers of the first and second rank, when walking, are always preceded by a pike carried before them which indicates that they hold the rank of *bumio*,[80] representative of the Emperor.

February 25, 1857

We are beginning today our official interviews with the two Governors. While we have been here we have already won quite a few points from the Japanese. These may seem trifling, but they really are of great importance to a people so isolated from the rest of the world, and whose suspicious diplomacy had caused the failure of all efforts at the time of Commodore Perry's arrival in these parts two years ago. At the beginning I couldn't take a step outside the consulate without having a *gobangoshi,* or police officer, dogging my steps, and following me like my own shadow. If I raised my cane, the man disappeared, but he was sure to reappear again behind another tree or another house. When we complained of it to the government, we were told that these people were for our own protection against the populace, and were a sort of guard of honor. Poor populace of Japan, whom they tried to make appear to us as so impressive and so fearsome! These poor people's hands were tied to such an extent that they did not dare look at us. And then the inhabitants of Shimoda had received the most rigorous orders not to communicate with us. If I appeared in the street, they would usually close their doors and windows. Women especially fled at a gallop at our approach. The young girls particularly ran as though the very enemy of mankind was at their heels; and if we were lucky enough to see a woman marching boldly towards us, it was a wrinkled octogenarian whose weakened sight did not enable her to distinguish those foreign devils from her beloved countrymen. Beasts of burden, usually quite indolent in Japan, came out of their lethargic state when we arrived, made pirouettes and somersaults and even though carrying a heavy burden they ran away at a gallop. Dogs, who had forgotten how to bark except at the moon, seemed to mistake us for that heavenly orb, for when they saw us they raised a frightful racket and a concert of all the dogs of the town, gathered together by the sound of the alarm gun, followed us to the limit of the city where they relinquished their privilege to howl to the dogs of the countryside. Only the cats did not seem to submit to the rigorous laws of Japan against foreigners, and watched us with indifference. And I had fallen so low as to call these aloof animals models of hospitality.

Secondly, the little house in the consulate yard inside the entrance gate was always occupied by two officers and soldiers who were relieved regularly every day.

Thirdly, if an officer came to visit us, he was always accompanied by half a dozen secretaries who wrote down every word uttered.

Fourthly, there were in Shimoda three imperial spies, accredited by the government.[81] These spies were empowered to enter the Governors' house at any moment, even in the night, and to attend all the conferences which the government held with us. These worthy people are supposed to report to their masters in Edo all that goes on here. If Japanese dignitaries came to see us, the spy was sure to appear later if he did not come with them. Spies stood apart from the other officers and observed all that went on between us.

Fifthly, all the letters the Consul-General addressed to the

Governors were never answered by another letter. The reply was always verbal. Every time the Consul-General complained of these indignities he received evasive answers, either that such was the custom in Japan, or that these measures were only taken in order to protect us, etc.

The Consul was aware that he had to change his attitude towards the Japanese, that his gentle and courteous remonstrances were of no avail. One fine day, he boldly addressed the Governors and told them that his government would never stand such outrages against the person of its representative, that the sacred character of a diplomatic agent was recognized by all civilized nations of the world, that when the Japanese had concluded treaties with foreign nations they had consequently subjected themselves to the general laws that rule all nations and that he could not be responsible for the reprisals and the indignation of all civilized nations which the government of Japan was about to draw upon itself by these outrages against the law of nations.

"I demand," he said, "that the guards posted at the door of the consulate and who treat like a prisoner a representative of the United States be immediately removed or I shall declare myself a prisoner and you will have to take the consequences." That speech seemed to make an impression, for when we returned to the consulate the guards were already packing and by sunset no one was left except those people directly attached to the consulate.

The Consul also said that if a Japanese dignitary wanted to visit him he would always be glad to receive him, but he did not want to see them hereafter flanked by secretaries who insulted him by writing down everything that went on and that the first time he sees a spy appear at his house he will eject him. Since that day spies and secretaries have ceased to come here, and even when we have interviews at the Government House they are absent. I do not doubt that during conferences at the *Goyosho* there are secretaries hidden behind the thin partitions of the chamber because with their usual tenacity they will conform to the ancient laws of the Empire as long as possible. I have no doubt either that there are among the Japanese officers secret spies who report all that goes on. In a word, every Japanese spies on another, and it is only by that system of mutual spying that the government can maintain itself in power. But, at any rate, appearances are saved and I do not doubt that communications established between the Japanese and civilized nations will gradually destroy this system of absurd, obsolete, and absolute laws that weigh heavily upon the Empire.

Now, when we walk about the streets police agents do not dare any more to follow us; I enter the houses freely; I speak with the common people without anybody daring to oppose it. Young girls are getting to be less shy when they see us and do not run away from us anymore; beasts of burden, formerly so imbued with Japanese doctrines against foreigners, can't distinguish them anymore from their lords and masters. The dogs alone remain faithful to their principles and bark just as loud and show their teeth just as fiercely as they did the day we arrived.

Now the Governors reply to us by letters.

March 1, 1857

We have many conferences with the Governors in order to add a few articles to the Treaty of Kanagawa.[82] The first point is that of the value of the dollar. Three silver *ichibus* weigh less than a dollar, and yet the Japanese insist that here a dollar should be the equivalent of one *ichibu* so that we actually pay more than three times the value of what we buy here. The Japanese say that all mines belong to the government, that the gold and silver in the mine have the same value as wood or stone, but that as soon as the government mints it with its stamp the piece of silver acquires its worth, that accordingly, all the money brought here by foreigners must be melted up to make *ichibus*. We reply that all the governments of the world give the minted silver of other countries its accurate rate of exchange, that they are even glad to receive it and that they do not charge anything for the expenses of minting and the waste of metal incurred in the melting. Thus, the Consul refuses to pay the Japanese what he owes them until the dollar has been accepted at its just value.

The Russian corvette, upon the Consul's advice, having also refused to pay at such exorbitant rates, paid the Japanese government only one third of what the latter claimed was owed and left the other two parts in the hands of the Consul, while the decision of their respective governments was pending on that question.

It is only through such arguments that the Japanese will learn. Finally, they accepted the proposal of the Consul to weigh silver against silver and gold against gold, but they wanted to charge twenty-five per cent for minting expenses. In reply they were told that these expenses in other countries were only one half of one per cent and it was proposed that craftsmen should be brought from the United States who would take care of all the minting business for ———— per cent.[83] Thus forced to recognize the unfairness of their demands they have come down to six per cent but will take nothing less. Thus, according to all appearances, the question of currency will be amicably settled.

Second, the port of Nagasaki, being open to the Russians, is open as well to American ships.

Third, the extraterritoriality of American citizens in Japan is recognized, which makes them answerable to American laws and liable to judgment by the Consul-General for all offenses they might commit while upon Japanese territory.

According to the latest information I have been able to get from the Japanese, it seems that Japan is governed by a State Council of five people chosen by the Shogun.[84] These five people have, subject to the Shogun's approval, absolute power. The greatest princes of the Empire must kneel before them. But the sanction of the Shogun is necessary on all laws passed by that Council. When a proposal of law is made by a member of the Council and is rejected by the Shogun, if the proposal is made a second time and is again rejected by the Shogun, the unfortunate member of the Council [making the proposal] is forced to commit hara-kiri, that is to say, to cut open his own stomach and die.

March 10, 1857

The American clipper *Messenger Bird* anchors here.[85] It has on board an assorted cargo. The Japanese show no enthusiasm to buy. From a cargo made up of all kinds of things, they would buy only weapons, woolens and cotton fabrics. But once they were quoted the price of these commodities, they claimed the prices to be exorbitant and they will buy nothing at all. The *Messenger Bird* is the first [ship] to take advantage of the change in the rate of exchange of the dollar which allows only six per cent and weighs the dollar against Japanese *ichibus*. The Japanese expected that since we now pay one third of what we formerly paid, the price of American goods would go down at the same rate, for they did not understand that they used to charge three times over and that American goods were always selling according to the just value of the dollar.

May 21, 1857

Today I find myself the happy owner of a horse—a thoroughbred—a horse that cost me no less than 128,000 *casch* [cash, Chinese coins] or $27.41. What an enormous amount for a thoroughbred horse! It looks as though my affairs are not going too badly. I started off in Japan by taking a valet. Here I am now, owner of a horse! If I go on this way why shouldn't I maintain my own carriage and ask in marriage the Emperor's only daughter? Satrap that I am. Oh! New York! Oh, days spent without dinner, and the fine chances I missed to sleep in the open air. Oh, black clothes, shining with old age. Oh, beloved shoes in which my heels and toes enjoyed perfect ventilation! Oh, trousers with holes worn in them! Where are you, old friends? Come and see his Very Serene Highness, Lord Heusken, parading on a horse. No, no, it is not a rented horse! That is an unworthy insinuation! No, gentlemen, there he is on his own horse, a horse that belongs to him and for which he has paid—or must pay, but that's the same thing—the enormous sum of one hundred and fifty francs.

May 23, 1857

The interpreter Matabe has arrived here in order to replace Tatsitsiro [Moriyama Takichiro] who is returning to Nangasaki [Nagasaki].[86] The office of interpreter is hereditary and is transmitted to the eldest son. Thus, all interpreters originate from Firando [Hirado] where the Dutch and the Portuguese had their first factories, almost three centuries ago.[87]

The Japanese have given pistols the name of a small island

called Tanegasima [Tanegashima] because that is where the Portuguese arrived and introduced the use of that firearm in Japan.

June 17, 1857

After ten months of patience the Consul-General has finally succeeded in having the Governors of Shimoda sign a convention.[88] The arguments have been heated and the delays invented by the government of Japan innumerable. The Governor, Bingo no Kami, has lost his job in that diplomatic scuffle, the Japanese government having recalled him and sent Nakamura, Dewa no Kami, in his place. The recalled Governor has been assigned the position of Governor of Reparations in Edo.[89]

The First Article of the Convention "opens the port of Nagasaki to American ships, where they can procure foodstuffs, coal if available, and other things they may need, and repair damages that their ships may have incurred." This will be most helpful for steamships which take on coal.

The Second Article "gives United States citizens the right to reside permanently in Shimoda and in Hakodate and the American government may send a Vice-Consul to the latter place. This article will go into force on July 4, 1858."

The establishment of a right of permanent residence already constitutes half a treaty of commerce, and since any American citizen will be able to avail himself of it, it will not be long until American missionaries arrive in Japan. The Japanese will not expect that, but it will be explained to them later that a missionary is a citizen just as much as a merchant or a ship's captain. Women, excluded so far from Japan, will be able to use that title; but the Japanese plenipotentiaries have affixed their signatures to the treaty, and unless they fail to honor the treaty, which would bring upon them numberless calamities, they will be powerless to oppose it.

Great victory!

The Third Article stipulates that "in payment of debts, gold will be weighed against gold and silver against silver, and the Japanese will get six per cent over and above for expenses of coinage." [90] The *ichibu* that used to cost us one dollar sells subsequently to this agreement for less than thirty-four and one-half cents.

The Fourth Article provides extraterritoriality for Americans who will be judged by their Consul.

The Fifth Article gives American ships that will stop at the ports of Shimoda, Hakodate, and Nagasaki in order to procure necessary supplies or to repair damages the right to pay in merchandise if they have no currency.

The Sixth Article: "The Japanese government recognizes the right of the Consul-General of the United States to pass beyond the seven *ri* limits, but upon its request that the exercise of that right be delayed, the Consul-General has consented."

The Treaty of Kanagawa gives Americans the right to freedom in the vicinity of Shimoda within a seven *ri* radius [sixteen English miles] of which Center Island in the Bay of Shimoda constitutes the center. The Government of Edo, having thus recognized that the Consul-General, by virtue of his diplomatic privileges, is not subject to the restrictions that apply to his countrymen, gives him, when it will decide that the period of delay has expired, power to penetrate [the interior of] Japan, to go to Edo, Miaco [Miyako-Kyoto], etc., etc.

The Seventh Article gives the Consul-General and those who belong to his household the right to purchase what they need directly from the merchants and to pay them in the country's currency without the intermediation of Japanese functionaries. If the government of Edo finally agrees to concede this right to all Americans who may come here to do business, we can state that we have a Treaty of Commerce with this Empire.

The Consul-General being endowed with full powers to conclude a Treaty of Commerce with Japan, deliberations are started to name a day when he and the Governors of Shimoda will formally present their respective credentials in order to start negotiations, because the provisions of the convention I have just quoted are considered to be only additional articles to the Treaty of Kanagawa.

July 4, 1857

At the request of the Consul-General the Governors this morning send the only two cannons they own to Kakizaki, accompanied by a few artillerymen. The Consul being ill, I go in my dress uniform, accompanied by a servant who carries the flag of the United States, to the beach where the two cannons are placed. The American flag receives a twenty-one gun salute in honor of the eighty-second anniversary of the independence of the United States.

July 9, 1857

Before the exchange of credentials by the respective plenipotentiaries, the Consul-General asks the Governors, who are specifically instructed by the Council of State to answer him on all questions contained in the letters the Consul had addressed to the Council on October 25, 1856, and on January 8, 1857, for a satisfactory answer concerning the letter of the President to the Shogun of Japan, of which he is the bearer. He had previously informed the Council of his desire to go to Edo to deliver the said letter.

The Governors reply that they have been empowered to receive that letter and that one of them will deliver it in person in Edo.

A few days earlier the Consul had been notified that the Governors of Shimoda had received a letter addressed to him from the Council of State, which would be handed to him at the next interview they would have with him at the *Goyosho*. He answered that the state of his health did not allow him to leave his house and he consequently requested them to give me the letter, whereupon the Governors answered that Japanese etiquette demanded that the letter bearing the signatures of the Great Council be handed to the Consul-General himself by the Governors or the Vice-Governors.

That incident afforded him an excellent argument to hasten his trip to Edo.

"What!" he said, "you yourselves refuse to hand my secretary a letter signed by the legislative power of this Empire and you demand that it be delivered only to the person to whom it is addressed? While I, bearer of a letter signed by the Chief Executive of a powerful nation addressed to the Sovereign of this Empire, am refused permission to hand it to the person to whom it is addressed? I demand that I may deliver the letter of the President to His Majesty, the Emperor of Japan, in person, and I can give it to no one else. I repeat to you at the same time that your refusal is a great indignity to the illustrious writer, to the United States, and to myself, their representative.

"I cannot compel you to grant what I demand, but it is up to me to inform my government of the manner in which the President's letter is treated here and it will be up to my government to react."

The Governors, in turn, ashamed and confused, said that their full powers—of which they had boasted so much—did not allow them to grant that for which the Consul-General was asking. Shinano no Kami has consequently left this morning for Edo to ask the Council of State how he is to act in this matter.

Thursday, June 25, 1857

We receive today a letter from Hakodate from a certain Mr. Rice who informs the Consul that he has hoisted the American flag there for he is in possession of a warrant as commercial agent for the United States at Hakodate.[91]

July 10, 1857

Today there is a cannon shot from atop the lookout mountain.[92] This shot makes me thrill with joy; finally, after four months we shall see again the inhabitants of the civilized world. After two years without letters, I imagine an immense packet. I shall soon see my mother's handwriting. I shall know how she is, whether or not she is now happy—if she can ever be happy in this world, poor dear soul! I shall hear from my friends. I shall soon know what is happening in the world. I leap from my chair; I dance and I sing; in spite of the heat of the vertical sun I climb at a gallop a neighboring mountain; I run to a certain promontory that juts into the sea and that affords an unlimited vantage point. Standing on the edge of the precipice I follow the line of the horizon, and penetrating the fog that floats over the waves, I discover far, far away the triple masts of a large ship. I return to inform the Consul of the happy results of my hike. We expect to see the ship enter the bay at any moment, but no ship comes. I climb again mountains and hills and scramble down again all day long, but the ship has disappeared, changing its course towards the northeast. The next day I resume my search, but no ship, no letters, no tidings.

And I return embarrassed and confused
Swearing, but a little too late, that it would
not happen again.[93]

August 1, 1857

I have my horse which was in the government stables at
Kakizaki brought here where I have rented a stable near the
consulate for the enormous sum of four hundred *seni* a
month [eight sous]. The reason I haven't used my steed yet
is that I have been expecting daily an English saddle from
Hong Kong, for the Japanese saddles do not suit me at all.
Tired of waiting, I have a cotton blanket, thickly quilted,
made here. It is to be attached under the horse's belly, in the
manner of our saddles. They bring me at the same time a
groom who costs me five *ichibus* a month [$1.72] and three
ichibus [$1.03] for his food.

I went horseback riding this afternoon. The roads are
abominable. Every dozen steps you must go up or down.
The roads are strewn with stones and holes. You can go only
at a slow pace and there are only three paths, the longest of
which does not exceed half a mile, where one can risk a trot
or gallop. My improvised saddle is even more uncomfortable
than the road and keeps sliding under the belly of the horse.

August 2, 1857

After another ride, I discover that the Japanese, in order to
tie the two ends of my so-called saddle, have used only one
rope, which, as you might easily conceive, has cut into the
back of my horse in a frightful manner. Since it is very hot,
one or two months will have to pass, possibly, before I can
use him again.

August 8, 1857

The Consul was kind enough to loan me his horse, while mine is incapacitated. To top off all my troubles that horse, while stepping down a steep grade (an ordinary thing on those abominable roads of Japan), slips and wrenches the muscles of his right shoulder. According to the opinion of the veterinary surgeon, he will be lame for the rest of his days. If things continue this way, I will need a new horse every day. Old wives say that trouble never comes alone and—but I have enough with my two horses and for the love of God, let us not bring in old wives' gossip to aggravate our misery.

August 25, 1857

Shinano no Kami arrived yesterday from Edo.[94]

August 27, 1857

We have an interview with the Governors at the *Goyosho*. The Prince of Shinano begins by saying that, after many objections and difficulties, the High Council has finally agreed to receive the Consul-General in Edo. But, he added, you cannot hand the letter of the President to the Shogun himself; however, the High Council will accept it for him.

The Consul answers that he must give the letter to the Shogun personally.

The Governors reply that it cannot be done, that the Shogun never treats personally, but that all business goes through the Council of State, that the eighteen princes of Japan (princes, independent, or at least halfway so) are opposed to it, that to grant what the Consul-General is asking for would create disturbances in the Empire. If the Consul is not satisfied with the last offer of the Council, then a letter will be written, addressed to the Secretary of State in Washington, in which the above-mentioned reasons will be set forth and the Consul will be asked to kindly forward said letter.

The Consul answers that he will gladly forward any letter they will be pleased to entrust to him. "But I can assure you," he said, "that it will be of no avail. I had always believed Japan to be a single united Empire and its government to have the power to command obedience. It would not be the first time that the head of the State receives an ambassador of a foreign nation. Among others, Father Valignani, bearer of a letter from the Viceroy of Goa, has been received by him."

The Governors answer that they have leafed through all ancient documents and archives but have not been able to find any such occurrence.

August 28, 1857

We have another interview. The Consul-General opens the business matters by giving the Governors a list of a few personalities who have been received by the Shogun, as ambassadors.

Today, the answer is that all that is correct, but that nobody has ever delivered a letter to the Shogun. The Governors then reiterate their request of yesterday: would the Consul please lay aside that matter of the letter and begin immediately to inform them of those important matters he has mentioned in his letter to the Council and which he promised to communicate in Shimoda. Shinano no Kami adds that he has assured the Great Council and His Majesty himself that the Consul-General, as soon as he received permission to go to Edo, would communicate important matters to them.

The Consul answers that he has promised nothing of the kind, that he has promised to communicate to them that to which he was entrusted by the President as soon as the Governors would give him in writing permission to go to Edo and *to deliver the letter into the Shogun's own hands.*

The Governors answer that they have never heard this last condition. The Consul turns towards me and asks me whether I have ever translated to the Governors his request to deliver the letter into the Shogun's hands.

I answer that I have done it many times, more than ten or twelve times. "And how," I said, "can they disclaim today any knowledge of the last clause of your proposal, when yesterday, in giving you the reply of the High Council, they said: 'You may go to Edo, but you may not deliver the letter into the Shogun's hands. The High Council will receive it for him.'? Why answer, 'You cannot deliver the letter into the hands of the Shogun,' if you have never requested it?"

The Governors have no reply to that and try to save themselves by saying that the Consul had mentioned nothing of it at their first interview following the arrival of Dewa no Kami, and that he had added this last consideration afterwards. They reiterate several times their request that the Consul be kind enough to inform them of that important business. "For," they add, "if you refuse, we may not be able to meet again in such a pleasant manner."

The Consul, angered by that answer, asks them whether they intend to threaten him? [and says] that threats make no impression on him. They could put him in a cage, [but] he will always remain faithful to the honor which he owes his country. It was explained to us later that these words: "We may not be able to see you again in such a pleasant manner" were not a threat but a Japanese idiom that refers to hara-kiri. In other words, the Governors will be forced to cut open

their own stomachs and die if they cannot transmit a satisfactory answer to their government.

August 31, 1857

Further conferences with the Governors. They reiterate
their prayer of last Friday to begin immediately the important business which the Consul has to communicate to them.
The Consul answers that it is impossible for him to do as
they ask, but that he has two proposals to make to them.

The first one is that, after having communicated the *important matters* to the Governors, he will go immediately to
Edo and will deliver into the hands of the Shogun personally
the President's letter.

The Second Proposal: The Consul will go immediately to
Edo and deliver the President's letter into the hands of the
Premier in the presence of the Shogun. He will address the
Shogun with a speech to which His Majesty will reply. (This
last condition is also a part of the first proposal.) After the
audience, the Consul will return to Shimoda and will then
begin the important business with the Governors of that
place. The Governors beg the Consul to come back tomorrow.

Today I am brought another groom called Sada Kitsuji. I
discharged the other one, Takeshiro, as he had been doing
exactly as he pleased and was not at all what I wanted.

September 1, 1857

The Governors begin by repeating all they have mentioned
during the previous interviews. They are charmed, gratified,
and happy that the Consul should have been kind enough
yesterday to make them such an important concession as to
declare himself satisfied with delivering the letter into the
hands of the Premier in the presence of the Shogun. But
(there is always a *but* which Japanese diplomats add when-

ever they give a favorable answer), but they beg the Consul to be kind enough to add one thing to what he has proposed: instead of communicating to them the important matters after having been to Edo, he should do it before leaving for the latter place.

We answer that whether they repeat what they have said today a thousand or ten thousand times, the deal will remain just as it stands. The Consul is unshakable.

"This is my ultimatum. There is nothing I can change about it."

In reply another allusion is made to hara-kiri. Shinano no Kami says that after having assured the government [authorities] that the Consul will open consideration of important matters before going to Edo, he cannot now return to them presenting a different story.

The Consul replies that there is no question about retracting statements, that he remains faithful to what he has said; if they are satisfied with the first proposal he will open business before his departure, faithful to his promise. But, by their making another proposal and giving another concession he is not forced to abide by his words, for these are given only conditionally. The conditions removed, he is relieved of his promise.

He offers them at the same time the two proposals in writing. The Governors refused to accept them and assert that it is impossible for them to submit to the Great Council a proposal such as the Consul has just made them.

September 2, 1857

The Consul writes a letter to the Governors in which he retracts the two proposals he had submitted for their consideration. The letter is just about to be sealed when Moriyama Yenosuke arrives, sent by the two Governors. He repeats yesterday's request, saying that Shinano no Kami will, perhaps, share the fate of Bingo no Kami if the Consul will not grant him that for which he is asking.[95] For an answer he is handed the letter I have just sealed.

Around four in the afternoon, Moriyama returns saying that the Governors have not rejected at all the two proposals, that they have only begged the Consul to reconsider their wishes for a few more days and would only like him to change that last little clause; they cannot understand the importance the Consul seems to place in communicating the important matters to them afterwards.

The Consul answers that in reality he has been dissatisfied with himself ever since he made the concession to the Governors—that he would communicate his business to them prior to the delivery of the letter—that he was sure he would be blamed for this by his government—that the letter refers to those very things he has to communicate—that it is the custom in all the courts of Europe to deliver the letter before opening negotiations—that the Governors, by refusing yesterday to accept his proposal, have done him a true service, because he is now relieved of his promise and may retract it honorably—that he had only yielded to the instances of the Governors to open business before the delivery of the letter in order to facilitate negotiations and to expedite business as soon as possible—that he would never have thought he would have to wait ten months only to see that point still not settled—that from now on, the Governors are to consider his proposals as void—that he does not have any more proposals to make and that it is now up to the Governors to come forth with suggestions.

September 3, 1857

Yesterday they celebrated the festival of lanterns.[96] The Bonzes [Buddhist monks] were busy all day repeating: Amida, Amida, Amida, before the statues of Amida, of Canon [97] and of Sesi.[98] A few candles cast only a flickering glow; in the temples, the altars strewn with flowers, the statues, the incense, everything made me believe I was in a Catholic church. A number of women came to make their devotions before the altars after first having pulled the cord of a small bell and made some small money offering. Some others came to place lanterns on the graves of their family or their friends.

It is noteworthy indeed that one always sees women at their devotions and so seldom men. Whatever may be the God to whom the temple is dedicated, be it the God of the Christians or the idols of the Heathen, women are the ones to crowd the places of worship. "The last at the cross and the first at the sepulchre." The festival of lanterns is here called *Bon*. Those who belong to the Shinto religion do not celebrate it.

What powers are those of circumstances! For the past five or six months I have eaten nothing but poultry. Since we finally succeeded in securing a small pig in Shimoda, lunch today consisted of two dishes: one, pork chops (Pork! the food of the peasant), and the other, a roast pheasant, worthy of being chewed and digested by the Emperor of Japan himself. The Consul asks what I would like to be served, pheasant or pork. By Jove! Who would have believed it? I answer, and without any hesitation: "Pork, please." A lowly pig thus triumphs over a splendid pheasant. Truly, my taste is becoming plebeian.

Today is the anniversary of the *San Jacinto's* departure and today is the first time we have received any mail. Who would have guessed that a year would pass before we would receive any news? A Japanese government officer comes on behalf of the Governors to deliver us a package which has just arrived from Hakodate. Two letters from my mother, Praise God! She is happy and fully recovered; she is alive; and seven letters from Hong Kong. There remains a large package of letters and newspapers that the mail refused to take because it was too heavy. Important news from China! The letters Mr. Harris has received from Sir John Bowring, Plenipotentiary of Her British Majesty in China and Governor of Hong Kong, are most important.

September 4, 1857

Further conferences with the Governors. Nothing but boring repetitions. They claim that they never rejected the proposals. They are angry with Moriyama, the chief interpreter. For that reason he does not attend the conference. They say that if the Consul claims they have rejected the proposals then the interpreter has not accurately translated their words. For this reason they have today two other interpreters who do not know, between them, as much Dutch as Moriyama alone. That is leading things from bad to worse! I believe, after all, that it is only a scheme of the Governors so that they might regain the refused proposals. Another conference next Monday.

September 7, 1857

Another conference with the Governors. It is finally agreed that they will send a messenger to Edo to ask the government for permission to make the Consul the following proposal: He will go to Edo and deliver the letter personally to the Premier in the presence of the Shogun, etc., . . . exactly as in the second proposal withdrawn by the Consul.

Upon our return to the consulate we hear a cannon shot from the lookout mountain. In spite of the precedent of the whaler I climb said mountain in my slippers under a burning sun. When I reach the summit I am gratified to see in the distance a large ship coming from the south and headed for the port. With the help of a telescope I seem to see it flying the Russian flag. I run down the mountain at full gallop. I regret it is not an American ship because, since the negotiations for our trip to Edo are still pending, we might lose the glory of being the first embassy ever to be received by the Shogun in his capital and of breaking the ice that surrounds the chief of that Empire like another arctic pole, if another foreign mission arrives in this country.

The sun has already gone down and it casts a reddish glow on the summit of the mountains that rise towards the west. I can't restrain myself; I take a boat and ten oarsmen; this time I want to be sure of my ship and should I row all night long, I just have to catch up with it; this time the ship will not escape us!

We have left the Bay of Shimoda; we are now on the open sea. It is very dark. For the past hour and a half we have rowed at random. Signs of discouragement are beginning to appear. I promise a tip to the oarsmen—in every country of the world a tip is effective—and the Japanese increase their efforts. One of them glimpses a light! Hurrah! We are saved. The moon is now slowly emerging from the clouds and casts a soft and welcome light around us. The steep coastlines and the reefs are covered by turns with a fringe, gleaming like snow under the sun of the Alps: it comes from the waves breaking against the rocks. The mountains that form the promontory of Idsu [Idzu] and the silvery waves of the Pacific Ocean stand out in the darkness. Near us a war frigate raises heavenwards her triple masts, and sways majestically upon the deep.

If we were still in the good old days one would think twice before boarding an unknown ship, but even if someone had assured me that this one was the famous *Flying Dutchman*, or a red pirate flying its grim flag adorned with the skull and bones, I would not have hesitated a moment to go aboard, so great was my desire to escape, were it only for a moment, my Patmos [99] or my St. Helena. Who can it be? Is it a Russian, a French, or English, or an American? But soon my uncertainty was dispelled, for I heard the familiar tune of "Yankee Doodle." A few moments later I was aboard the corvette *Portsmouth* and was greeted by Captain Foote and the officers.[100] I am led into their quarters and there I spend two hours, the most pleasant two hours I have spent since the *Olivuzza* left. I can assure you that conversation did not lag. I did not need to draw upon stock phrases! "How warm it is today! We are going to have some rain," etc. We have so many questions to ask each other. I, poor ignoramus, who hardly knows whether the world still exists, and on the other hand, the officers of the *Portsmouth* who want to know in turn how things are going in Japan. Finally I leave, carrying a huge package of letters and newspapers which I begin to read by the light of a Japanese lantern once I am back in the boat. At two in the morning I am back at the consulate.

September 8, 1857

The corvette anchors at the entrance to the harbor. The Captain and a part of his staff come to pay us a visit.

September 9, 1857

Today we have dinner in the Captain's own room. The first lieutenant attends. He is Mr. McCombe, son of the famous general of that name.[101]

September 10, 1857

The Consul introduces the Captain and his staff to the Governors at the *Goyosho*. Afterwards we have dinner in the officers' quarters.

September 12, 1857

The corvette weighs anchor and departs for Hakodate. What with the dinners, helping the officers at the Bazaar and writing letters to the government I have had almost no time to think of my own affairs. After nine months an occasion appears to write letters—I have a mountain of them before me to be answered—but I can't do it. The corvette can stay only five days here and all my time is taken up with dinners and official letters. I have been writing all night and still have been able to write only three of my personal letters.

Complete harmony seems to prevail among the officers of the *Portsmouth*. Captain Foote is a charming man, simple, open, sincere, generous, a true naval officer. At the dinner table he was telling us about his battles with the Chinese (I love to hear an old sea dog tell of his feats) and the capture of the Barrier Forts. He was commander-in-chief of the fleet after the departure of the Commodore.

He related to us in such a candid and animated manner how he had bombarded the four fortresses, how he had landed at the head of two hundred eighty men and routed the Chinese who numbered more than twelve thousand able-bodied men, and how he had taken the fortresses armed with one hundred fifty cannon. There was one enormous cannon, twenty-three feet long.

Captain Foote promised me to use his influence with the government on my behalf and to request that my salary be paid to me starting on the day that I left New York.

September 23, 1857 [102]

Another conference at the *Goyosho*. Dispatches arrived from Edo granting the Consul everything for which he is asking. We will be received in Edo with the greatest honors. We will be granted an audience with the *Taikun* [title of the Emperor which means "great lord." In time of war he takes the name of Shogun, which means generalissimo; at other times his subjects address him with the title of *Kubo-sama*].

The plenipotentiary will deliver a speech, after which I shall hand him the letter of the President. He, in turn, will give it to Hotta, Bitchū no Kami, President of the Great Council. Several other points of lesser importance are arranged, some of them absurd, mere trifles, but demanded by Japanese customs. There is a fruitless attempt to make the Consul pay his respects in the Japanese manner; that is to say, on his knees with his head bent low—which he positively refused. He is willing to pay the same homage to the Taikun of Japan as is presented by an Ambassador to the most powerful monarchs of the West, but nothing more. Shinano no Kami and Moriyama will leave in a few days for Edo.

October 21, 1857 [103]

Moriyama returns from Edo. The day of our departure is decided upon. It is Monday, November 23. They inform us of a multitude of arrangements, most of which are exceedingly childish. Japanese diplomacy has gone to great lengths of accuracy and clarity, even to giving us two maps of the Imperial Palace and indicating to us the different rooms we are to occupy on the day of the audience, the stairs, the corridors we will have to pass through.

On the day of the audience we will leave our Embassy Hotel in a *norimon*. Once we arrive at the outer enclosure of the palace, I am to leave my *norimon,* as will the Vice-Governor of Shimoda.

At the inner wall, where the greatest dignitaries of the

Empire must leave their *norimon,* the plenipotentiary shall leave his, as will the Governor of Shimoda, the Prince of Shinano, and we will walk together towards the great staircase of the Palace.

The Consul, having asked if anybody ever left his *norimon* at a place more convenient to the entrance of the Palace proper than that where he was to leave his when on his way to pay their respects to the sovereign, was at first told no. But when he asked for a positive answer, they replied that everybody must leave his *norimon* at the spot where he is to leave his, except the three brothers of the King who leave theirs a little further on; but the highest princes of the Empire and other Princes of the Blood must take the walk from the inner wall to the entrance of the Palace.

When we arrive at the top of the stairway, we are to be greeted by two *Ometsuke* [spies-in-chief], but we are told that these are officers of the very highest rank who are to act as masters of ceremonies.

We will be led into a room where the floor is covered with matting. There we will remove our soiled shoes and replace them with brand new ones. The Consul has no objection to this because the matting is at once table and bed to the Japanese who keep them scrupulously clean. We can count ourselves fortunate that they don't insist that we go shoeless, since the Japanese never wear shoes inside their houses.

We will agree in advance on the speech of the Ambassador and on the reply of the Taikun, so that the Ambassador will speak directly to the monarch in English, and the latter will reply in Japanese, without the intermediation of an interpreter, etc.

Yesterday I nearly killed myself. While I was riding a horse on these miserable roads of Japan, my steed stumbled, fell, and I was projected over his head to the ground. I made a complete somersault and landed head first on the rocks strewn on the road. I might have wrenched my back or fractured my skull in those acrobatics! I jumped back on my horse and came back to the consulate, to the great surprise of the inhabitants of Kakizaki, with blood dripping in great drops from my hat. It seems that a sharp stone on which I had fallen had made a rather deep cut. It was precisely at the same spot where the Catholic clergy wear the tonsure. "Wretched you," I thought, thinking of my tonsured skull. "They are going to mistake you for a Jesuit or a Franciscan in disguise, and if they don't cut off your head immediately, the alarmed authorities of Japan will lock you up in a cage for the rest of your days!"

November 13, 1857

It seems that the Japanese do everything they must do at the same time, prescribed by law. They take their breakfast, lunch, and dinner all exactly at the same hour. They change clothes four times a year on the same day. One day everybody is busy drying fish; another day is to dry fabrics woven by the women. Apparently they go even further, for today everybody without exception has a cold, certainly by order of the government.

November 23, 1857

This morning between six and seven o'clock the yard of the temple fills with a crowd of people, litter-bearers, soldiers, coolies, etc., etc. Kikuna Sennojo comes on behalf of the Governor to tell the Ambassador—that's how we now style the Consul-General—that everything is ready and that he has been appointed to head the party and to see that everything proceeds in good order as far as Edo.

Having entrusted the care of our household and possessions

to our four Chinese (I thank Heaven that I can always carry my belongings, movable or immovable, on my person), we mount our horses in order to avoid for as long as possible being enclosed in our *norimon*. Kikuna, an Imperial officer of the second class, precedes us followed by a soldier bearing his pike, and the other persons of his retinue; then comes the Ambassador on horseback, preceded by a standard-bearer and followed by two samurai, a man armed with a huge umbrella and a shoe-bearer. Then comes his Excellency, the Most Serene Mr. de Heusken on his steed, followed by two samurai, etc., etc.

Upon arriving in front of the Governor's palace in Naka-mura where the Japanese retinue which is to accompany us to Edo is waiting, we dismount and greet the Vice-Governor of Shimoda, Wakana Myosaburo, who had left his *norimon* and come to greet us. After having exchanged the usual com-pliments—and the Japanese does not lack for those—we start again in single file, Master Kikuna always at the head, then the Ambassador, myself, the Japanese officers—the Vice-Gov-ernor's *norimon* terminates the procession.

We skirted the river which waters the Valley of Shimoda and admire the rich crop of rice, which, after having embel-lished the countryside around Shimoda, covering it with green when young and with gold when ripe, has just been cut by the sickles of the harvesters and will soon fill the Imperial warehouses and those of the Princes of the Empire.

After having traveled two *ri,* we rest for a half hour in a *miya* [Shinto temple] to smoke a few pipes of tobacco and drink the ever-present tea.

A few people attached to the Imperial Bazaar of Shimoda who had accompanied us that far, following an ancient Japanese custom, are led to the Ambassador. After paying him a number of compliments they hand him pieces of paper on which their names are written. Informed by the interpreter that these people expect some kind of reward for their reiterated expressions of friendliness and respect, he has tips given to them and they depart.

We resume our journey and cross a mountain about three thousand feet high. Nature here appears less fruitful and offers a striking contrast with the fertile valley we have just left behind, when a lovely waterfall about sixty-five feet high fills this gloomy and monotonous scene with life. I love waterfalls.

At 2:30 P.M., we arrived at Nashimoto at the base of Mount Amagi. We have covered six miles today. After this, I need not add that railroads have not yet been invented in this country.

A *tera* [Buddhist temple] situated upon an eminence from which one enjoys a lovely view of the neighboring countryside has been prepared to receive us. The temple is built on a terrace and a lane lined with magnificent pines leads the weary traveler to it. Two hundred feet below one sees a lovely little brook cascading its clear and limpid waters from stone to stone and flowing into the sea a couple of leagues in the distance.

Kikuna comes to make his apologies for not having been able to do better because the district we are crossing is quite poor and isolated and is lacking in good hotels because there are so few travelers. The other officers come in their turn to present their respects to the Ambassador.

One is always making compliments in this country. They say the weather is fine; they hope the Ambassador will sleep well; they are sorry the lodgings are not better, but there will be an improvement as we near Edo; they are glad they were chosen to accompany him, etc., etc.

Since the mats which cover the floor of palaces and cottages alike are at once table, chair, and bed to the Japanese, we have been compelled to take with us two chairs, a table, mattresses, etc. These good Japanese! They are full of attentions. They have built a bathroom expressly for us!

I find the countryside so beautiful that I take my cane and leave for a walk through the neighbourhood leaving at the temple my retinue of soldiers, valets, shoe-bearers, etc.—to the great stupefaction of the natives who cannot understand why a man traveling with a *norimon,* a horse, and a number of servants should go walking all by himself, like a peasant going to work in his field. After having crossed two hills and a stream I see two soldiers running after me, while two others, out of breath, run to me from another direction. The poor fellows are exhausted; they have had a hard time catching up with me. They tell me that the Vice-Governor, having arrived at the temple, wants to pay his respects to the Ambassador and that I am needed to interpret what he has to say.

Although I have no doubt that all this has been done to interrupt my rural wandering, I retrace my steps and find the Ambassador and the Vice-Governor trying to outdo each other, gesticulating, speaking respectively English and Japanese to the interpreter who understands only Dutch and his native tongue. The Vice-Governor, of course, has nothing more to say than the eternal, "The weather is nice; I am charmed by this, and desolated by that."

After his departure I take a cold bath which refreshes me greatly, and after dinner I read a few strophes of Corneille and go to seek rest in the arms of Morpheus.

November 24, 1857

This morning at eight o'clock we set out to ascend the summit of Amagi, a mountain about five thousand feet high.[104] We climb steep paths above deep chasms. Sometimes there are steps hewn out of the rock like a genuine staircase, because the path follows an almost vertical grade. The paths are so narrow that four men cannot walk there abreast and the curves of the route are so sharp that our *norimon* can hardly negotiate them.

In crossing the mountains of the promontory of Idzu I understand only too well that when the Japanese chose the port of Shimoda for the Americans, they gave them a piece of land that was more inaccessible from Nippon's side than an island, because the obstacles placed by nature between the aforementioned town and the rest of Japan make any extensive traffic by land an impossibility.

The descent is even worse than the way up. It seems an abyss is opening under our very steps ready to swallow us; and then the sharp outcropping of rock pushing through what little sand and turf there is on the road offers no foothold for a horse's hoof.

I dismount, preferring to walk, my two samurai, the shoe-bearer and the umbrella-bearer still following me like my own shadow. I am beginning to realize that grandeur has its disadvantages and that Sancho Panza was right when he divested himself of his governorship.

What wouldn't I give to be an ordinary traveler and go through these mountains leisurely, stopping at attractive spots, or stretching myself out on the grass according to my fancy?

Now, if I stop, the whole procession must stop and I run a chance that the persons of my retinue will step on my heels, and in spite of my immense importance and my present exalted grandeur, I could then very well establish an intimate relationship between my nose and the mud of the road.

The skies, fair so far, are getting overcast. Ah! That's my own fault! Why do I have that person with the umbrella always by my side? I am sure that umbrella will bring me bad luck. The cypress groves are becoming thicker and line the road on either side. I see vast expanses covered with horse-radish or wild turnip.

Here and there through a clearing in the foliage or through the ravines that cut through the surrounding hills, we can glimpse in the distance the hazy blue waters of the Pacific which we have not seen since we left Shimoda.

On the summit of the mountain there is a small inn where we rest for a half hour. Wherever we go it seems that a kind genie supplies the Japanese with food and drink. In a wink, without us knowing from where it comes, they are supplied with all kinds of victuals, and take their dinners, suppers or lunches as comfortably as they would at home. Descending the mountain we stop again after an hour's travel at another inn where the Japanese take a second dinner.

The road is exceedingly muddy here so that my shoes sink constantly into the mire and through the attraction of two bodies in contact, atmospheric pressure, lack of skill of the tanner, and the lack of professional conscience of the shoe-maker, the leather tears. That presents me with the distress-ing necessity of placing myself under torture, seeing my limbs crippled or my muscles stiffened, in a word, enclosing myself in my *norimon.*

As we near the valley and emerge from the clouds that hover over the summit of Amagi, the countryside begins to unfold; valleys of ravishing beauty upon which the sun casts a gentle glow appear before our eyes. Rounding a mountain, I sight through the foliage of a few pine trees a white peak that gleams in the sun. In an instant I realize that I am look-ing at Fujiyama. Never in my life will I forget the sight of that mountain as I saw it today for the first time, and I don't think anything in the world will ever equal its beauty.

There are mountains three times higher than Fuji; the glaciers of Switzerland are, no doubt, impressive and mag-nificent; the summit of The Himalayas, the sublime Dawalaquiri,[105] raises its venerable brow to immeasurable heights, but one cannot see it until one has climbed other mountains that hide it from sight in the plains; one sees but ice and glaciers; snows surround you wherever you may turn your eyes. But here, in the midst of a smiling countryside covered with abundant crops—with pine groves and giant camphor trees that seem to vie in longevity with the very soil where they were born, making shade with their majestic foliage for some *miya,* or chapel, dedicated to the ancient Gods of the Empire, and as a backdrop for this theater of plenty and serenity—the pure outline of the unique Fujiyama rises like two symmetrical lines toward the sky, whose pale blue seemed dark, compared to the immaculate snows of the mountain that reflected, like another Kohinoor, the rays of the setting sun.

In spite of myself I pulled the reins of my horse and, carried away by an outburst of enthusiasm, I took off my hat and cried: "Great, glorious Fujiyama!" Glory forever to the mountain of mountains of the Pacific Sea, which alone raises its venerable brow covered with eternal snow amidst the verdant countryside of Nippon! Jealous of its beauty, it will not suffer a rival which might lessen its splendor. Its crown of snow stands out alone above the highest mountains of Nippon, and Amagi, which we have just passed after a most difficult day, seems only a small hill, hardly worth mentioning.

Ah! Why don't I have about twenty of the friends of my younger days around me! The surrounding hills would soon repeat the echo of a thrice repeated *hip, hip, hip, hurrah* in honor of the sublime Fujiyama.

Never, anywhere, have I seen that mountain as beautiful as it appears from here. A few steps from this point we reach a temple, the Temple of Yugashima, where we are to spend the night. From the windows of my room I can enjoy an excellent vista of my favorite mountain. I draw a sketch of it, and I can assure you that it is a detestable sketch, one that resembles anything but Fujiyama.

We have covered six *ris* today.

Wednesday, November 25, 1857

This morning we leave Yugashima. The fact that the road was rough had kept us until now within the bounds of Japanese respectability, progressing at turtle's pace with all the dignity of a funeral procession, but now the temptation of a level road, leading through the plain to Fujiyama and recalling to our memories the well-paved roads of Europe, prevailed over our regard for the etiquette of Dai Nippon, and, spurring our mounts, we soon left behind samurais, *norimons,* emblems of decorum, Vice-Governors, etc., etc. They all disappeared in the distance, except Kikuna who was on horseback, two soldiers and a standard-bearer who kept pace with an emulation worthy of praise. The whole spectacle greatly surprised the poor Japanese, who watched us with an abashed expression, unable to understand why people of so high a station, extravagant enough to have umbrellas borne behind them under a perfectly clear sky, should let themselves be carried away by speedy horses like poor plebeians, instead of reclining comfortably in their *norimons* like true sons of Daimyos.

Poor Kikuna, unaccustomed to this speedy progress, finally falls from his horse and makes a rude acquaintance with our common mother. Fortunately he was not hurt. He says that the blame should be put on the horse, and if the horse could speak, he would doubtless put the blame on his rider.

We arrive at a Buddhist temple built by Yoritomo [106] where we have a rather interesting conversation with an octogenarian who has preserved all the spirit of his youth and whose dark black hair does not betray a single white strand. Everywhere along the road and in the fields gatherings of people watch us go by, all kneeling, their hands placed on the ground as a mark of profound respect.

Soldiers, upon our arrival, push people to the roadside, ordering them to stand in the fields at a respectful distance. The Ambassador has Kikuna informed that he does not want people to be dispersed, and upon his insistence the soldiers desist.

About nightfall we arrive at Mishima, a city of twenty streets on the Tōkaidō, or great highway of Japan. We like the hotel where we pass the night very much. It is extremely well kept. The quarters are convenient and very clean, overlooking a garden which contains artificial rocks, ponds, shells, firs pruned into bizarre shapes, small lanes with stones laid on the pathways so as not to soil your shoes. Today we have covered eight *ris*. After having rested for a half hour, we go to see a *miya* [temple]. We go there afoot, passing through an immense crowd of people gathered on both sides of the road. The grounds of this Shinto temple are very extensive, divided by lanes bordered by majestic fir trees. At the entrance stand two towers, or wooden pagodas, three storied and painted in red.

The temple itself was ruined by an earthquake three years ago.[107] Along the lanes one can read the names of the charitable people who have contributed to the rebuilding of the *miya* written with ink on small boards. There are so many names that, if the donations are in the least substantial, there should be the wherewithal to build an edifice which would outdo that of Solomon. The Ambassador having contributed his part to the collection for the temple, the priests come in full costume to thank him.

There is also a huge pond filled with goldfish, the largest I have ever seen, but they have this in common with the goldfish of civilized countries that when you throw them something to eat they come to you in great numbers, fighting among themselves in order to get the delicacies which you offer them.

Mr. Harris is handed a letter from Mr. Donker Curtius, Commissioner from the Netherlands to Japan.

Thursday, November 26, 1857

This morning we are leaving the good town of Mishima. A hard day lies before us since we must ascend the mountain of Hakone which rises to about six thousand feet above sea level. I prefer to climb it afoot with Wakana Myosaburo, officer first class, and Gohara Isaburo, officer second class, with whom I begin a conversation in Japanese which lasts for a long time because it takes me about ten times longer to express a thought in Japanese (than in my native tongue) and after all my pains I often fail to make myself understood at all. But the satisfaction I feel from speaking Japanese is so gratifying to me that I keep on talking, and if my words do not sound too clear I throw in a word of Latin or Greek to the great edification of my audience.

I also take pleasure in quoting to them a few verses by Racine or Corneille and I have myself the pleasure of making the mountain of Hakone echo the imprecations of Camille.

The great highway, or the Tōkaidō, on which we are now traveling is bordered by terraces which rise about ten feet above the road, and upon which are planted magnificent cypresses and pines, probably the same trees which shaded good Kaempfer on his way to Edo; Kaempfer has given us the best available history of the Japan which I recognize again at each step, in each village, in each custom of the Japanese which he has so admirably described. The physiognomy of Japan has not changed since the time of Kaempfer. No civil wars have come to devastate its territory. Its fertile fields have not suffered under the trampling of horses or the weight of guns, the humble dwellings of peasants have not been set afire by undisciplined soldiers.

Each year the harvest has been reaped and stored in warehouses designed to receive it and the sweat of peasants has not been sacrificed to the fury of Mars or of Bellona. The same odd coiffure covers the heads of the Japanese. Their clothes are cut in the same manner as those of their ancestors. Their feet are protected by the same straw shoes. The same common people till the soil and prostrate themselves in the dust before the same masters who glory in the possession of two swords as in days of old, while the innate politeness of the Japanese, which the old authors mentioned, keeps shining with all its original splendor.

If we now turn and look to the Occidental world and consult the history of the past, how many pages are written with letters of blood, how many fertile countries have been turned into inhospitable deserts, how many peoples erased from the list of nations, how many thrones overthrown, the heads of those who called themselves masters of the world, who in the insolence of their power proclaimed "l'état c'est moi," falling under the blade of the executioners.

With what surprise the Japanese must have contemplated the few representatives who from time to time requested his hospitality! I can imagine the proud Portuguese and Spanish, sometimes pirates, sometimes merchants, sometimes propagators of the faith, moving along in the shade of these very trees which are now spreading their green foliage over the writer of these lines. Their plumes fly in the breeze and their shining armour reflects the rays of the sun, while the stones which are strewn along the route resound against their long swords carried in belts slung from their shoulders. The Jesuits, wrapped in their cassocks, are filled with ambition and love for their nascent order and with pride in planting the cross in the Buddhist monasteries and the Shinto temples of the Empire. Then come the officers of the Dutch factory at Deshima with their dress wigs and their three-cornered hats, watched by the satellites of the Shoguns whose suspicious policies cause them to see the germ of new trouble or of another rebellion in every foreigner whom they still allow to remain. [Heusken's manuscript is mutilated on the ensuing page by someone who probably removed a sketch by the unfortunate expedient of cutting the page with scissors. The first legible line begins with the end of a sentence "lui semble" and resumes] . . . , while, despite all the changes and all the revolutions which have taken place among us, I see, when looking around me, the same Japanese who, three centuries ago, saw from the heights of their isolated island the first European ship draw near the coasts of Dai Nippon.

In climbing the mountains of Hakone and suffering all that the worst of roads—the most uneven and pitted, strewn with rocks and covered with mud—may force the traveler to endure, one finds oneself richly rewarded by the superb vistas which are offered from time to time.

The industrious Japanese have made the most of these places by building there small inns. . . . [At this point the manuscript is again interrupted due to the loss of the half page. It resumes with a line of text which has been partly obscured by the marks of the scissors.]

. . . In the Ocean because . . . of Amagi which we crossed two days ago, and behind us the Bay of Suruga and the city of that name, so famous in the annals of Japan, where the founder of the present dynasty had his fortified castle.[108] After having climbed for about four *ri*, we reached the summit of the mountain, and after having descended a half *ri*, we arrived at the village of Hakone of about three hundred houses.

Upon our arrival at the inn of this village we were shown into our apartments which overlooked a small lake, the waters of which were of a deep blue color and the bed of which had certainly been formed by a dead crater. The lake is surrounded by steep mountains, covered by vegetation, behind which Fujiyama can be seen.

Here I must confirm the observation of Kaempfer, that it is very cold here in winter. The wind which blows from the lake and from beyond the snows of Fuji make this place much colder than the surrounding area.

At the far end of this village there is a station or barrier where, from time immemorial, those going to or returning from the capital are searched by Imperial officers. This barrier is placed in a defile so that, since the surrounding mountains are very high and steep, anyone who wishes to go to Edo is compelled to go through this very passage.

The Ambassador was told that when passing through the aforementioned barrier, the officers on duty would open the door of his *norimon,* or he could have it opened by his servant, and after having glanced at the inside they would close it immediately. If he had any objection he could go through the barrier on horseback or afoot. (He was told that the most powerful Princes of the Empire, the Prince of Satsuma himself, submit themselves to this right of inspection.)

The Ambassador replied to them that in his quality as a representative of the President he could not subject himself to such treatment, that he would go through the barrier in his *norimon* or he would not pass through it at all, that the Prince of Satsuma, for all his exalted rank, is still a liege going to pay his homage to his lord, but that for himself, since he enjoyed full rights of extraterritoriality, he could not submit to any right of inspection.

After two hours of delays and consultations between the Vice-Governor of Shimoda and the Commandant of the Guard, it is finally agreed that Mr. Harris will go through the gate in his *norimon,* the door of which will not be opened, but they reserve for themselves the right to open mine.

Upon arriving at the barrier, Takizo, Mr. Harris' valet, opened the door of his *norimon* and closed it immediately. Mr. Harris was furious, believing with reason that the Japanese had broken their given word; but it appears, after all, that the only person responsible for this was Takizo, who, having heard Ikizo being ordered to open the door of my *norimon* and knowing that everyone has to submit to this custom, and being ignorant of the rights of general extraterritoriality of ambassadors, believed that he was subject to the order as well and obeyed it.

Because of the aforementioned delay, we arrived at Odawara around nine o'clock in the evening, after having covered today a distance of eight *ris.* After sunset we lit countless lanterns and also torches called *taimatsu,* made of very thin bamboos bound together. I observed along the route a great number of waterfalls having their source in the lake of Hakone, located at about five thousand feet above sea level. It is through them that the lake discharges its excess of water. They finally form a river which flows into the sea near Odawara.[109]

The descent from Hakone is as difficult as the ascent. The huge stones, everywhere on the road, do not make things easier for the traveler; but they are obliged to leave them there to preserve the road and make it passable during the heavy rainfall of the rainy season which changes it into the bed of a torrent whose waters wash away everything except the aforementioned stones which offer resistance.

The finest hotel I saw during our trip was at Hato, about

one league from the village of Hakone. The apartments were extremely clean, but this is the usual thing in Japan. They were very well tended and overlooked a dainty garden studded with all kinds of flowers, artificial rocks, dwarfed trees trimmed in all sorts of shapes, three lovely waterfalls (due to the proximity of Hakone Lake) which, falling from rock to rock, made an extremely lovely effect, miniature grottoes, ponds filled with goldfish and carp, etc. Everything, even the pebbles, had been scrupulously cleaned.

When it was dark the light of the torches and of the lanterns, following the irregular turns of the road, made our procession look like a luminous serpent; the sound of the unseen waterfalls pleasantly strokes our ears while the booming of the sea resounds dully in the distance.

As we approached Odawara, the pure sea air felt cooler and cooler. Before entering this town a detachment of police, carrying lanterns on the ends of poles, pounded on the street iron rods provided with rings of the same metal to do honor to the American Embassy. Thus escorted we cross the pleasant town of Odawara and finally stop at a good-looking house where we put up for the night.

Friday, November 27, 1857

This morning at about eight-thirty we set out for Fujisawa. I have never heard the waves breaking on the shore with such violence as at Odawara. The whole house, although at a fair distance from the sea, was trembling, and I believed that I heard an earthquake.

After a trip of eight *ri* we arrived at Fujisawa, where we we will spend the night. Hakone is the last mountain that we have to cross. From Odawara the Tōkaidō traverses a plain which extends to beyond Edo, and we see the mountains only in the distance. The road is perfectly tended, smoothly leveled, and would be suitable for carriages, which are not as yet used in this country.

On both sides of the road, as far as the eye can reach, one sees rice fields in which countless flocks of storks walk with measured tread, heedless of everyone, or take wing to settle again in the next field, now running, then flying, or running and flying at the same time. Great numbers of wild geese streak across the sky, and their honks, although not at all melodious, please me because they are familiar to me and remind me of other times and other places.

In all the places through which we pass, a deputation of the authorities comes to meet us and escorts us through the place, acting, so to speak, as a guard of honor. Before the entrance to the place the deputation is lined up in order; they pay the usual compliments, bowing their foreheads to the ground, which they repeat when they leave us. The officials are accompanied by policemen armed with iron rods. In this way an open passage is always made in the middle of the road. Before the houses the people are gathered in groups in order to let us pass. They are all sitting in good order, not uttering one word, hands towards the ground as a sign of the deepest respect. Not only the ground floors but also the second floors are packed with people assembled here to watch us pass.

The government had ordered that no one should be on the road while we were passing, but should stop in towns or villages until we had passed. The Tōkaidō, the great highway of Japan, usually crowded with a multitude of travelers, *norimons*, horses, priests and mendicants, *samaburi*,[110] *bicouni*,[111] and with the immense retinues of Princes, was absolutely deserted, and I met, at the most, two or three *norimons* and five or six men on that great highway of Japan from Mishima to Shinagawa, a distance of about eighty miles.

For this reason the towns contained many more people

than their respective populations, without mentioning those who had come from every part of the Empire solely to see us pass. Undoubtedly they may have paid an enormous price for a window overlooking the street where we would pass. The government had given orders to render the Embassy all possible honors during our entire trip. Temporary bridges had been thrown over the rivers which we had to cross; roads had been repaired in several spots.

Some people, walking ahead of our procession continually shouted: *"Shita ni iro, shita ni iro,"* kneel down, kneel down, and all the common people, men, women, and children, knelt down and remained in an attitude of the deepest respect until we had passed. I traveled from Shimoda to Shinagawa, a journey of seven days, amidst a kneeling population, while our heralds continually repeated the *"shita ni iro,"* kneel down, even in the remotest parts of the forests or on the tops of the mountains where there was no one, as if the trees and plants should pay homage to the Embassy of the Republic Par Excellence.

The sight of all these human beings, as good as I am or even better, on their knees began to disgust me. Here a white-haired old man bent his trembling knees and lowered his venerable brow; there a young girl turned her lovely face towards the ground and remained in a humiliating posture.

It is certainly an excessive honor to see all the beauties of Japan on their knees before oneself; but this honor did not please me; if I had been allowed at least to kneel with her, this thing would have had a different complexion.

Fortunately, on the day of our arrival at Edo, the order ceased to be effective, and everyone stood erect and looked us straight in the face. This relieved me very much. I must still add that the order to kneel was applicable only to the [common] people; those rejoicing in the possession of the two swords [samurai] were exempted from it. What an immense power the government must wield here to order all the people to bow down before two foreigners.

Saturday, November 28, 1857

This morning we visit a Buddhist temple and then leave for Kawasaki, where we will spend Sunday. We pass through Kanagawa, a town consisting of an extremely long street built along a bay which opens into the inner bay of Edo. There I see two corvettes and a schooner, the first two, it is said, were built at Satsuma and Mito two years ago. They were constructed from rather old-fashioned models in this enlightened century of steamships and clippers. A little farther on I discover a third corvette, and in the distance before Shinagawa, the paddle-wheel corvette, the *Soembing,* now called the *Kanko Maru,* given by the government of the Netherlands to the Japanese government.[112]

At Kanagawa we stopped in a lovely little inn, which luckily does not reek of the Daimyo, the rooms overlooking a lovely little garden washed by the waves of the bay. We enjoy here a magnificent view of Edo Bay, the village of Yokohama, where Commodore Perry concluded the treaty of friendship with Japan while the aforementioned corvettes provide a somewhat European aspect.

In the evening we arrive at Kawasaki, where we will stay tomorrow to pass the Sabbath since Mr. Harris does not want to travel on that day. Once at the hotel, Mr. Harris objects to staying there. The hotels on the highway are called *Honjin.* The establishments are invariably provided with a carriage gateway and other daimyoesque attributes which are opened for only persons of quality.

The government gives an appointment to whoever will build the *Honjin* with his money, and the right of keeping such an establishment is hereditary and passes from father to

son. Since persons of quality are obliged to go there, it sometimes happens that the owners of these establishments, being
assured of their aristocratic clientele, neglect to keep them
in good condition, so that the public hotels in many instances
are better maintained. We found the *Honjin* of Kawasaki in
a deplorable condition.

Despite the conspicuous honor of spending a night in a
room, the floor of which is six inches above the floor of the
others, where only Daimyo and Shomyo have exchanged their
august breath, Mr. Harris prefers to sleep in a house where
the cracks in the wainscoting do not let in the cold air of a
November night and from where the eyes can rest on more
interesting things than partitions and draperies decorated
with the Imperial colors which protect the Daimyo from the
rays of the sun, the azure blue of the sky, and other common
and vulgar things, because in Japan, the greater a man is,
the more secluded he is, the less he moves, and the less he
speaks.

I believe that the greatest honor that can be paid a dignitary of this Empire would be to wall him up alive in a niche,
as was done in other times to the nun who was unfaithful to
her vows. *Vade in pace!*

They hastened to procure us another lodging. It was a little
white pavilion, detached from the main house (a public
tavern), with two apartments on the first floor overlooking
the environs of the town and the rice fields where the storks
were strolling peacefully. This establishment is called the
Mannenya [House of Ten Thousand Years], but despite this
antediluvian name it is rather comfortable.[113]

Sunday, November 29, 1857

This afternoon we go afoot to a Buddhist temple, the most
beautiful I have seen in Japan.[114] The temple is built in the

shape of a cross, the roof of copper. There was a great quantity of vases, lotuses, and other ornaments, all in copper. They were made with a great deal of taste, some bearing the signs of the zodiac in bas-relief, devils, satyrs, and beautifully simulated flowers.

Before the main altar there was a copper lotus of a colossal size. Tapers and lamps burned before the images of Amida, Kannon, and Seishi. The Bonzes were in their sacerdotal habits. Mr. Harris, having made a gift to the priests, the leader among them thanked him with a majestic bow. With his head entirely shaven, his rosy cheeks puffing on both sides, he resembled one of those jolly, good abbots of the Middle Ages receiving the tithes from the faithful. The Bonzes of other Asiatic nations never express gratitude when they are given a gift. These gentlemen accept everything they are given, but thank no one but God for having moved the hearts of men to charity.

Monday, November 30, 1857

We depart early this morning. The Mannenya is quite near the barrier of Kawasaki. A few steps from the barrier we embark on small boats to cross the Logo River.[115] After a short ride we reach Owari where we rest in a plum-tree garden. We are served plums and other fruit preserved in salt. Near Shinagawa we pass the place, mentioned by Kaempfer, where the executioner does his duty. It is a small field which borders the road with two or three trees and a big stone, like those of Japanese tombs. Otherwise one cannot see anything. All the horrible implements of this kind of place, the heads, the bones, the crows picking the corpses, which Kaempfer mentions, I could not see at all. Perhaps the government had ordered the clearing of the place upon our arrival.

At Shinagawa we fall again into the abominations of a

Honjin. From the renowned room with the elevated floor, a tiny garden adorned with two or three dwarf pine trees, with stones representing rocks and a small hill topped by a dwarf tree, all this surrounded by sublime walls and eternal flags, regales the eyes.

Here we prepare ourselves for our entry into the capital of Japan with all the solemnity possible. Though I would have preferred to go on horseback, Mr. Harris judged it proper to enter by *norimon,* as (he thought) more suitable.

The procession was opened by the Vice-Governor of Shimoda, Wakana Myosaburo, in a *norimon* surrounded by four soldiers, and preceded by a man carrying his pike; then came another one carrying his bows and arrows, two others carrying his travel chests, etc., etc. Then came Mr. Harris, in his *norimon,* surrounded by ten guards [samurai], and preceded by the flag of the United States. The *norimon* was carried alternately by twelve men; then came his umbrella-bearer, his shoe-bearer, his horse led by the bridle by a stable boy, and a man carrying a basket for the horse. Then came my *norimon* in which I was suffering all kinds of tortures, not knowing what to do with my legs, then three guards, one of whom was my valet, one my shoe-bearer and one my umbrella-bearer, and then my horse led by the bridle by my stable boy, a man carrying the basket of my horse. Then the *cango* [Kango, palanquin] of the Japanese interpreter. The interpreter himself, Namura Tsunenosuke,[116] walked beside the door of my *norimon;* then Wakana Myosaburo, officer first class, Gohara Isaburo, officer second class, Saito Sennojo and Takahashi, officers third class, the first two in *norimon* and the others in a *kango,* with the men of their retinue, one hundred thirty men, not overlooking the cook, a man who is in Japan more indispensable than the air we breathe.

On the coast of the bay, Shinagawa is protected by five batteries, the first four on islands, preventing thereby any

communication with the capital, and the fifth one at Shinagawa.

A continuous throng of people borders both sides of the
highway which leads from Shinagawa to our hotel. It was a
distance of about seven miles, and I do not believe I exag-
gerate in estimating the assembled multitude at a million.
Despite this immense number not a voice was heard, a respectful silence reigning over all, except that when we passed
they stooped down one over the other in order to glance into
our *norimons*.

The streets of Edo are divided into sections of ——— feet
each.[117] At the end of each section there is a barrier which
was opened at our approach and would be closed as soon as
the last of our procession had passed. Thus we found ourselves always in a sort of tiny fortress, which prevented too
many people from collecting at one spot. The police of one
section would accompany us from the entrance gate to the
exit gate where the police of the next section came to take
their places. The people were garbed in a kind of dark blue
blouse with figures of white and red like harlequins; they
were holding in their hands an iron rod, the head of which
was adorned with rings of the same metal, which they would
resound upon the street at each step.

Among these thousands of faces, of men, women, boys, and
young girls, not one showed signs of antipathy, anger, or
even of indifference. All seemed happy that the gates of Edo
had been opened to foreigners; and I am convinced that the
sole reason why Japan had excluded itself from the commerce of other nations of the world is the profound veneration which people of this nation have for ancient laws, for
one law that was issued at a time when necessity seemed to
call for it, and the obstinacy of some Princes of the old school
whose hatred for the Christians was transmitted from father
to son and which they regard as a family possession.

One might, perhaps, reply to me that the majority of those

Gyokusenji Temple, first Consulate of the United States in Japan

Heusken's room in the Consulate. All sketches were done in pen and ink by Henry Heusken.

The Cathedral of San Lorenzo at Macao

The Grotto of Camoens at Macao, to which the Portuguese poet Camoens retired to work on the verses of his *Lusiad*

Watt Pho, Siamese temple containing a 175-foot-tall statue of Buddha

American officials have an audience with the King at the court of Siam

The Menam River, gateway to **Bangkok** and the commerce of Siam

Townsend Harris and Henry Heusken in conference with the two Governor of Shimoda in the Goyosho (about June 17, 1857)

assembled on the highway were only the people sunk in the slumber of servitude, docile and obedient people who regard anything their masters wish to demand as orders emanating from divinity. For this reason I wish to add that among all the officers and Nobles, from the highest rank to the very lowest, whose acquaintance I had the pleasure of making, not one of them gave me the feeling that we were unwanted here; on the contrary, all without exception have welcomed me with the most open friendship, with the most scrupulous politeness.[118]

I was indeed swept with admiration in viewing the order which reigned over this vast multitude. If people pressed too far forwards, thereby preventing the free passage of our procession, an officer shaking his paper fan sufficed to cause hundreds of persons to step back.

If one of our great capitals found itself in the same situation as the city of Edo today, how many children would have been crushed under foot, and how many women would have died from lack of oxygen! How much profanity seasoned by a liberal use of spiritous beverages! What a tumult; how many hurrahs and shrill cries! And I have no doubt that rotten apples and even stones would have been thrown, aimed at the sacred features of the members of the Embassy.

Seeing, from the recesses of my *norimon,* all these people gathered about me, these glances animated by the most acute curiosity, this chaos of human heads lost in a single mass, my thoughts involuntarily take me back to the days of my childhood, when I considered the annual arrival of His Majesty or the presence of some illustrious person in the city of my birth to be a noteworthy event. I would disregard the rain and the cold, I allowed myself to be shoved and jostled by the multitude, all that in order to see for two or three seconds

> The King in his golden carriage
> The Queen and her ladies in waiting.

Ah, I was once envious of even stable boys, and today here I am in the position of the aforementioned personages. An entire people are shoving and jostling each other, leaving their daily occupations, dying of hunger and fatigue. And for what? In order to be able to glance into two *norimons* containing two children of Japhet.[119]

I have already mentioned that in Japan the greater you are, the less you expose yourself to the eyes of the common people. For this reason, when entering the fashionable district and passing the palaces of the Daimyos, I was not allowed to see the young and noble Japanese girls because the bars and the blinds behind which they were hiding their charms gave me the chance of perceiving only the vague outlines of a throng of heads, except for a few very rare exceptions when the slats of a charitable blind, opening more than usual, allowed me to see for an instant a pair of black eyes, worthy of belonging to the favorite of the Sultan, or a small hand, as white as the snows of Fujiyama.

At the gate of our hotel, situated within the third enclosure of the Imperial Castle, where we arrived at four in the afternoon, Mr. Harris was welcomed by Shinano no Kami, Governor of Shimoda. We were shown to our chambers. Mr. Harris had a room and an alcove for sleeping, and I had the same. They had made chairs, tables, and bedframes, things unknown in Japan, especially for us. Each of us had a bathroom.

In spite of the fatigues of our trip, Shinano no Kami asked Mr. Harris to give him the letter destined for the Minister of Foreign Affairs, announcing his arrival in the capital, etc. Mr. Harris yielded to his entreaty and gave him the letter, already prepared at Shimoda. I had only to add the date.

In the letter he asked the Minister to indicate to him the day of the audience with His Majesty. Shinano no Kami thereupon informed us that the Taikun had appointed an

Ambassador Extraordinary to greet him [Mr. Harris] upon his arrival and to deliver to him a gift on his behalf. He said that it would be desirable for us to conform somewhat to the Japanese ceremonial and that he would indicate to Mr. Harris what the procedure would be. Then they had us go through a regular theatrical rehearsal.

First, we were led to the entrance of the house where Mr. Harris was to receive the Ambassador Extraordinary; then, a number of bows in the vestibule; then, change places in the chamber as in a quadrille, make a bow, go forward, then another. By Jove! I don't know what. I have only confused ideas about the matter. All I can recollect is that when the Ambassador Extraordinary, and by Jove, he was quite an extraordinary man, when he spoke in the name of the Taikun, he was wont to stand at a certain spot in the room, and when he spoke in his own name, he would first change places. Mr. Harris was begged to abide by the same formalities and to change places as the other [the Ambassador Extraordinary] did.

December 1, 1857

The affair mentioned yesterday, the reception of the Ambassador, has taken place today. Mr. Harris received him at the door. One step lower than himself were Shinano no Kami and a few others kneeling; on the lowest step of the flight of stairs were the Vice-Governor and other officers of high rank, and in the courtyard a multitude of officers, all kneeling.

After the fatigues of this horrible reception, a reception such as can take place only in Japan, Mr. Harris hastily opened the box which contained the gift from His Majesty. The box, my dears, contained a great quantity of bonbons. There was enough to fill the shop of a confectioner and make ill an infinite number of children.

Tuesday, December 1, 1857

Eight Commissioners have been appointed in order to see that Mr. Harris wants for nothing, that he be properly received everywhere, and that all his business pass through their hands. They are Hayashi, Daigaku no Kami, ——— Hizen no Kami,[120] and Inoue, Shinano no Kami. Toki, Tamba no Kami, is their chief. Before the reception of the last of them, who was the Ambassador Extraordinary, all these gentlemen were introduced to Mr. Harris.

Wednesday, December 2, 1857

We receive the reply from the Minister of Foreign Affairs informing Mr. Harris that the audience will take place on the seventh of this month at nine o'clock in the morning. At the same time he felicitates him [Mr. Harris] upon his arrival.

Thursday, December 3, 1857

Mr. Harris writes to the Minister that he will come on the appointed date and at the same time also advises him of his desire to pay him [the Minister] a visit. In the same envelope he sends a copy of the President's letter to the Emperor. This same day we receive a reply, saying that he will be happy to see Mr. Harris tomorrow at his home.

Friday, December 4, 1857

About one o'clock in the afternoon we betake ourselves to the minister's home in our *norimons*. After following along the walls of the castle for a half hour we enter the castle. Then we go through a wide street lined on both sides by the palaces of the Princes, which look like huge barracks. We reach another moat and another gate. From there on, we go to another street and we soon find ourselves at the carriage entrance of the palace of the Prince of Bitchū.

A great number of officers are seated in good order on mats by the entrance door, and when we go by all this multitude of heads bend to the ground, as if at a given signal.

At the end of a suite of rooms, we exchange bows with the eight commissioners. Then we are led into a reception chamber where two chairs, two tables, tea, tobacco and pipes are laid out for us.

After having waited for a quarter of an hour, a door is opened leading into a huge chamber called the Salon of Forty-Five Mats. The Prince of Bitchū is standing near the door, and, after exchanging bows, he shows Mr. Harris to the other end of the salon where we take our seats. The Prince places himself upon a taboret on the one side, and we sit on the other side on two chairs. He congratulates Mr. Harris on his arrival, and the latter reciprocates with the usual compliments. Moriyama Takichiro is kneeling beside Shinano no Kami. All that Mr. Harris says is then repeated by Moriyama to Shinano no Kami, who repeats it to the Prince.

Mr. Harris hands them a paper containing the speech which he proposes to deliver at the audience with the Emperor.

The Minister and his retinue retire, leaving us alone. Then servants enter with some chairs. Everything they carry is held aloft with both hands at the level of the head; they advance with measured steps, letting their feet drag on the mats.

The Minister re-enters. We seat ourselves again.

The servants, a dozen of them, enter, carrying in the fashion described above, tables, some tobacco, some fire, pipes, and sweetmeats.

I have omitted mentioning that before sitting down, the

minister gives to Mr. Harris a paper through the intermediation of Shinano no Kami. It contains the answer which the Taikun will make to Mr. Harris' speech on the day of the audience.

The Minister, after some further conversation, conducts Mr. Harris to the entrance of the apartment. Thus was concluded the first interview between the first dignitary of Dai Nippon under the Emperor and the representative of the United States.

The Minister, Hotta, Prince of Bitchū, is a man of most charming manners. He has a very gentle countenance and he smiles with a great deal of charm. He is forty-five years old. He stammers a little when speaking. I believe that inwardly he was quite ill at ease, at least he should have been. He, who had up to now seen everyone prostrate at his feet, or at least been shown the signs of highest respect, saw in himself the first instance of a President of the Great Council granting audience to foreigners who were occupying seats of the same level as his own and who did not pay him any of the homages customary when he honored with his presence the powerful lords of Japan, or the ambassadors of the foreign countries.

Sunday, December 6, 1857

Mr. Harris receives today a letter from Mr. Donker Curtius, containing another one for me from my good mother. It turns out to be a good St. Nicholas after all.[121]

December 7, 1857

At nine o'clock in the morning we set out en route to the Imperial Palace. First [comes] Shinano no Kami, Governor of Shimoda in *norimon* with his retinue, then Mr. Harris preceded by the flag of the United States and followed by his retinue, then myself, then Wakana Myosaburo, Vice-Governor of Shimoda, all in *norimons.*

The sky was most serene. After skirting the walls of the second enclosure for about twenty minutes, we cross the moat and enter the enclosure through a double gate forming a square in the walls of the enclosure. After passing over another moat and through another gate, we find ourselves within the last enclosure in the true Imperial Castle.

This enclosure is much more picturesque than the others, having been kept in a splendid condition. The walls are adorned with entirely white, three-storied pagodas. Where the walls protrude, and along them, there are plastered galleries. All this together with the trees provides a most picturesque effect.

At this gate all of us leave our horses, *norimons,* flags, etc., with the exception of the Ambassador who remains in his *norimon.* After having reached the fourth bridge, the Ambassador also leaves his *norimon,* and after having passed through four other gates flanked by walls, we reach a courtyard in which the Imperial Palace stands.

Once at the entryway we exchange our soiled shoes for others and climb a staircase of seven steps. We are received in a kind of vestibule by the two Ometsuke, Tamba no Kami, and another one who precede us into an antechamber. About eight feet above the floor the paneling is carved in openwork representing trees, flowers, parrots, etc.

Here the Commissioners come to pay their respects and to offer their services. One of the dignitaries carries kindness so far as to ask the Ambassador if he does not wish to visit the men's room. Thereupon we are shown into the great hall of the Palace. The ceiling, which is thirty feet high, is supported by wooden pillars. We are then led into the audience room in order to see it and to rehearse what we are to do. Then we return to the hall and are offered chairs behind a screen.

Finally, the Taikun is on his throne. We hear people make the sound so well known throughout the world in order to enjoin silence.

The two Ometsuke come to inform us that everything is in readiness. They precede us, then comes Shinano no Kami, then the Ambassador, then myself carrying the letter of the President wrapped in the American colors. On our right we pass a crowd of court nobles (about six or seven hundred) on their knees in court costume, which consists of a kind of square-shaped lacquer cap perched on the very top of the head, and of garments with very wide sleeves of hemp of a pale yellow color. On the ample sleeves of their costumes they carry their coat of arms. They wear a belt of white silk tied like the rabat of a Protestant minister, in which is their scimitar. They carry only one for this occasion. They wear trousers which, being twice as long as the leg, completely conceal their feet and the remainder of the trousers trails behind, giving them the appearance of walking on their knees. There reigned the most profound silence despite the great number of courtiers.

On arriving at the paneling which partitions the hall from the chamber where His Majesty can be seen, the two Ometsuke fall upon their knees, as does Shinano no Kami. Making a half turn to the right we find ourselves facing His Majesty. Shinano no Kami precedes us, dragging himself on his knees; then the Ambassador follows him, walking normally and bowing; he ascends one step, proceeds the length of two mats, bows a second time, and a third on the fifth mat, where he halts. On his right are the five members of the Great Council, on his left five other dignitaries [all] on their knees. Otherwise there was no one who could rejoice in seeing His Japanese Majesty.

From the place occupied by the Ambassador the floor rose another step; at the rear of this chamber on a platform about three feet high, His Majesty, the Taikun of Japan, was seated on a kind of stool; but the place where he was was so dark and remote that I could hardly see him, the curtain hanging from the ceiling hid his face. Those who were on their knees could see him very well, but for us, standing erect, it was more difficult.

Then the Ambassador delivered his speech saying that he appreciated the honor of having been chosen by the President to carry a letter to His Majesty, and the honor of being appointed plenipotentiary to His Majesty's court, and that [it was for him] his greatest pleasure, and finally in English: "May it please Your Majesty, in presenting my letters of credence from the President of the United States of America, I am directed to express to Your Majesty the sincere wishes of the President for your health and happiness and for the prosperity of your dominions.

"I consider it as a great honor that I have been selected to fill the high and important place of Plenipotentiary of the United States at the Court of Your Majesty, and as my earnest wishes are to unite the two countries more closely in the ties of enduring friendship, my constant exertions shall be directed to the attainment of that happy end."

Upon the conclusion, the Taikun seemed to stamp his feet three times and answered in Japanese: "Vergenoegd met eenen brief gezonden met den afgezant van een verafgelegen gewest en tevens met zyn gesprek. Eeuwig zal Gemeenschap gehouden worden."

This is the Dutch of the interpreter, Moriyama Takichiro and means: "Pleased with the letter sent with the Ambassador from a far distant country, and likewise pleased with his discourse. Intercourse shall be continued forever."

At the end of that speech—in which there are no personal pronouns because the Taikun is too great to use the small word "I"—I, who had remained at the entrance of the Imperial chamber, come forward, and making the compulsory three bows, I present the President's letter to the Ambassador who opens it, shows the President's signature to the Minister of Foreign Affairs, and hands it to him; he, in turn, puts it on a small table before the throne. Then the Ambassador takes his leave, walking backward and observing the compulsory three bows.

This took place in the presence of the grandson [descendant] of the monarch who banished from his Empire everything foreign or Christian, and that persecution in Japan came to an end only with the death of the last Christian. The Imperial edict still existed which proclaimed that anyone who carries a letter from abroad will be put to death with his entire family.

But let us not reproach too much the poor Japanese with the cruelties perpetrated on a nascent religion, whose disciples, forgetting the precepts of their divine master, took part themselves in the civil wars which were laying Japan waste. If we cast a glance at our own annals, we shall see that the fires of the Inquisition have hardly been extinguished, that Calvin put Servetus to death, that the members of the Leagues massacred the Huguenots on St. Bartholomew's Eve, that we Europeans who boast about our superior enlightenment, who call ourselves the servants of Christ, have not ceased killing one another because of difference of faith, and have been so fanatical as to proclaim that all those cruelties, those fires, those gallows were required for the service of this Lord of Kindness and Mercy, who taught us only love and benevolence.

The Court of Japan is certainly not conspicuous for its luxury. Not one diamond sparkled among the crowd of courtiers. A small gold ornament on the handles of their swords was hardly visible. I have seen the nobles of the Siamese Court trying to hide their savage condition behind a barbarous luxury, covering themselves with gold and gems. But the simplicity of the Court of Edo, the noble and dignified bearing of the courtiers, their polished manners which would do honor to the most illustrious court, cast a more dazzling splendor than all the diamonds of the Indies.

From this kneeling throng two men move forward going upright towards the throne of the august monarch of Dai Nippon, this grandson [descendant] of Ieyasu, descendant of a long line of Princes, all equally hostile to the foreigners and the Christians. Not one sword is unsheathed; not one guardian of the throne among this legion of nobles rises to impede the progress of those two profaners; not one cry of sacrilege is heard. They remain mute and immobile, like marble or bronze statues.

Has the Court of Edo suddenly been struck powerless? Did some well-disposed goddess take them under her protection? Does an awesome army guard them? Not one bayonet follows them; they carry no other weapon than two swords which would shatter into a thousand pieces at the first stroke. No, it is the sun of civilization, the star of progress which has risen again in Asia; the darkness of ignorance and seclusion is disappearing and the proud rulers of this Empire begin to feel their own weakness and the power of the peoples of the Occident, and this Empire, which like a coquettish queen has scorned up to the present time the advances of all the mighty peoples of the world, is finally going to respect the rights of men and enter into the great family of nations.

However, Oh country which has become so dear to me, is the progress really progress, this civilization really civilization for you? I, who have admired the artlessness of your inhabitants as well as their simple customs, who has seen the abundance of your fertile fields, who has heard everywhere the happy laughter of your children, and has never been able to discern misery, I fear, Oh, my God, that this scene of happiness is coming to an end and that the Occidental people will bring here their fatal vices.

A few minutes later we go to another chamber where the Great Council is assembled. Fifteen robes are brought in on two tables. Hotta, Bitchū no Kami, then says to the Ambassador: "His Majesty, the Taikun, gives you this present;" then he added: "His Majesty, the Taikun, gives this present to Mr. Heusken."

After we had thanked His Majesty, Hotta speaks again and says: "His Majesty presents you a dinner."

We go to an adjacent chamber. The Ambassador and the Great Council bow again to each other. We return to the antechamber where we had been welcomed. There the eight Commissioners bid us farewell. In the vestibule at the top of the staircase we again exchange bows with the two Ometsuke and return to our residence in the same manner in which we had come.

There we are served the dinner from the Taikun.[122] Everything is served on little tables made of plain wood. We are told that it is a great compliment because all these wooden plates can be used only once. We are also told that all the plates and dishes are for us. On the Ambassador's tables are two small figures beneath a fir tree, a likeness of a very famous fir tree that lives for a thousand years, all admirably fabricated from paper, as are the artificial flowers.

The figures represented persons, Banzioe and Yakousin,[123] who had lived more than one hundred years. In Japan this is called a compliment of longevity. The Ambassador's present consists of fifteen silken robes, mine of five rolls of silk.

Tuesday, December 8, 1857

The Ambassador writes a letter to the Minister of Foreign Affairs and informs him that he is now ready to send important communications to him or to the Great Council. He asks him also to thank His Majesty for his gracious reception and for his presents. Hotta, Bitchū no Kami, sends the Prince of Shinano expressly to inquire about the Ambassador's health and to tell him that he will answer his letter tomorrow.

Wednesday, December 9, 1857

This morning Udono [124] came here to inquire about the Ambassador's health. This afternoon the Prince of Shinano brings the reply of the Minister advising the Ambassador that he will be ready to hear the Ambassador's communications next Saturday.

Tamba no Kami comes here at the same time to inquire about the Ambassador's health. Ieyasu, when he usurped the throne, added three hundred princes to the Japanese nobility. Since that time the Taikun names the five members of the Great Council. Besides these three hundred hereditary princes there are eighteen princes whose lineage goes back for seven or eight hundred years. The independent princes, although of a rank higher than the three hundred others, are never appointed members of the Great Council. The members of the Great Council are the highest ranking officials of the Empire, and even the aforementioned eighteen princes have to bow before them.

Because the Ambassador has ordered two maps of Edo, the Prince of Shinano tells him today that the Great Council is deliberating about this order and has not as yet given a final answer. He tells us at the same time that twenty years ago Mr. von Siebold had procured two maps of Japan, and that the Director of the School of Astronomy, who had provided them, had undergone the most severe punishment in Japan, namely crucifixion. [He said] that von Siebold had been forbidden to stay in Japan. Light earthquake.

Thursday, December 10, 1857

Every night I hear the honking of flocks of wild geese returning to their abode. In the morning they leave for places where they seek their food. Between Kanagawa and Edo I have seen a great number of storks. These storks are of a grand stature and a whiteness of plumage which is unmatched. Killing them is forbidden.

I have observed a rather peculiar way the Japanese have of warming themselves which corresponds so well to their frugal manners. They normally sit around a brazier in which there are some embers. In order to benefit from the heat radiated by these embers, the poor people place themselves almost on top of the braziers, because in their open rooms protected only by paper-covered windows from the hardships of winter, these braziers do not raise the temperature of the apartment by one degree. They put into the brazier a small square stone, and after having heated it well, they put this stone in a wooden case and wrap the whole in a handkerchief. Then they place this contraption on their stomachs.

Our table is better provided than it was at Shimoda. Every day we have excellent very fresh oysters, geese, ducks—open your eyes, be all ears, you American gastronomes! Even the celebrated canvasback [125] of the United States, the true canvasback is served at our table, [as are] quail, ortolans, etc., etc., venison, wild boar, etc.

Friday, December 11, 1857

Apart from the officers and soldiers who have accompanied us from Shimoda, there is a multitude of officers from Edo who are quartered at our hotel, and the very same spies who were so shamefully expelled from Shimoda have their quarters here very near the entrance gate. Therefore, everything that enters or leaves our residence is subjected to their inspection. The Japanese officers are extremely polite, but there are a few who show a certain haughtiness or indifference towards me when they see they are being observed. But as soon as these same officers are able to talk to me alone, they apologize, saying that they have to act as they do because the house is full of spies, and that everything one does is reported to the government and if they happened to be on even the least friendly or confidential terms with me, this might have fatal consequences for them. The Ambassador, having been quite ill since the day of our arrival here, and not having wished to press these matters, wants to end all this, feeling that he cannot endure these things any longer.

He tells the Prince of Shinano that only today he has been informed that beyond question spies have quarters in his house, that as long as he resides here this house is his, that he is the master of it, that no one can be allowed to enter it without his permission, and that he demands the immediate expulsion of the spies and officers of Edo who fill his home.

They reply to us with the same song that we received in Shimoda: that these people are here to pay us honor, to protect us, that the spies are not here in order to watch us but in order to keep the Japanese under control and that the demand of the Ambassador cannot be granted.

The Ambassador replies to them that this is an insult to the honor of the President whom he represents and that from today on he designates himself their prisoner, and that he will not leave his house prior to the settling of this matter, and that in consequence he refuses to go tomorrow to the palace of the Prince of Bitchū to present his communications to the Minister, and that all this is a sufficient reason for the United States to declare war on Japan.

Here our poor Prince of Shinano is really embarrassed!

Poor Shinano! I feel sorry for him. There he is caught between two fires. He is responsible to his government for the actions of the American Ambassador and if he wishes to execute the orders of the Great Council he must stand the commotion caused by the justifiable indignation of the Ambassador.

He beseeches him [the Ambassador] to go tomorrow at the appointed hour to the palace of the Minister. He says that his position is at stake and that afterwards he will do everything in his power to settle the matter in an amicable fashion.

The Ambassador finally yields to his pressing entreaties, but only on the condition that afterwards matters will be satisfactorily settled. He promises to do everything possible.

Saturday, December 12, 1857

This morning about eleven o'clock we set out for the palace of the Prime Minister who receives us at the entrance to his apartments. We seat ourselves on chairs and the minister and the nine Commissioners and the Prince of Shinano seat themselves on stools. The interpreter, Moriyama, is kneeling and the interpreter, Tsunenosuke, behind him is kneeling, head lowered and hands placed flat on the floor. The poor man remained motionless in this position as long as the conference lasted. He was not accustomed to being in the presence of persons of such exalted rank as the President of the Great Council and the aforementioned Commissioners.

This conference with the President of the Great Council seemed to be much more important than the audience with His Majesty, the Taikun. The Ambassador made him an eloquent discourse concerning the present state of Japan; that steamships had established bonds between the most distant nations; that all the nations of the world formed but one family.

It was a sublime moment when he touched the topic of religion. It was the first time, since the cruel persecutions had succeeded in crushing Christianity, that a voice ventured to raise itself in favor of the persecuted religion, the very name of which breathed of high treason, and this in the palace and addressed to the first dignitary of the Empire, to the President of the Great Council.

The time has passed, said the Ambassador, when one endeavors to propagate a religion at the point of the sword. The Spanish and the Portuguese who landed on these shores two hundred years ago were cruel and lawless people. They combined with their lust for gold a desire to propagate their religion at the point of the sword and to make conquests. This belongs to the past. Mankind has finally learned that freedom of conscience is the great principle which should govern all nations, and in America one can see a temple of Buddha rising next to a Christian Church.

Not a sign of displeasure could be seen on the faces of these Japanese noblemen. The President of the Great Council seemed to take much interest in the eloquent words of the Ambassador, and the word Christianity, this terrible word, this word which seemed like a phantom besetting and undermining the present order of things and the existence of the dynasty of Ieyasu, did not bring the slightest cloud upon the peaceful features of the Minister. And the Imperial edict of 1638 was still in force, the edict which promised a reward of five hundred pieces of silver to whomever discovered a priest, and for a Christian the reward was in proportion.

At that moment I felt as though I could see an image of the Imperial edict of 1638 written in letters of blood on the paneling of the Council Chamber, this edict which promised a reward to whomever discovered a priest or a Christian, which threatens with prison everyone who propagates the Catholic religion. Whoever bears this scandalous name or who bears a letter from a foreign priest will be put to death and with him his entire family.

The letters of blood seemed to vanish and I fancied I heard a hymn of praise intoned by the sacrificed martyrs of Shimabara at the moment when freedom of conscience found its advocate in the apartment of the President of the Great Council, and found that advocate in the person of the Ambassador of the United States. After having revealed the advantages of free trade, and all the paths by which its fruitful course may be interrupted, he said that his discourse was at an end.

The Minister, after having asked him whether there was anything he wanted to add, answered that he was pleased by the communication which the Ambassador had been kind enough to make to him.

Seeing that I was not smoking, he asked whether I didn't smoke. They served us grapes and oranges, as well as tea.

One remark by the Ambassador caused a murmur and seemed to caress the self-esteem of the Japanese who whispered in approval. He was remarking that if one stands atop high Japanese mountains, the searching eye can visualize a great number of ships, flying the American flag, which have covered thousands of miles in order to find whales along the Japanese coasts so far from their native country. Why, he added, should not the Japanese who are courageous and not lacking in personal energy send their ships to take their flags to the distant American coasts?

The Minister, having shown us to the door of his apartment, we bade farewell to the eight Commissioners in another chamber and departed.

Monday, December 14, 1857

Having remained in our house for an entire week, except for the visit to the Minister and the audience, the Ambassador asked for a place where he could get some air and ride on horseback. We are given an adjacent court just wide enough to permit a horse to turn around and of a length not exceeding fifteen metres. Not being satisfied with this small enclosure, I am finally shown today a large square area surrounded by hedges and trees and located atop a hill which enables us to enjoy from here a beautiful view of the entire city of Edo.

January 2, 1858

About one o'clock at night I was engaged in reading *Les Femmes Savantes* by Molière and the following lines spoken by Trissotin:

> I came to apprise you of great news
> While we were asleep, Madame, we were
>   lucky to escape a great danger.
> A world has been passing along ours
> And fell through our vortex.
> And had it, on its way, met with the Earth
> It would have shattered it to pieces, as if it
>   were glass.

—when suddenly the house began to tremble in a terrifying manner. The lamp on the chair by my bed almost fell to the floor. Well, it was a sample of the earthquakes which occur from time to time in Japan. The shock was rather severe and had an undulating motion which gradually increased and then diminished and concluded with a terrible convulsion. The whole took about twenty-five seconds.

The earthquake of 1855 destroyed one sixth of Edo and killed ten thousand persons in the city of Edo alone.

The normal rate on loans in Japan is ten per cent. A man sentenced by a judge to pay a debt does not pay interest for the time elapsed since the debt was due, because it is said that this person is already sufficiently punished by the reputation that he has lost, that he is, so to speak, dead and no one will trust his word any more and that shame is enough of a punishment in itself. Also, because the rich loan to the poor who take their money, it would be favoring the rich too much if the other party were sentenced to pay this interest (Judaic Law).

A man is never sentenced until he has confessed his guilt. If the circumstances sufficiently proved his culpability, he is put to torture until he confesses.

The most severe punishment is death by crucifixion. They fasten the condemned to a cross with ropes and kill him with spears thrust through his body. They continue thrusting spears through his body until death occurs. Sometimes the condemned does not die until eleven spears have been thrust through his body.

This punishment is for the great political crimes, for patricide or matricide, and for servants who have killed their masters. In other cases criminals are beheaded. Flagellation is in use. The criminal is whipped with very thin bamboo strips bound together. He is given from fifty to one hundred lashes.

January 10, 1858 [126]

Mr. Harris had requested the government [for permission] to visit the university and the mint of Edo.[127] After many delays, he is brought the following reply: that no person, however exalted his rank, is admitted to the mint, except the persons attached to that establishment; that he, the Prince of Shinano, himself cannot enter it; that the law may seem ridiculous but that one should obey it, and that consequently the government begs Mr. Harris not to insist upon his request. The request to visit the university is granted.

However, there is in the university a temple containing a statue of Confucius, to which divine homage is paid. His Majesty, the Taikun, pays to this statue the same homage as he does to his own ancestors and prostrates himself before it. All of those who visit the temple pay the same homage and genuflection to the statue of Confucius, as the Ambassador has seen paid to the Taikun by the courtiers during the audience, and Mr. Harris is requested to pay it the same homage as he did to the Taikun.

Also, in visiting the temple the Japanese noblemen wear their court dress.

Mr. Harris replies that he does not bow before statues and that in all the temples he has visited he has never been asked anything of the sort. Shinano answers that the Japanese are perfectly free not to pay homage to a certain god, and to believe in another one, but that Confucius is honored everywhere in Japan because of his virtue, and that all those who visit his temple must pay him homage and that he is honored as if he were a god.

Mr. Harris declines the invitation to visit the university.

It appears that in this university only the history of China and the works of Confucius are being taught. Those who can recite by heart all these books at the examinations are taken by the government into its service. One of the Commissioners of the Treaty of Kanagawa is the head of this establishment. He is called Hayashi, Daigaku no Kami. This means Hayashi, his family name, Kami, "chief," no, "of," Dai, "great," gaku, "school." The history of Japan is not taught there.

January 16, 1858

Since Mr. Harris made his important communication on behalf of the President to the government of Japan on December 12th, the time has been passing with unbearable slowness while we await the reply of the government. Mr. Harris has judged it proper not to cause a useless sensation by going out to see the city of Edo, before he had obtained the terms of the treaty which he has been planning to conclude with Japan; we, in consequence, have been staying at home all the time, except for two hours daily during which we go riding on horseback in the open air in the area allotted by the government, located about ten minutes from our residence.

Today we have a conference with Hotta, Prince of Bitchū, President of the Great Council, who informs us that the proposal to have a resident minister has been accepted, but that we will have to enter into negotiations with regard to the time when he will be received, the place of his residence and other regulations regarding this matter. The government at the same time grants free trade, and consents to substitute another harbor for that of Shimoda; additional ports are refused because three have already been granted.

January 18, 1858

The Commissioners appointed by the government of Japan exchange their full powers with Mr. Harris, who, having handed over his full powers, is given them back once they have inspected the signature of the President, the seal of the United States, and the signature of Secretary of State Marcy.[128] Wakana Myosaburo, Vice-Governor of Shimoda, places in Mr. Harris' hands the full powers of the Commissioners endorsed with the red seal of His Majesty, the Taikun. After having examined them, Mr. Harris returns them to the Vice-Governor. He then gives to the Commissioners a treaty which he has drafted and which he submits for their consideration. The Commissioners are: Inoue, Prince of Shinano,

Governor of Shimoda and Iwase, Prince of Higo, Imperial Inspector of Nagasaki.

Monday, January 25, 1858

The draft of the treaty having been translated by Moriyama Takichiro assisted by Doctor Kansai, the Commissioners are coming here today to express their views.

A diplomatic agent can be sent to Japan, but he must reside between the towns of Kanagawa and Kawasaki, and he can come to Edo only when he has business in the capital.

The United States would dishonor itself by ratifying a treaty containing such a clause.[129] A diplomatic agent must reside in the capital.

Additional ports cannot be granted. The government must take public opinion into consideration and treat it with caution. The people are still prejudiced against foreigners. Americans residing in the ports open to commerce will become better known and appreciated by the Japanese; prejudices will gradually diminish and then the Empire will be opened more and more to commerce. Thus the people will be reconciled to foreigners and the Empire will be gradually opened. The Port of Kanagawa will be given in exchange for that of Shimoda. Diplomatic and consular agents can travel in the Empire of Japan on their official duties. Merchants cannot travel in the Empire because when the above-mentioned officials travel the Government can protect them from the attacks of hostile persons, but the government cannot provide these precautions for the benefit of every individual who travels.

Then the Commissioners tell us the following story: In Japan each official head of a family upholds his family. The eldest son inherits the position of his father, the younger sons learn the military arts but have no position. But many of these people, sons and relatives of officials, behave badly and on account of their bad conduct their fathers or relatives no longer wish to provide for their needs. These people, thus abandoned by their families, are called *loo-nin* [130] (men floating upon the water), what one would call in French, scoundrels, vagabonds. Three of these men have been arrested recently. They had plotted to do harm to the Ambassador of the United States.

Upon the inquiry of Mr. Harris whether they intended to kill him or only to harm him, they replied that they did not know, the reason being that the culprits had not yet been brought to trial. They then gave us the names of these three men. Then they added that the government is in great uneasiness for the Ambassador, that our residence is surrounded all night by guards and that the people in our household could hardly sleep for fear of an attack; therefore, the Ambassador could easily understand that if Americans should be given the right to travel through the Empire they would find themselves exposed to accidents which might have fatal consequences and disrupt the amity which exists between the two countries.

Mr. Harris replied to them that he was not in the least afraid, that he knew the Japanese to be fine people, that naturally there are bad ones everywhere, but that he was eternally grateful to the government for its solicitude for the safety of his person.

The Eighth Article concerning religion has been accepted. As for houses, buildings, etc., they wish to assign to Americans a certain place in the open ports where they can live together, because if the Americans have their residences among Japanese dwellings, this would create confusion.

With regard to commerce, they wish to grant the same things which they accorded to the Dutch and the Russians. They do not wish to give coins to Americans but only paper money, as set forth in the treaties concluded at Nagasaki. After some years they will grant this demand, but the government wishes first to experiment with the treaties just concluded and later to make more liberal concessions.

Tuesday, January 26, 1858

The Commissioners have begun to request a delay of three years before the treaty becomes effective.[131] We reply to them that now is not the time to discuss that matter, that first of all the treaty should be concluded, and then the effective date of the treaty may be considered, and that we are now on the first article dealing with the residence of a minister in Edo.

The Commissioners agree that a minister will reside in Edo, but they demand a delay of three years for this.

Mr. Harris declares that he is unwilling ever to insert such a clause in the treaty, and that this reveals a reluctance on the part of Japan to receive a minister.

Finally it is agreed that a minister can come after July 4, 1859, and Mr. Harris promises to write his government that the government of Japan would prefer that the minister not come to Japan before three years have elapsed.

Then, they also wish to add to the clause "that the diplomatic and consular officials can travel anywhere in the Empire," the words "for official business."

Finally they agree that the minister and the Consul-General can travel whenever it pleases them to do so, but the Consuls only for official business.

Mr. Harris tells them that he will consider this.

The Japanese assert that the words "for official business" have quite another meaning for them than for us, that all officials of Japan when they go out always do so for official business, whether they go out for their pleasure or not; that, as Mr. Harris says, if the minister when it is hot says "I wish to take a trip to climb Fujiyama," it is always considered official business, because the life of a high official is dear to the people. He goes to Fujiyama for his health; by so doing he takes care of his life, and by living he serves the interests of the people as an official; therefore, he travels on official business.

Mr. Harris then made a long discourse about the ports which he desires Japan to open. [He said] that the more ports are opened to commerce, the more trade will increase, that the merchants must display their merchandise to the people and create a demand, etc., etc., that the more trade increases the more revenue the government will receive.

Thursday, January 28, 1858

Another conference.[132] The Commissioners repeat the same objections to the proposal to open more ports. [They assert that] the government intends to make an experiment with the three open ports on the basis agreed upon with the Dutch and the Russians, that public opinion must be appeased first of all, that merchants are always desirous of making money, that they will not object to trading with foreigners, but that merchants do not constitute the whole nation, that among the Daimyos and the military there are still strong prejudices against foreigners. [They say] that the President of the Great Council has done his utmost to cause the Daimyos to be favorably inclined. [They say] that he has spoken personally with the one half of the Daimyo corps which is stationed in Edo, that the other half is stationed on their estates; that he has communicated with them by letters, but that many of these Daimyos are still ignorant; that the subjects of the Daimyos share the opinion of their masters, that now the government wants to experiment with the opening of the three ports, that later on the Daimyos will see for themselves by the effects of trade that it is advantageous for the Empire and they themselves will grant more privileges to the foreigners.

Coal mines have been discovered at three *ris* from Nagasaki. Therefore the port on the island of Kyushu is not necessary. Mr. Harris no longer insists upon it. He also withdraws [his request for] Hirado, and instead of two, he asks for only one harbor on the occidental coast of Nippon.

They reply that they will open the port of Niigata in Ietsigo [Echigo], a town of sixty thousand inhabitants. It appears from reports which are supplied that this harbor is not safe, being only an open roadstead. Japanese barks can sail up the river one *ri,* but this cannot be done by American ships because the mouth of the river is only nine *sjaku* [shaku] deep, about nine feet.

It is agreed that the Americans and Japanese will inspect the coast and that a convenient port will be opened on January 1, 1860, on the west coast of Japan, and that Kanagawa will be opened on July 4, 1859, while Shimoda will be closed six months later.

They assert that Miyako is very small—one *ri* square—that those who have written books about Japan have lied about the grandeur of Miyako, that there are many errors in Kaempfer. There are only twenty houses where silk is spun, the city is very poor.

To Mr. Harris' remark that since the Mikado and his court reside there the town must be very rich, they reply to him in amusement that he seems to talk with great discernment of the spiritual head of Nippon, the son of God, the ancient autocrat of this Empire. Then they say that Miyako belongs to the clergy, that the Daimyo themselves have no power to command any thing in Miyako, etc., etc. With regard to Osaka, this [place] is so near Miyako [that] the government cannot allow it.

Mr. Harris proposes to them the opening of Edo within five years from January 1st, 1858, Osaka within three years, and that he will speak of Miyako later on. He adds that without these ports the treaty will not be satisfactory and that the nations of Europe would not accept it.

Since tomorrow is a feast day for the Japanese, they will return the day after tomorrow.

Mr. Harris requests as a favor the pardon of the three *loo-nins* who have planned to harm him. He says that he has come to Edo with the most friendly intentions in the world, that his mission is one of peace and friendship, and that he would not want his visit to Edo to cause suffering to anyone. He adds that he would like the government to make public his request to set these men free, that this would make a good impression on the people who would see from this [act] the friendly intentions of the United States. He is told that his request will be transmitted to the government, but that these three men have not injured the Ambassador of the United States, but rather the government of Japan which wishes to be as friendly as possible to the Ambassador.

Mr. Harris agrees that this is true, but that he did not wish to prove that he has the right to interfere in this matter, that he is only asking it as a favor, that the purpose of punishment is not to punish men because they have committed crimes, but in order to prevent others from committing them, that many times clemency has proved to have greater effect than severity.

The Japanese also add that it is not certain as yet whether these people planned an attack on their own volition, or whether they had been incited by others. These three men are now being tried. They are appearing before the court of the Governor of Edo.

They also assert that if the Ambassador is not content to have commerce on the same conditions as the Russians and the Dutch, they will endeavor to grant him this under some other conditions.

Upon his assertion that the United States does not threaten, that it does not wish to force anything upon the Japanese government against its will, but that he has requested them to make proposals acceptable to France and England, that the commerce will produce greater advantages for Japan than for the United States, that this commerce with Japan will be of great importance to the United States, they reply that all men are equal and that they will say to the plenipotentiaries of these nations the same things which they are now saying to the Ambassador.

Saturday, January 30, 1858

The Commissioners open the meeting by inquiring about the size of the house to be occupied by the minister and the number of persons in his retinue.[133]

Mr. Harris replies to them that one [minister] will wish a larger house than another, that is a matter of personal taste, that one minister may have a household of one hundred servants, while another has no more than three.

The government has done everything possible, say the Commissioners, to settle the matter of the ports, and is willing to permit the opening of Edo after five years (January 1, 1863) to American traders, but they must reside at Kanagawa.

The reply is made to them that the distance from Niponbas[134] to Kanagawa is seven *ri*, that a man can hardly cover this distance in one day and be back at Kanagawa since he is not permitted to stay overnight in Edo. In order to do business the one who sells and the one who buys must be in direct communication, that half of the Daimyo are residents in Edo, many of the articles of luxury and of utility can be sold only to these Daimyos.

They reply that the wholesale trade will take place at Kanagawa, that many merchants will endeavor to establish themselves there, that the government has permitted construction of merchant ships along European lines, and that these ships cannot sail any further up the bay than Kanagawa because of a sand shoal. Therefore all wholesale trade must be conducted at Kanagawa. The wholesale merchants are called *toyas* [tonya]. The government has decided to establish trade on other terms than those granted to the Dutch and the Russians, the Americans will be allowed to go to Edo and to enter the markets there and to buy and sell as they please without any interference from the government; all this has been granted at the remonstrances of Mr. Harris.

Higo no Kami says that he hopes very soon to visit the United States, and that he does not doubt that this moment will soon arrive. The Americans who wish to visit Edo may sleep at Kawasaki.[135]

Monday, February 1, 1858

The Commissioners tell us that they intend to permit American merchants to occupy one or two streets or as many as they need in Edo for their business, that the merchants can go there for their business, but that their residences, their wives, and their children must remain at Kanagawa.[136] They can stay in Edo as long as they need to for business purposes: two days, one month, one year, two years, or five years.

Mr. Harris replies that their sole objection seems then to be against receiving the wives and children in Edo.

They reply that they have no objections at all to the wives and children but they will put in the treaty: "Edo will be opened on January 1, 1863, for trade;" and that at the same time Mr. Harris should give them a letter promising that the Americans will go to the place assigned for business purposes when the time comes, but will leave their families at Kanagawa, that there is probably no difference [in this] for the Americans, but there is a great one for them [the Japanese]. If the people read in the treaty: "Edo will be opened for trade," they will be satisfied with that. But if the Americans take their families with them, then Edo will be opened for permanent residence to the Americans, because a man in Japan who lives with his family in a city resides there in fact, whereas a merchant who comes to the city only for business is there only temporarily in order to conduct his transactions.

Mr. Harris suggests the insertion of the following words: "On January 1, 1863, the city of Edo will be opened to American citizens to conduct trade. The place which they will occupy for their business will be assigned by the diplomatic agent of the United States and the government of Japan."

The Commissioners agree to consider this and everyone retires.

Tuesday, February 2, 1858

The Japanese Commissioners say that Mr. Harris has suggested: "Edo will be opened for business," that it is for all kinds of business, good and bad business, and that for this reason they wish to substitute "for trade" [107] for it.

Mr. Harris replies to them that a man going to Edo cannot take his American cook with him, or if he is ill, he cannot be visited by his doctor.

The reply is made that naturally a merchant can be accompanied by the people whom he needs, because these people go to Edo indirectly for trade purposes, because they are needed by a man who engages in trade.

Seeing that an endless discussion will stem from this matter, Mr. Harris proposes to leave this article and to deal with

article number seven which allows Americans to travel in
Japan under certain restrictions.

To this the response is negative. They say that it is impossible to grant this, and that there are provinces of Japan
which even Japanese are not allowed to enter. All this will
change in the course of time. The government will soon allow
the merchants to build ships after our models and visit foreign
empires. By then the Japanese themselves will modify their
customs when they see those of others, and of their own
accord will ask for the entire country to be opened to
foreigners. But, at the present time, it is impossible to allow
foreigners to travel over the entire country, or to admit them
to Miyako or Osaka, because in both of these cities there are
temples of great sanctity, and this [the admission of foreign-
ers] would assuredly be the cause of confusion and rebellion.

Upon the urgent request of Mr. Harris regarding Osaka,
they finally tell him that they will give him Sakai, three *ris*
from Osaka, or Hyogo,[138] thirteen *ris* from Osaka, both on
the Bay of Osaka. The port of Hyogo is one of the best har-
bors of the Empire, even better than Kanagawa. The city of
Sakai is three times larger than Nagasaki, and public opinion
will not be so offended by the opening of Sakai because in
ancient times this city had been opened to foreigners. Many
Spaniards had resided there and had temples.

They produced at the same time a map upon which was
shown these two cities as well as Osaka. Ships cannot go
further than three *ris* distance from the mouth of the river,
and they must ascend this river yet another ten *ris* before
reaching Osaka.

The President, they asserted, has charged Mr. Harris to
come here and deliver communications to the government
of Japan for the benefit of this Empire alone. The President
is concerned only with the advantages of Japan. Why now
this insistence upon points which will be the cause of rebel-

lion in the Empire? These disorders are certainly not advantageous to the country; the country is opening, has already
opened [its doors] a great deal and by degrees all obstacles
will be removed, but it is not possible to do everything at
once.

The President mentions of dangers from the nations of
Europe if Japan refuses to do certain things as [specified] in
the treaty. But calamities are calamities, and whether they
come from without or from within, these calamities remain
the same. The privilege of traveling in the Empire for the
merchants is for their sole material advantage. Now compare
this venal objective with that of plunging this Empire into
disorder. (This speech is one of the most sensible made by
the Commissioners during the negotiations, and they were
correct. Japan is in a dangerous position. On the one hand,
she is threatened with war and conquest if she does not
grant certain privileges. On the other, her people will revolt
if she does grant these privileges.)

Mr. Harris resumes his speech in a dignified manner on
the things of which the plenipotentiaries had spoken. He
points out that their Excellencies have said many things that
are true, that he is of the same opinion with regard to many
of their objections, but that they erred on one point, the
advantages of trade.

The President has not sent him here for the purpose of
attempting to throw money into the pockets of certain individuals, the merchants. He has not come here in advocacy of
merchants, for their profits. No, he came on the orders of
the President to paint to them the dangers which menace
Japan, and to propose means for avoiding these dangers,
and of experimenting with commerce for the benefit of
Japan.

Your Excellencies deceive yourselves, he said, if you think
that commerce exists only for the acquiring of money by

those engaged in it. If a place is thriving because of commerce, not only those who live in that place, but all who live in the vicinity and who are not involved with trade, profit by it indirectly.

Commerce is the blood, the great source of life of an Empire; look at England. Without trade the people who live in that small country would starve. What is it that has made her the master of two hundred million human beings? Trade! What is it that has made her the mightiest country of the world? Trade! Look at Holland, another country which occupies a land barely taken from the sea. Holland, that small parcel of land, constitutes a nation worthy of esteem. And why? Because of trade.

For more than two hundred years Spain and Portugal were the most powerful nations of the world. Now they enjoy a mediocre position. Why? Because they neglected trade! I therefore pray that your Excellencies will not believe that trade is conducive only to the sordid purpose of filling the coffers of a few individuals. No, commerce is conducive to a higher, more sublime purpose. It is the life, the great activity of nations, and if Japan in employing its resources is opened for commerce, there is no reason why it would not end in a most fortunate condition, the England of Asia.

He asks the Commissioners to take the question of travel under consideration tomorrow. He asserted that the question of Edo could be settled in a satisfactory manner, and asks how they would regard the opening of Sakai for permanent residence by Americans, with the right of going in the daytime to Osaka where they would have their business establishments and of returning to their families at night.

The Commissioners state that they will reflect upon what His Excellency, the Ambassador of the United States has said, but that it is unnecessary to take the question of travel under consideration, because that is impossible in the present state of affairs, and it is unnecessary to take under consideration anything which is impossible.

However, the following day is a festive day in Japan, and they cannot come because on this day one casts out the devil [*oni*] by throwing peas at him. At night the people extinguish their lights and throw peas in the dark and beat the air with rods to chase away the devil. It happens many times that in the dark one hits his best friend or his wife instead of the devil and throws peas in their faces.

They produce also a map of Miyako to prove that the city is small. Immense plots of land are occupied only by temples, the palace of the Mikado, and the castle of the Taikun, so that there is very little ground left for the inhabitants of the city.

To the remark by Mr. Harris that everywhere the government of Japan was believed to be one of the most absolute, that the Great Council had the greatest powers and did not concern itself with the opinions of a few individuals, they reply that the government has such powers insofar as it follows faithfully the ancient laws and customs of the Empire, but if it suddenly deviated from these laws and opened the Empire to foreigners, there would be a mass uprising in opposition to the violation of these laws, that the power of the government lies in the profound veneration of the Japanese for their ancient institutions and customs.[139]

Thursday, February 4, 1858

This morning Shinano no Kami called privately on Mr. Harris. He begged him, in the name of their old friendship, not to insist upon Article Seven, which grants the right of travel throughout the Empire. It is quite true, he said, that we not only think but are completely convinced that this will cause a rebellion. You stand between us and the President of the United States, and if you communicate to him our arguments, the President will communicate them to the other powers, the United States being one of the most powerful nations of the world.

Mr. Harris promised then to modify Article Seven, but for this he wishes a slight concession to the United States.[140] They are willing to grant to him, as agreed, permanent residence for Americans in Sakai, with the privilege of going during the day to Osaka to transact their business at the place where they will have their establishments, and of returning at night to Sakai, Sakai being only one Japanese hour from Osaka. "Now," he [Harris] said, "I demand permanent residence for Americans in Osaka."

Shinano no Kami repeats that this presents serious difficulties. He reasserts that when the people read in the treaty that Osaka will be open to foreigners for residence, this will cause the greatest confusion, Osaka being so near to the Dairi [141] [Imperial Palace], etc., etc.

This afternoon another conference with the Commissioners. Higo states that he heard from Shinano that you will modify the seventh article. He is very pleased and grateful for this. The proposal regarding Osaka will be taken under consideration.

Then the Consul again takes up his treaty. The first article is in order. The second, of course. The third needs many changes. It is agreed that the Americans can build houses, rent ground (the government being the sole owner of all the land in Japan, the Americans will naturally have to lease land from the government), etc., in the ports and cities opened for their permanent residence. The Consul and the local authorities will agree on the places where the Americans will have their dwellings. If these officials cannot reach an agreement, the matter will be referred to the minister of the United States and the Central Government. The places designated for the residence of Americans shall not be surrounded by walls, fences, and gates which would prevent access and egress.

[To the passage] "that all articles imported into Japan upon which import duties have already been paid can be transported to all parts of Japan without paying other duties," etc., they propose to change these words to "can be transported to all other parts of Japan," because [as the statement stands] this would grant Americans the right to accompany their merchandise. They concede that this seems ridiculous, but that there are in Japan some members of the opposition party who in reading the treaty will try to explain these things in their own way and to convince the uninformed of this, and that this possibly would bring confusion.

Mr. Harris said that he is willing to add [this], although American wares are not American persons; but it will not be possible to explain all that, with the result that this article will give the Right to the Americans. They will travel everywhere in the Empire.

The Japanese government agreed that when it has a surplus of copper it will notify the merchants a year or a half year in advance of selling this copper to the highest bidder in public auction. They say, at the same time, that the government will not have copper coins for sale.

We agree to except rice, wheat and other staples which are for exclusive use in the lives of the inhabitants and will not sell them for commerce, but only for the needs of ships and of residents, because Japanese merchants, if they knew that they could sell rice at a higher price to foreigners, would accumulate it in their warehouses and there would be a shortage of food staples. The people, reading this article, would immediately exclaim: "What! They are going to export our rice, our food! Shall we have nothing to eat? Doesn't everyone in Japan eat rice?"

Saturday, February 6, 1858

The Commissioners say that they have thoroughly considered what Mr. Harris said to them concerning Osaka, and concerning his objection that if an American becomes ill in Osaka and the sun sets, the Governor will say to him, "You must return to Sakai," and will force him to take a *norimon,* [then] this man may die en route.[142]

"Here is a matter of the greatest importance," says Mr. Harris, "and what will be the consequences thereof?"

With reference to this, the Commissioners today propose that Sakai be opened in 1860 and later in 1863, the city of Osaka, where the Americans can go during the day to transact their business, returning at night to Osaka. [Heusken's pen has slipped here. The entry makes sense if we read Osaka as Sakai.] To meet the objection raised by Mr. Harris they will construct a hotel between Osaka and Sakai where a sick person can pass the night. Mr. Harris replies immediately that they would do better to close the city completely than to say: "You may be here in the daytime, but you are too vile, too low to be permitted to sleep within our walls; however, if there is an emergency you may spend the night in a tavern outside our walls. You treat Americans like lepers or like that class of yours which works with leather, etc.,[143] etc." They say that the name of the Taikun is Minamono Ijesada.[144]

Monday, February 8, 1858

They say that it has been finally decided to open Osaka in the same manner as Edo and insist that Osaka will be opened one year after Edo, that is to say, in 1864. Mr. Harris gives them a happy idea: open Edo in 1862 and Sakai and Osaka in 1863. This is accepted. The two places will be opened to the Americans for business and only for business. Their families will not accompany them there, but will remain at Kanagawa. This had been agreed upon for Edo. Now they make a proposal themselves for the third article and say that these places will be opened for the residence and commerce of Americans.

Thus, in their great fear of granting free residence, they have made a proposal themselves, in which, without knowing it I suppose, they actually grant by these words the residence of everyone, even though it had been agreed before, between the Commissioners and Mr. Harris, that Edo would be opened only for business.

Last Saturday they had also said that since the United States had already sent Ambassadors to Japan three times, Japan should this time send a Japanese Ambassador to Washington in order to exchange ratifications of the treaty, but that they will talk more about it day after tomorrow. At first I had thought it was idle chatter, but they talked about it so seriously that I believed them. Today they confirm what they had said and tell us that the government has decided to send an Ambassador by Japanese steamship. He will go to San Francisco, California, and from there he hopes to take the American mail to New York and then to Washington. The sixteenth article is modified so that the treaty will be ratified in Washington.

Tuesday, February 9, 1858

Today they assert that since Mr. Harris assured them that the commercial regulations had been proposed for the sole purpose of assuring the revenues of Japan, and that they are upon the same basis as those of America and England, they accept them implicitly.[145]

Mr. Harris delivers them a discourse on the folly of demanding duties on tonnage and exports and offers them at the same time the tariffs which he proposes on imports. They say that these matters must be referred to the bureau of audit for decision and that everything that Mr. Harris has said will be repeated to that office.

Yesterday they had spoken about the matter of the limits around the places of residence, that [it] had already been decided for Hakodate and Nagasaki, that for Kanagawa they propose approximately two and one-half *ris* radius, and that for the other [places] they must first send some persons to inspect the localities, that it is better not to mention these limits in the treaty, and to allow the questions to be settled by the local authorities, and that they are very surprised that Mr. Harris proposes to them a radius of ten *ris*.

Mr. Harris replies now that it would be better to put the Americans in a prison then and there, that in the Treaty of Kanagawa the seven *ris* from Shimoda and the five from Hakodate were meant for persons residing in the country only temporarily, and now that the ports have been opened for permanent residence you offer me only two and one-half *ris* radius. Well, then, we shall say nothing in the treaty concerning limits [of travel], but then you will see that the Americans will demand to be permitted to travel everywhere, because limits have not been mentioned.

The Commissioners say that they must examine the matter and send agents to those territories, about which they will bring reports.

Mr. Harris says that in that case the treaty will be delayed one or two months.

Today they say that they cannot give an answer about the limits [of travel] and the tariff before four days, that the fifth day is their first day of the year, that one usually does nothing for seven days. However, considering the importance of the treaty, they will celebrate only for three days and will, therefore, return in eight days.

Concerning a proposal by Mr. Harris yesterday to have the port of Hyogo instead of the port of Sakai, they say that this is very difficult because the way by land from Hyogo to Osaka crosses the territory of a Daimyo.

Friday, February 12, 1858

This morning Moriyama was here. He did not think that there would be any more difficulties concerning the regulations and the tariff.

"With regard to money," he said, "there is no difficulty. The Daimyo are not concerned with money, taxes, and customs. They do not mention these matters at all. We understand nothing about commerce and we are compelled to believe you who have assured us, on your honor, that those regulations are for the welfare of Japan. But when it comes to the major concessions of the treaty, these are the matters where the danger from the Daimyo lies."

This afternoon Shinano no Kami came to pay us a visit. He says that Hotta, Tamba and Shinano himself will entertain him [Mr. Harris], as he has requested, at their homes on the New Year's Day.

Then he mentions that what Mr. Harris has asked him about images, such as that of the Taikun's; that is a most serious matter. With entreaties that we remain silent about it, he then informs us of a fact of the greatest secrecy,[146] that is, that images of the Taikun are made only after his death. It is only then that one is made for his tomb.

Then he said that he and Mr. Harris were friends and that I also was his friend, and therefore he asked me not to insist upon my plan of going into the streets of Edo on the second day of the year, that all the Daimyo [then] visit the

Taikun, that on this day men who usually travel with a retinue of thirty men, then take one hundred, that when one
happens to get in the middle of the procession of a Daimyo,
then they shove aside the intruder who broke the train.
The castle is so full of people that they are all pressed close
together. People of a lower rank yield the right side to people
of a higher rank whom they encounter. But if Daimyo of the
same rank meet each other, there is sometimes some jostling.
The officers who bear two swords do not do this, but rather
the other followers of the Daimyo who are of a lower station,
such as the bearers of *norimons*. Eight years ago, on the day
of a festival of the Taikun, there had been a fight between
the people of two Daimyo who had met. The coffer-bearers
hit each other with their coffers which were suspended from
poles. The servants feel the same way as their masters, and
are even more eager to defend the honor of their house than
the masters themselves. The *ronin*, although they are rogues,
always wear two swords because of their noble birth, even
though their hearts are depraved. Having lost their reputa-
tions as honorable men, they wish to regain respect by gain-
ing an evil reputation. They wish to demonstrate everywhere
that they are brave and the man who has the most scars is
looked upon as their chief and is honored accordingly.

Shinano, when he was a judge, condemned a man who in
two years had committed eighteen murders. He was crucified.
One man who had been attached to the cross and pierced by
two spears said "Wait," and then composed a Japanese poem:
"that the world meant nothing to him now and that they
could do with him as they wished." He died only after the
thirteenth spear thrust.

Japan had its Erostratus,[147] a *ronin* who, to achieve renown,
cut down all the pine trees [Matsu] he could find. These pine
trees are very much venerated and appreciated by the Japanese. They say that, when a man becomes a rogue and debases

himself more and more, it is usually the fault of his evil wife.

"Our historians," Shinano said, "bid us to obey the maxims, to follow in the footsteps of our ancestors, to change nothing in them. If you do this, you will prosper; if you change anything, you will fall into decay." He added, "This is so strong that if your ancestors bid you to go by a roundabout way to go to a certain spot, even though you discover a route which goes directly there, you may not follow it. You must always follow the path of your ancestors." [148]

Sunday, February 14, 1858

New Year's Day for the Japanese. The weather is admirable. The Daimyo and the great lords of the Empire pass by in their *norimons* or on horseback, followed by their escorts. The chief of the retinue marches first, then the two equerries on either side of the horse's head. The nobles on horseback come next in full ceremonial dress [*kamishimo*] surrounded by their samurai, who are at the same time a kind of servant and bodyguard. (They are permitted to wear the *kamishimo* and the two swords.) All these people wear the robe and the [illegible] above the knees, etiquette requiring them to march barelegged despite the cold of a February day. Then come the spear-bearers, near the tail of the horse and others depending on the rank of the lord. They usually have three to five samurai. I see also three or four *norimons,* decorated with weird figures and high colors or gilt. These are *norimons* for ladies and in these *norimons* I catch sight of lovely ladies draped in vermilion robes worn over white dresses, all made of silk.

This morning Higo no Kami came to pay us a visit, but he departed when he was told that I was still in bed. He left five fans as a present for Mr. Harris and three for me.

Many aspects of Japanese society were puzzling to the representatives of the western powers in the first years of the new intercourse. None were more so than the status of the Imperial institution and its relationship to the Shogun. The sacerdotal attributes of the Emperor were quickly appreciated, but since these men had no opportunity to learn of his historical position (a position misunderstood by most Japanese at the time) they could have no real appreciation of the position of the Shogun.

At no period in Japanese history had the Emperor enjoyed a full exercise of authority. In the remote past the priest-chief of the Yamato clan had gradually won a position superior to other clan priest-chiefs in a loose association of clans. In the mid-seventh century the priest-chief of Yamato was raised to Imperial status as the Japanese sought to create in Japan a new state based on the T'ang Chinese model. The Imperial regime even then exercised full authority over only a fragment of the Japan we know today and the Emperors themselves were seldom dominant figures in their own courts. There quickly developed the practice of relegating the Emperors to only their priestly functions, while the temporal authority was exercised by others in their names. At the same time such real authority as the Imperial Court enjoyed in the nation's affairs gradually disappeared as autonomous authority grew in many areas where local leaders sought to achieve security through local and regional arrangements among themselves. This nascent feudalism finally developed into a fully elaborated system by the end of the twelfth century when one feudal family won hegemony over the remainder.

The natural culmination of this rise of a local leader to real power over the entire country was the establishment of the Shogunal system, whereby the Imperial Court was deprived of even the nominal temporal authority it had enjoyed. Henceforth Shoguns received formal commissions from the Emperors to govern the country. This system of government by delegation of authority persisted, but with great fluctuations in effectiveness, down to the establishment of the Tokugawa Shogunate in 1603. With the rise of the Tokugawa family to supremacy, the Shogunal system achieved its most efficient expression, but the Tokugawa system of administration was far more important than the personalities of the individual Shoguns.

By the nineteenth century some Japanese had begun to study their own national history and, as a consequence, the Imperial institution emerged from virtual obscurity, but this emergence was not accompanied by any real understanding of the historic role of the Emperors. Men, mainly representing families and regions unreconciled to the Tokugawa domination, began to talk and write, usually *sub rosa* and at great personal risk, about the Tokugawa "usurpation" of Imperial authority. The fact that Emperors had never really ruled in Japan was misunderstood or ignored. The interpretation of the Tokugawa position as a "usurpation" provided their enemies with a theoretical basis for attack upon the Tokugawa and for rallying about the Imperial institution. The emergence of the Imperial institution as a vital force in Japanese politics was perhaps the most significant domestic development in the years after 1854.

Wednesday, February 17, 1858

Conference. The Commissioners begin with a preface which threatens to have no end. They say that after having ascertained the opinions of the Daimyo, Hotta, Bitchū no Kami, grants to Mr. Harris the three points demanded by him to form the basis of the treaty, but that he refuses to open additional ports, that in the negotiations with the government they [the Commissioners] had made more concessions than Hotta had authorized, that the Daimyo had been called together at the castle and that they had informed them about the treaty (provisions) as it existed at that time.[149] There ensued great confusion. The majority of the Daimyo would not agree to give their approval to concessions beyond the three points. The government anticipated revolt if they concluded the treaty. The subjects of these Daimyo always share the opinions of their masters, and some of these Daimyo have fifty to sixty thousand subjects. But the government does not wish to take back what has already been agreed upon by the Commissioners in their negotiations with the Ambassador of the United States. There are only points of minor importance yet to be settled. Because the President had sent Mr. Harris for the benefit of Japan, Mr. Harris certainly could not insist upon something of which a rebellion would certainly be the consequence. The government will honor everything already agreed upon, including dates, but wants only to delay the signature of the treaty. In the interval it will endeavor to soothe the ruffled feelings of the Daimyo who did not want to listen even to reason and said: "We have no regard for life; it does not matter to us; but we wish to remain faithful to the ancient laws of our ancestors."

In order to pacify them the government is sending a member of the Great Council to Miyako to demand the concurrence of the spiritual leader of the empire. He will need thirteen days for his preparations, fourteen days for the journey [there] and fourteen days for returning, in addition to the time he will have to spend at the court of the Mikado.

"And if," Mr. Harris says, "the Mikado does not consent; if he makes objections?"

"The government will not receive objections from the Mikado," was the response of the Commissioners. "To make the treaty acceptable to Japan we want to organize as many ceremonies as possible, and if the government at that time should have succeeded in opening *one* hand of the Daimyo, it will open the other hand by the decree of the Mikado." Thus Japan needs also the sanction of the church to achieve its end and by means of the [existing] superstition, which it will employ to the utmost, will convert the rebellious and obstinate hearts of the Daimyo of the Empire.

Mr. Harris, having replied to them that it is unheard of in diplomatic history to negotiate a treaty and afterwards not to sign it, says that if the government complies with what has been agreed upon, the government can keep secret the signature of the treaty, that he has no objections to that. He cannot force the Commissioners to sign the treaty, but, on the other hand, he cannot consent to this proposed delay. The President would certainly disapprove of this. He [Mr. Harris] proposes to put this question aside but he wants it to be understood that he has not abandoned it. He will persist and continue the negotiations on those points which have not yet been agreed upon.

The Commissioners then start again objecting to things, mere trifles. They want it mentioned in the treaty that diplomatic agents could be sent only by those nations to which the Japanese government sends one. Mr. Harris says that their objections all seem to be related to the fifteenth article which grants the same privilege to all nations which wish to make a treaty, that this article is meant for the sole interest of Japan and if they want to withdraw it they may, that he does not mind in the least.

Then they say it is all right and they have nothing against it. But they begin talking about the term "diplomatic agent." They say that they do not have such a word in their language and that the Japanese will not understand, and can they not employ the expression "a high officer will be sent to Washington" and "officer" in lieu of "consular agent"?

Mr. Harris thinks that the aim of the Commissioners is to prolong the negotiations indefinitely by weighing each word and by objecting to trifles right up to the signature of the treaty in order to observe how things develop or to await the chapter of chances.

They also say that Dutchmen and Americans are now

known in Japan, but that even the names of other nations
are unknown to many Japanese, and that they will be amazed
at seeing a Minister residing in Edo to represent a nation,
the very existence of which these Japanese are unaware.

Thursday, February 18, 1858

This morning Mr. Harris sends a note to Shinano to bid
him come and see him today. This afternoon he comes, and
Mr. Harris informs him that he cannot remain any longer
in Edo, that he will die of it, that he has lived all this time
like a prisoner in his house, that he had not wanted to go
out for fear of damaging the negotiations, that on his way he
might have met one of those Daimyo, that some accident
might have occurred, and that this might have caused suspicion and trouble. But now he proposes to conclude the
treaty, to copy it, and complete it finally for the signatures,
and that then Hotta or the Great Council should write him a
letter saying that the Commissioners appointed to negotiate
a treaty of commerce between the United States and Japan
have agreed on the treaty, that the treaty is ready to be signed,
but that for important reasons the government will postpone
the signature until the return of the Embassy to the Mikado,
that in two months or earlier the treaty will be signed. Mr.
Harris says that, everything being ready for the signature,
he will return to Shimoda by steamship, that he will finish
his dispatches to his government, that when the government
[of Japan] is ready, they will send the steamship again to
Shimoda to bring him back to Edo for the signature of the
treaty.

Shinano says that of one hundred Daimyo, thirty are in
favor of the treaty, and of eighteen ancient princes of the
empire, six [150] [are in favor of it], but that the others still
obstinately refuse, that among them, some are on their estates

and the opinions of these are not known. There are eighteen ancient princes and three hundred other Daimyo.

Friday, February 19, 1858

The proposal made yesterday by Mr. Harris has been fully accepted by the government. Final negotiations are thereupon begun. The first article states that consular agents will be permitted to go everywhere in the Empire. They repeat their objections: that there are territories belonging to the Daimyo where not even [other] Japanese people are allowed to enter. There are seven or eight principalities among the eighteen great principalities whose princes refuse entry to anyone and if a person should enter then he would immediately be decapitated. In order to prevent any difficulties or accidents which might occur, it should be added to the treaty that they [Americans] will have the right to travel in all parts of Japan where there are no obstacles. Among these principalities there are those of Kaga, the chief of the most powerful of the Daimyo, and the Prince of Satsuma in the third position, his principality having remained in the same family for seven hundred years. Even the Japanese government sends an Ometsuke to his territories only when the Prince dies and another succeeds him. This is the only time the government sends an official. The Daimyo control all the affairs of their principalities without the slightest interference by the government, and, in short, reign there as suzerains. Everything is done to placate these Daimyo so that the treaty will not upset them so much. These Daimyo will be enraged upon seeing that a traveler is allowed to go anywhere. Japan is now on the verge of rebellion.

Finally, it is agreed that the diplomatic agent and the Consul-General will be permitted to travel everywhere and consular agents are omitted. On the question, if the government does not have the power to permit consular agents to travel in Daimyo territories, how can it have the right to tell the Prince of Satsuma, for example, that the Minister is allowed to cross his territory, they reply that the Minister and the Consul-General have a much higher rank and must therefore be treated with the greatest respect possible such as is due their rank. For this reason they will be allowed to go to Satsuma, but Consuls, being ordinary officials, will not be permitted to do this. A Consul in Nagasaki, for example, will be permitted to go to Satsuma if a ship goes aground on that coast, after the government has notified the Prince of Satsuma that the Consul will cross his territory because of an emergency.

Articles One and Two are agreed upon. Mr. Harris also says that he would rather that the clause about the freedom of travel for the diplomatic agent and the Consul-General was not granted, that it does not mean much to him and that [in his opinion] they could leave out the whole clause which grants the right of travel to the diplomatic agent and the Consul-General, since they could always claim this right under the law of nations.

Saturday, February 20, 1858

Today M. [Moriyama] tells me a very interesting thing about Japan. Taiko Sama [151] had united all Japan under his rule. When he died, he left the throne to his son, Hideyori, under the regency of the Prince of Kaga, the Prince of Sendai, and the Prince of Mikawa. But Hideyori would not rule wisely. He wanted to return to the Daimyo the power taken from them by Taiko Sama, and he wanted to go to Korea and conquer China.[152] Because of this, the regents deprived Hideyori of his power, and the Princes of Kaga and Sendai, being allied with him, agreed to give the sovereign power to Mikawa,[153] who reigned very wisely and was thereafter worshiped as a god under the name of Gongen Sama.[154]

Now, when the Prince of Kaga read the treaty as it is at present he went nearly mad and said: "It would be better to fight immediately than consent to such things."

As long as the Taikun governs wisely the great Daimyo obey; but now they say, "We are not your subjects, we are your friends." Proud Kaga no Kami, besides his other subjects, has ten thousand officers who serve him. The three hundred petty Daimyo are not by themselves to be feared very much, for were they to oppose a measure taken by the government, the government would soon order them to submit; but these petty Daimyo put themselves under the protection of one among the eighteen great princes and tell him, "Let us be friends, we are entirely yours."

Now there is a superstition in Japan: when one is in doubt, one writes two characters on two pieces of paper and offers them to God (Dieu) (to the Mikado), asking him which of the two is to be adopted. The Mikado opens them and everyone submits to his veto.[155]

For this reason the government has decided to send a member of the Great Council to Kyoto to ask for the concurrence of the Mikado.

"But," I then ask him, "what if the Mikado has an opinion contrary to that of the government?"

"Oh," he says, "we have several recourses. We give money to the officers of the Mikado, who himself receives a great deal of money from the Taikun. But he has resolved that the treaty is for the benefit of *Japan,* and he wants it signed. The government is very puzzled as to how to bring about the submission of these Princes. Hotta, Bitchū no Kami, does everything possible. Whenever he and the Council of State does something that is not good or that does not succeed, they must all commit hara-kiri. What is to be done now, when the treaty is signed, if a rebellion breaks out and it cannot be put into effect?

The Princes of Owari, Kishu, and Mito are called the three brothers of the Taikun. They are not so in reality, but it is a title attached to their dignity as Princes of Owari, Kishu, and Mito.[156]

Saturday, February 20, 1858

Today one of the most alarming, boring, tiring, erratic, ignorant, and childish conferences we have had so far with the sages of Japan. They reconsider the treaty and start again to argue, reconsider, delete, and change the clauses on which fourteen days before they had agreed and which they had proposed themselves. First, in the third article, they had been the ones to propose and Mr. Harris had accepted, "the place to be occupied by the Americans will be decided by the C. [Consul] and the A.C. [Consular Agent]. If they cannot agree upon it, the problem will be referred to the diplomatic agent who will settle the matter with the Japanese government."

Moriyama with his great knowledge of the Dutch language says that *the place* can mean *a place* and *many places;* he bases this on a quotation he has found in an old grammar book, written by an old schoolmaster. "The definite article *de* [Dutch for "the"] sometimes means *een* [Dutch for "a"] and sometimes *alle* [Dutch for "all"], for example, *de mens is sterfelijk* (human beings are mortal) means that all men are mortal and that one man is mortal, and, he concludes triumphantly, therefore *the* place means *one* place and *all* places. Therefore they propose to insert a *certain* place.

Mr. Harris says that he does not wish to make grammatical

errors, that "the" means "a" place and no more, that if the Commissioners cannot translate this into Japanese, it is because the interpreter does not understand Dutch, and that Mr. Heusken, born a Dutchman and being a well-educated gentleman, should understand thoroughly his mother tongue.

Shinano replies that if Mr. Harris trusts Mr. Heusken, he has equal faith in Moriyama. It seems that in "special" port, they wish to have something through which to turn the residence of the Americans later into a kind of Deshima. Thereafter [it is agreed] that this matter will be referred to the diplomatic agent and must be referred equally to the Japanese government.

Then, that Edo and Osaka will be opened for the residence and commerce of Americans, a clause which they had been the ones to propose, they now add that these places will not be places for permanent residence; also that the Japanese munitions of war can be purchased only by the Japanese government.[157] Japanese can be employed as domestics or in any other capacity only after the government has been notified. Also the copper coins of Japan may not be exported, etc. Then, they give the limits [of travel] of the open ports.

Saturday, February 27, 1858

Mr. Harris falls ill.[158] He vomits and complains that he has an awful headache and that all the bones in his body ache, his back, his legs, his arms, etc.

Monday, March 1, 1858

Shinano calls. Mr. Harris is ill. I receive him alone. He brings up a multitude of objections to the articles [of the treaty]. I remove them to the best of my ability.

Tuesday, March 2, 1858

The two Commissioners come today as they promised to complete the negotiations. They still make some objections in conference with Mr. Harris. I make a few minor changes in the treaty. Finally, they decide that the treaty is concluded and that a final copy of it may be written.

They tell us that Hotta, Bitchū no Kami, himself will go as the Ambassador to Miyako with Higo no Kami.

They will leave on Saturday, March 6. They submit the copy of a letter which they will address to Mr. Harris in which they ask the government of the United States to notify the Russian and British governments of the treaty concluded with the Americans.

Friday, March 5, 1858

Mr. Harris feels so ill that he asks me to propose to the government that the steamer take him to Shimoda today, and that I would come when the other copies are ready. Not knowing what may happen, he will sign the two copies which are ready, and if any accident should occur, a copy signed by the two Commissioners could be transmitted to me for forwarding to the government of the United States.

This afternoon Shinano comes and says that the Ambassador cannot leave alone, that I should go with him, that two copies are enough and that two other copies can be written at Shimoda and signed when we return to Edo. With regard to the signing of the two copies by Mr. Harris the Commissioners say that the treaty cannot be signed [by them] before it is shown to the Mikado, but that they have no objection to Mr. Harris signing the treaty. Today preparations cannot be completed, but tomorrow the steamer will be ready to receive him and depart for Shimoda. Tonight the two copies are finished in the three languages. I bind them together and affix the United States' seal. Then Shinano comes into his room. Mr. Harris signs in his presence the two English copies of the treaty and the two copies of the regulations. He gives one to Shinano and keeps one for himself. Then Shinano gives him a letter from the President of the Great Council promising that the treaty will be signed in two months counting from the fifth day of their first month.[159]

Saturday, March 6, 1858

We leave this morning around seven o'clock by *norimon.* There is a terrible snowfall. On arrival at the embarcadero Mr. Harris goes aboard the boat [a launch]. He is so weak that I have to support him so that he can walk. I lift him from the *norimon* and put him in the boat. At about ten o'clock in the morning we arrive at the steamer.[160] We depart at 2 P.M. and arrive at Shimoda at two o'clock the following morning.

Sunday, March 7, 1858

At eight o'clock we leave [the steamer] in a boat. I have to support Mr. Harris from the landing at Kakizaki to the consulate because he cannot walk very well. This evening he comes to the table but he eats very little.

Monday, March 8, 1858

Mr. Harris is now worse, I believe, but he keeps to his chair most of the day. He moans a great deal at night.

Tuesday, March 9, 1858

The Governor sends word that he would like to know whether Mr. Harris does not wish to see the doctor whom the government had sent to Edo especially for him. He replies that he does not. He is very weak. This evening he falls and is unable to get up. I help him up and lead him to his chair.

Wednesday, March 10, 1858

Last night Mr. Harris moaned horribly. He fell from his bed this morning and could not get up. He cries: "Assist me. I am lame." This morning he sits in his chair and tells me that as soon as I have finished with a copy of the treaty, he wants to check it with me. He will take the English and tells me to take the Portuguese.[161] He speaks so irrationally that on my own responsibility I summon a doctor, despite his orders. The doctor comes. He says that it is a rheumatic disorder of the intestines and that it will be very difficult to cure him. Mr. Harris scarcely recognizes me and asks me the date of the month and although I shouted as loudly as I could, he did not hear me. Assam [Harris' butler] has the idea of showing him ten fingers and he understands. It is very difficult to give him medicine. When the doctor comes, I tell him, "Mr. Harris, the Governor has sent a doctor," but he closed his eyes. Afterwards he became very manageable. "Do you wish it, Mr. Heusken?" he asked. "Yes, sir, I wish it very much." "All right then, I agree," he responded.

I make him take four doses of ipecac at four different times. He does not want to take these decoctions. He repeats endlessly, "Water, water." I try to give him a concoction of camomile and elderberries instead of water. He brings it to his mouth but rejects it. He cries: "Tell Mr. Heusken I want water, water, fresh water."

At five o'clock I go to bed. At three o'clock in the morning two officers and the doctor who had left for Nakamura return, accompanied by a doctor from Shimoda. They say that they have orders from the Governor to stay here so that should Mr. Harris need something they will be there to carry out his orders.

Thursday, March 11, 1858

This morning the doctors think that he is worse than yesterday. They had hoped yesterday that they could make him perspire. Today they say that it is a nervous fever. Doctor Kanai of Edo had predicted that Mr. Harris would have a nervous fever if he did not take care of himself. He had given him two doses of pills which had purged him very effectively while at Edo. At night he could not stop getting up to go to the bathroom and back to bed.

The doctor here now says that it was very dangerous to have given him a purge. He says that it will be very difficult to cure him. At noon brown spots begin to appear on his legs. They say that it is the rot. His body is also covered with purple spots from rot and they say again that it is impossible to save him. I try to speak to him but do not succeed in reaching him. Then as loud as I can [I say], "Mr. Harris, you are very ill," but he does not understand me. Then I repeat several times, "Mr. Harris, would you not pray, pray to God?" He replies, "Pay you?" "Oh, P-R-A-Y." "Oh, yes! I will pray to God bye and bye," and he goes back to sleep. I cannot make him understand anything. What am I to do? I am entirely alone here. My God! This is a terrible thing.

The Vice-Governor comes with a gift from the Governor,

a box of sugar and one hundred eggs. He tells me again that if I should want anything, I have only to ask for it.

Today he eats a cup of chicken broth. At four o'clock Dewa no Kami, Governor of Shimoda, comes here to inquire in person about the condition of the Ambassador. He repeats the offers and declarations of friendship made this morning by the Vice-Governor and the other officers. He asks me, if I should see a crisis coming, to inform him immediately, and, even though it be in the middle of the night, he would come immediately in person. He was accompanied by Wakana Myosaburo and other officers.

This evening I succeeded with difficulty in making myself understood a little. I explained his plight to him and asked him if he would not like to pray a little with me. He replied, "Yes, Mr. Heusken." Then I took the book and read him some prayers. He gave most of the responses and the Amens in a very distinct voice and with nods of his head without my assistance. I said the Lord's Prayer again and again. This was most comforting to me, and inspired by the circumstances, I read the prayers as movingly and convincingly as I could.

I asked him, "Mr. Harris, have you nothing to say to me?"

"No," he replied.

"You have nothing to say to Mr. Drinker?"

"No."

"Nothing to Mrs. Drinker?"

"No."

"Your attorney?"

"No, you can write him."

"Nothing to Senator Whitman, Governor Marcy?"

"No, no."

"You have no relations, Mr. Harris?"

"Oh, she is English!"

"Well, you may perhaps now see your God face to face. You have something more to say?"

"Mr. Heusken, I have no secrets. I have always led a life of great simplicity. I have never been encumbered with many estates. I am ready to see my God (or something to the kind). In my letter I have provided for these things. The cloth that is here you may keep or give away. I always thought of making a will."

I told him that he should not think of me, but did he have nothing more to say? I could not restrain my tears.

"Heusken," he said, "wipe your nose not so near my face. Heusken you are a good boy and a true friend. I leave the care of my soul to you."

Friday, March 12, 1858

This evening he was carried to his chair by the servants where he rested for an hour. In the morning I succeeded in getting him to swallow a spoonful of camphor and musk. His pulse is a little stronger this morning. A little later he sent for me, certainly improved by the dose I had administered to him. I spoke very distinctly, but his hearing was very weak.

I said to him, "You sent for me. You have something to say to me?"

"No. I sent for you to ask you how you are, Heusken. You are very pale, very thin, you even have lost a lot of weight and your color is very sickly. Well, what do you think now? Yesterday you were quite alarmed and did not these doctors think I was going to die? Well, what is my temperature today? Average? Lower? Higher? The letters I have written, you can look them over. If they are not good, destroy them. If so, send them, and write that, taken by a violent indisposition, I apologize for this letter. This Eastern state of affairs is very bad. Hereditary power, bodies in a state. I want you to write to the President that, if he approves of my conduct here, he exhibit me as minister upon my return."

A few minutes later I return with paper and pencil to ask him whether he did not have anything else to tell me. "No. Yes," he said. "Yes." I expected to hear something of importance when he told me "yes." "These warm undershirts, put them against my feet."

Saturday, March 13, 1858

This morning he is much better. He sits in his chair. He wants to have the barber. I tell him that this is not the thing to do. Having left the room, I see upon my return that he has been given his razor and that he is shaving himself. Assam took the blade and finished shaving him while he sits. He asks for clean linen. They bathed him completely and he looks a hundred times better. (I believe the danger is passed. The doctors say that today is the crisis. He asks me to open the window and says while he looks at the trees and nature, "I thank God now, since to see nature is to see Him.") He reaches the door of his room, and while supporting himself on me he walks the few steps to the entrance, has it opened, and after contemplating nature for a few moments, comes back in.

The Vice-Governor pays him a visit.

Sunday, March 14, 1858

He is much better. He drinks some broth. Wakana pays him a visit.

Monday, March 15, 1858

He is better. The Governor pays him a visit.

Tuesday, March 16, 1858

The Vice-Governor pays him a visit. He is much better, but refuses to take any more medicine.

Wednesday, March 17, 1858

He eats nothing today. All he does is smoke opium.[162] [Heusken has inserted four lines of writing between the original lines of the manuscript. For all practical purposes these lines are illegible.]

Thursday, March 18, 1858

The Vice-Governor, Wakana, comes here. He brings a letter from the Great Council and a present from the Taikun for Mr. Harris. The letter says that the Taikun has been informed of Mr. Harris' illness and he sends a present. Whenever a present from the Taikun is being delivered, they always shout *"shita ni iro"* in the streets and everyone kneels before it.

And here is another book that I am going to entrust to the care of Her Majesty, the Queen of the Low Countries, in my name to administer during the long months from September 6 to the eighth of this month. We cannot hope for more in a day which is not going to last beyond —— [illegible].[163]

[The ensuing lines are under the above date, but it is logical to assume that some time has elapsed.]

Mr. Harris feels so strong that he wishes to return to Edo. He has me write the Governor that he wants to leave on April 2.

Wednesday, April 7, 1858

The Governor comes here and says that he has received a letter from the government [saying] that the government has done everything possible to restore the health of Mr. Harris, that it sent him three doctors, and that the doctors have said that it is dangerous for him to travel. For this reason it would be better for him not to leave before May 13.[164] Mr. Harris won't hear of this and says that he must be there [Edo]. The Governor then says that Hotta has not yet returned and that it has been agreed that the treaty would be signed when Hotta had returned or they had heard from him. Mr. Harris shows the letter in which Hotta gives his promise that the treaty would be signed in two months. He does not want to postpone [his departure] for a day, although the Governor asks him for a delay of one week.

Ten days ago a great fire in Edo destroyed 128 streets and about five thousand houses near Nipon bas [Nihombashi] in sixteen hours.

Thursday, April 15, 1858

This morning we go aboard the steamer. The captain says that he cannot leave today because of the bad weather. Mr. Harris insists. We depart. The steamer cannot move against the tide and the wind from the southeast, and we return. The captain knows nothing of tacking about.

Friday, April 16, 1858

We depart. We have traveled about twenty miles when a squall strikes. The captain is frightened by it and puts about for Shimoda. He puts about again to spend the night in another harbor. He is still fearful and puts about again for Shimoda. Then he changes his course once again and we arrive at nightfall in the small bay of Ajiro.

Saturday, April 17, 1858

We leave Ajiro early this morning. We pass Uraga off the American anchorage under a most serene sky. The captain puts about in order to spend the night in Uraga, saying that he cannot reach Shinagawa before nightfall, and that the American anchorage is unsafe and that the bay is very dangerous because of reefs.

We arrive at Uraga about three o'clock. I want to go ashore. The Vice-Governor says that he must first ask the permission of the Governor. After the permission arrives he says he will notify me. I state that I do not wish to go ashore after the permission of the Governor. I will go immediately or not at all.

Sunday, April 18, 1858

We leave Uraga quite early and arrive at Shinagawa about 8 A.M. We take a launch and go ashore. I mount a horse and we go to our hotel. [We cause] much less sensation [than before]. The fire of [blank] April has passed here, and [the damage] already has been somewhat repaired. Moriyama receives us at the hotel and takes us to our rooms. He gives us presents from the government, lovely potted flowers, a dwarf cherry tree, a double camellia, etc., all magnificent.

Monday, April 19, 1858

Shinano no Kami gives us a letter from Hotta, which came from Kyoto in four days, saying that he cannot keep his promise to have the treaty signed on the appointed date, but that it will take longer. Toki Tamba and Yudono Mina-boro [165] also come to pay a visit to Mr. Harris.

Thursday, April 22, 1858

Today a prestidigitator came. There was a clown who was doing funny tricks and beating two drums; there was also a flute player. Then came the prestidigitator, a man with a completely shaven head. He also performed very extraordinary tricks. He seemed to make small butterflies appear, flutter about in the air, rest on flowers or on his fan—and did this for over an hour, letting them flutter around himself, all this with the sole aid of his fan.[166] Truly remarkable!

April 23, 1858

Tonight Mr. Donker Curtius arrives in Edo, accompanied by his secretary, Mr. de Graeff van Polsbroek. The latter writes me a letter in the name of Mr. Donker Curtius asking me to please inform Mr. Harris of his arrival.

Saturday, April 24, 1858

This morning I go on horseback to pay a visit to Donker Curtius to compliment him on his arrival.

Sunday, April 25, 1858

Donker Curtius and his secretary pay us a visit. We are being sent a gift of wine, cigars, arak, tea, and coffee.

Monday, April 26, 1858

Today we pay a visit to Shinano. His Excellency receives us and gives us a Japanese dinner with all the formalities. First there is a cup of tea, then some fish, some chicken soup, and then quail very nicely arranged with their plumage, and sake. He then shows us his home and his official chambers. He owns a half-dozen guns, bayonets, two or three old muskets of the Spanish school, a dozen bows and a great number of arrows. His garden was charming, extremely well kept, with a small pond full of goldfish, all kinds of flowers and shrubbery, a Shinto shrine, an area for riding horseback and for archery, and a small house [for protection] against fires.

He tells us that Japanese custom forbids women to be present. They are allowed to see only other women, boys whose hair has been completely shorn, and men whose heads have been completely shaven like scholars. They look through apertures in the windows in order to observe us.

Tuesday, April 27, 1858

Mr. Harris and I pay a visit to Donker Curtius.

Wednesday, April 28, 1858

This morning I pay a visit to Donker Curtius. This evening I pay another visit, returning by the beautiful light of the moon. I have ten lantern bearers. In the quarter of the two castles I meet men with lanterns who light my way, their weapons in their belts. In the merchants quarter twelve lanterns, half red and the other half blue, come to meet me and show me the way through this area, while police officers of the quarter walk before me with iron staffs which they clang on the stones with a lovely effect. In the clear waters of the moat, the walls of the castle, surmounted on both sides by magnificent cypresses, reflect their dark outlines.

Thursday, April 29, 1858

This morning Mr. Harris and I go to the temple of Kannon [Vishnu].[167] There was a great crowd there. At the entrance to the Temple there were two statues, one was the God of Casks and the other the God of Wine. Passing through this portal which opens in a double swinging door, we came to a wide avenue which was bordered on each side by rows of shops. It was, in short, like a fair. Having walked for about ten minutes we reached another gate; then, finally beyond that, the temple proper. After having ascended a stairway of approximately thirty steps, we enter the temple. Because of its sanctity this temple is visited daily by great crowds of people. There was a toe of [illegible] and a statue which, having been touched so many times by the worshiping faithful, had lost its nose and its eyes and showed only the faint contours of a [illegible] with a faint trace that a mouth had existed. The temple is very beautiful, but very dirty. There were a number of idols, a lantern, curious objects hanging in the air or [placed] below, a painting depicting some twenty young ladies representing the beauties of the Yoshiwara, the quarter of prostitutes.

In a temple the Japanese carry their religion to extremes. The grounds belonging to this temple are enormous. There are trees, great cypresses, and several booths full of curiosities. In one of them there were figures made of tortoise shell, men, women, crows, and, especially, two magnificent storks. There was also a man who greatly resembled a Dutch burgomaster of the seventeenth century, probably one of the presidents of the factory at Deshima. In another booth there was a big ship with —— [illegible] figures, and a quantity of life-sized figures, men reading or smoking their pipes, an apartment with ladies busy with their toilets, some coolies, a merchant, and men writing, all very well made. A last one shows nudity, an enormous collection, one of the greatest of nude women with a drapery around their loins. An old woman resembling Mme. Musch sold sea shells. The gardens were filled with cherry trees, all in bloom and of such a beauty on a small scale as I have never seen. There are dwarf trees, etc., etc., and other kinds of plants.

Friday, April 30, 1858

Mr. Donker Curtius pays us a visit.

Saturday, May 1, 1858

We go today to Ōji Asukayama.[168] We pass the palace of Kaga no Kami and soon reach the open country. The scenery is very picturesque. There is a very level road. We visit Ōji, the temple of the God of Foxes.[169] Asukayama is the place where the population of Edo goes for pleasure and to hike in the hills which overlook immense rice fields. There were a number of men, women, and small children running as quickly as possible in order to see us, crying sometimes "Americans," but more often *"tojin"* [Chinese].

In that village there are shops where they sell things disconcertingly exposed to public view. Great [male] genitals made of paper on a mask in lieu of the nose, or also [made] with the private parts of a woman.

Thursday, May 13, 1858

We lunch at the residence of Mr. Donker Curtius in the Javanese manner. Then a prestidigitator [comes].

Tuesday, May 18, 1858

Today a conference with Shinano and Higo no Kami. The latter has just arrived from Kyoto with a message from Hotta.

He says that matters are not progressing too well, that there is so much opposition from the Daimyo that followers of theirs have posted placards in nine different places: "We shall kill Hotta, Bitchū no Kami," that the Mikado has finally given as his reply, because he himself is rather fearful of giving his consent because of the Daimyo, that he will attempt once more to convince the Daimyo, and as soon as they will give their assent, his own will follow without delay. Hotta is still constantly in Kyoto trying to settle matters. If he is not successful, he will return to Edo to consult with the Taikun and the government on what is to be done. They assure us constantly that the government will issue orders to have the treaty signed, but that in the present state of affairs, this is not possible. We having said that refusal to sign the treaty would have the most regrettable consequences, they reply that the government knows all this very well, but, if they should sign the treaty now, a rebellion would certainly follow and they repeat, what difference does it make whether the danger comes from without or from within, if danger must come.

On last Saturday, May 15, Mr. Harris wrote a letter to Shimoda to be delivered to the first commander of a warship arriving at that port, requesting him to come with the ship to Kanagawa. This has been done with the knowledge of the Japanese government and the latter has raised no objections.

Monday, May 17, 1858

We go to a temple today to watch some wrestlers. Mr. Donker [Curtius] had ordered a splendid lunch to be prepared near the temple, which we ate with the greatest relish in the world.

Tuesday, June 1, 1858

Hotta returns from Kyoto.

Saturday, June 5, 1858

Conference with the above-mentioned, who says that despite all his efforts he has not been able to arrange matters in such a way that the treaty can be signed. However, the government remains determined that the treaty will be signed, but he does not know when this will be. It will not take so very long. At the same time he presents his views on paper and says that the Commissioners will consult with him later.

Monday, June 7, 1858

Conference with the Commissioners. They repeat the same objections that signature would immediately place the Empire in a state of full revolt. Pressed by Mr. Harris [asking] what delay they request, they finally answer: "Three months."

Mr. Harris says: "What guarantees do I have? You have given me your promise to sign after two months. Now four

months have elapsed and these three make it seven. If the
Mikado and the Daimyo persist in their attitude, what is to be
done?"

They say that, if after some time they have not managed
to persuade these gentlemen, they will force their compliance
by means of their power, and the treaty will be executed in
spite of them.

Mr. Harris suggests the postponement of the signing of
the treaty until after the arrival of an American warship,
or to sign tomorrow, dating the documents three months
hence. They say that the signing of the treaty is the same as
the completion and execution thereof. Mr. Harris says: "If
you cannot sign, you must have some secrets. The Daimyos
know that you have given me your solemn promise to sign
the treaty now within such time. This promise is the same for
them as if the government has signed."

They say they will put these propositions before the Council so that they will be presented to the Imperial Court.

Tuesday, June 8, 1858

I am with Mr. Donker [Curtius]. He has had a conference
with the Japanese. The Japanese have given him a copy of
our treaty and have offered him the same advantages. He tries
to get a treaty before that of Mr. Harris, by asking only for
Shimonoseki and Uraga, diplomatic residence at Edo, the
export of coins and some minor privileges. He will have the
privileges of the American treaty, obtaining them as soon as
the treaty is signed. However, he does not tell me what the
Japanese have told him.

With this entry for June 8, 1858, Heusken ceased keeping his journal. For two and one-half years thereafter we
have nothing from his pen. Then on January 1, 1861, he

began again. Why he should have resumed his journal at this point just a few days before his death remains a mystery. Was it some premonition of the doom soon to overtake him?

Except for a few minor fragments, Townsend Harris had ceased keeping his journal at the end of February, 1858, just prior to his near-fatal illness. Thus within a few months both Harris and Heusken ceased keeping private records of the diplomatic activity in which they were engaged. We can only speculate on their motives for so doing. Was it the press of diplomatic activity? This seems hardly likely since their records had been faithfully kept during the periods of most active negotiation with the Japanese. Both men must have had abundant time for their private observations on passing developments, had they wished to do so. Professor Cosenza, who published *The Complete Journal of Townsend Harris*, has speculated upon the possibility that Harris did keep a complete journal, portions of which subsequently disappeared. While this must be regarded as a possibility in the case of Harris, who kept his journal in a number of record books, it may be virtually ruled out in the case of Heusken, who resumed his journal on January 1, 1861, in the same record book which he had been employing since his departure from New York in the autumn of 1855.

Fortunately neither Harris nor Heusken disappear from view in the period following the conclusion of their diaries. The treaty over which the two men had labored for so long was finally signed on board the *U.S.S. Powhatan* in Edo Bay on July 29, 1858. This came as a great relief to Harris who was not unaware of the position he might occupy in history. The preceding few weeks had been a period of considerable anxiety for Harris who was fearful that the Dutch, by making more modest requests of the Japanese authorities, might win from him the honor of having negotiated the first real commercial treaty with Japan. Heusken seems to have shared this anxiety. Harris outlined the problem for the State Department in a dispatch dated July 8, 1858, reviewing recent developments in Japan.

"The Japanese had given the Dutch Commissioner a copy of the Treaty they had negociated with me, and he was aware of the desire of the Japanese to postpone the execution of it. He openly avowed his intention to negociate such a Commercial Treaty as would not be objected to by the Daimios, and said that if subsequently the American treaty was signed, the additional privileges would accrue to the Dutch, and thus Holland would secure the great credit of having made the first Commercial Treaty with Japan. I have no doubt that, had I broken off the negociations, a Treaty would have at once been made as desired by the Dutch Commissioner.

"In addition to the loss of credit to the United States, I had also to consider that the fact of the Dutch, having made such a Treaty, would greatly embarrass any future negociations for the obtaining of the provisions omitted in the Dutch Treaty, if it did not entirely defeat them.

"After mature deliberation, I determined to accede to the request of the Japanese, provided they would also pledge themselves in writing, not to sign any Treaty or Convention with any Power, until the expiration of thirty days after signing the American Treaty.

"This proposition was accepted by the Council of State, who subsequently wrote me a letter, expressing the conditions already stated."

Despite the conditions to which the Council of State had agreed, the Japanese authorities in quick succession negotiated similar commercial treaties with the Netherlands on August 18; with Russia on August 19; and with Great Britain on August 26; all within thirty days after the signature of the American treaty. Harris, himself, contributed to this technical violation of the agreement by placing the services of Henry Heusken at the disposal of Lord Elgin in the negotiations leading to the British treaty of August 26, 1858.

Lord Elgin acknowledged this assistance in a letter to Harris on August 27 in which he said:

"I have found Mr. Heusken not only well qualified as an Interpreter, but in all other matters which I have had to refer to him, both intelligent and obliging in the highest degree, and I shall not fail to convey to Her Majesty's Government my sense of the importance of the aid which you, Sir, and your Secretary have rendered to me at this conjuncture."

Harris also offered the services of Heusken to Baron Gros, the French plenipotentiary who negotiated a commercial treaty in October, but he declined, preferring to rely on the services of a Frenchman who had some knowledge of the Japanese language.

The new treaties came into effect on July 1, 1859, but before that time Harris had negotiated the Convention of Kanagawa of March 19, 1859, which provides further evidence that Harris was not unmindful of his potential place in history. It provided, among other things, that no Japanese embassy would leave Japan for any other foreign capital before the mission bearing the Japanese ratification of the Harris Treaty reached Washington. In these negotiations Heusken as usual played an indispensable role.

More than a year had elapsed since Harris' near-fatal illness. When the *U.S.S. Mississippi* visited Shimoda in late March, 1859, Harris placed himself under the care of the Naval Surgeon, John S. Fox, who treated him for a now chronic dyspepsia. Since the *Mississippi* was to stop at Nagasaki en route back to the China coast, Harris decided to take a much-needed rest from his labors by combining a visit to Nagasaki on official business with a vacation on the China coast. While in Nagasaki, Harris inspected the city to determine the most eligible sites for residences of Americans, some of whom were already there in anticipation of the commercial opportunities soon to be afforded. While there he also appointed John G. Walsh as Acting Consul for that port.

The *Mississippi* left Nagasaki on April 27, 1859, for Shanghai and while in Shanghai, Harris was officially informed of his elevation from Consul-General to Minister Resident. Two months later Harris was back in Shimoda much improved in health and preparing to move to Edo.

Harris arrived in Kanagawa on June 30 and appointed E. M. Dorr as Acting Consul there. He entered strong objections to the plans of the Japanese to substitute Yokohama for Kanagawa as a residence for foreigners envisioning the former as a probable "new Deshima."

Whether Heusken accompanied Harris to Nagasaki and Shanghai is not revealed in the records. It seems likely that he remained behind to handle routine matters at the Shimoda consulate. If that was the case, Harris' conversations with the Japanese authorities at Nagasaki must have been handled through the agency of other interpreters. If Heusken was left behind it would help to explain a puzzling development in the relations between these two men. The irritations Heusken must have felt in his solitude at Shimoda would explain the breach between the two men which occurred on July 4, 1859. On that date Harris wrote the Department stating:

"I regret to inform you that Mr. Heusken, my Dutch interpreter, left me this afternoon without giving me a single day to provide a substitute.

"I have strong suspicions as to the means that were used to induce Mr. Heusken to act in a manner so contrary to the rules of propriety and integrity, and to leave this legation at a most important juncture, and in a manner so well calculated to embarrass and injure the interests of the United States; but as they are only suspicions, I do not feel warranted in giving you any particulars until what is now suspicion shall become ascertained fact. I cannot obtain an interpreter at once, but I shall use all possible efforts to procure such temporary aid as will prevent injury to our affairs in this country.

"I feel greatly grieved at this sudden parting with a person to whom I had become much attached and who had been my sole companion during my weary solitude in this country."

In Harris' private papers we find a laconic note from Heusken saying: "I received your note this evening and will call on you next Thursday, the 14th instant." This was dated July 8, 1859, and is obviously in response to a letter from Harris requesting an explanation for his behavior.

Harris had meanwhile established his residence in Edo where the British Consul-General, Rutherford Alcock, offered him the services of his interpreter, Mr. Cowan. Harris accepted the offer but fortunately Heusken soon returned to his former employment.

The account which Harris sent to the State Department of the manner in which Heusken rejoined him at the American Legation in Edo has a most curious ring. He stated, in effect, that it was all a misunderstanding and that Heusken had left his employment under the impression that he had Mr. Harris' consent to do so and that he returned to service the moment he appreciated that his impressions were wrong. Harris then continued with a long argument for a salary increase for Heusken whose income was well below that of other western interpreters in Japan.

After describing the better compensation and more secure status of other interpreters, Harris further wrote:

"Mr. Heusken was engaged by me on the 1st of October, 1855, but his salary did not commence until the 1st of March, 1856, he losing five months of his time thereby.

"Since the 1st of January, 1857, Mr. Heusken has been

employed in the important business of interpreting all my negociations with the Japanese, which resulted in the Convention of Shimoda, the Treaty of Yedo and the Convention of Kanagawa.

"His labors in these negociations were the more arduous on his part from the fact that he had to be the Instructor of the Interpreters on the part of the Japanese, who were ignorant of all the more important words, necessarily employed in the preliminary part of those negociations, particularly in those that preceded the Treaty of Yedo.

"These services were beyond the legitimate duties of the Interpreter to the consulate, and I respectfully submit that they form a just claim for extra compensation. . . .

"By Mr. Heusken's experience in Japan he has added much to his usefulness by a considerable knowledge of the Japanese language, and also by his complete knowledge of the Dutch as used by the Japanese, which is a peculiar patois, which has grown up among them during the last 200 years.

"I think it an act of justice to Mr. Heusken that he should be allowed a consideration for his extra services and that this allowance should be not less than $1500.

"I respectfully inform you that I cannot retain the services of Mr. Heusken or procure a competent person in his place for less than $2500 per annum, and I trust that you will be pleased to authorize me to pay that sum."

We can only speculate on what actually happened. Harris' version of the incident as merely a misunderstanding is unconvincing. It is entirely possible that what occurred was the climax to a long development. We cannot overlook the fact that Heusken and Harris were twenty-eight years apart in age and worlds apart in temperament. They must have worn on each other's nerves at times. In addition, Heusken had served Harris for more than three years with no increase in compensation. He had served, as Harris noted, in capacities beyond those of interpreter and was, beyond question, the most accomplished man at his craft in Japan at the time. The superior status and compensation of other interpreters must have galled him greatly, particularly in view of the fact that Heusken was by this time something of an "old Japan hand."

Did Heusken make an increase in his salary a condition of his return to service in the American Legation? Was his precipitate departure on July 4, 1859, a calculated move on his part to force the issue of a raise in salary? Was Harris' rather lame explanation of what had transpired and his argument for an increase in Heusken's salary simply his method of intimating diplomatically to his superiors what the real issues were? We cannot answer any of these questions with finality. It is, however, interesting to note that Heusken's salary was raised to $2500 per annum on January 1, 1860, and that he served Harris from that time until his death in January, 1861, with no further incident.

The period following Heusken's reconciliation with Harris was to be a happy time for him. In contrast to the nearly three years which had gone before, Heusken found many congenial companions among the diplomatic and commercial communities in Edo, Kanagawa, and Yokohama. He was now first Secretary of the Legation in Edo and so well informed on things Japanese that he became the guide and companion for many visitors to Japan who subsequently published accounts of their travels. All mention the warm affection they came to feel for him. He was frequently loaned out to foreign missions in Japan and was, in fact, assisting a Prussian mission to negotiate a treaty with Japan at the time of his death.

But this same period was one of growing difficulty for all foreigners in Japan. The signing of the various treaties had aroused many Japanese who were sincerely opposed to abandonment of the traditional policy of seclusion. In addition there were many Japanese who had no strong antipathy to foreigners but who were hostile to the Tokugawa regime and sought to find in its policies means whereby it might be overthrown. When Heusken met his death in January, 1861, he was but the seventh foreigner to be assassinated in Japan in the eighteen months since the treaties had gone into effect.

These same months which saw the growth of hostility to foreigners saw the development of increasing problems for the existing regime. The Tokugawa authorities had carried the treaties into execution despite the opposition of powerful feudal lords. The chief minister of the Shogun, the Tairo, Ii Naosuke, who was primarily responsible for this action, was assassinated on March 24, 1860, at the very gates of the Shogun's palace by retainers of one of the xenophobic feudal lords. Thus, as the regime sought to honor its commitments to the foreigners, it was at the same time compelled to face the hostility of powerful groups within Japan. Harris appreciated the dilemma of the authorities and this appreciation led him to take a different position from his diplomatic colleagues in Edo when his own secretary, Henry Heusken, was cut down less than ten months after the Shogun's chief minister.

When Heusken resumes his journal he had already been assisting Count Eulenberg, the Prussian representative, for some time in the negotiation of a treaty similar to that enjoyed by the other major powers of the West.

January 1, 1861

Today I went to see Mr. Harris who was at the home of Mr. Dorr,[170] the American consul at Kanagawa. Mr. Harris is informed by message that a Governor of Foreign Affairs wishes to speak to him. The Governor says that he has been sent expressly by the Great Council to tell him in confidence that the government of Japan has learned of a rumor that five or six hundred *ronin*, probably of the Prince of Mito, are embittered against foreigners, the reason being that, because of the export trade, the price of food staples is rising constantly, and that they want to burn Yokohama to the ground. The government fears that they might also attack the legations in Edo and the consulates in Kanagawa. The two Japanese steamers have been ordered to stand by near Yokohama. Two Daimyo have already sent about six hundred men in order to protect the foreigners of Yokohama. The government asks the consuls to leave their isolated residences at Kanagawa and go to Yokohama. The ministers and their attachés should retire to a house situated within the compound of the Imperial Palace. The government has not yet mentioned this matter to any of the other ministers. They ask for the opinion of Mr. Harris, who tells them that he does not think the matter so serious, but he immediately sends me to Edo to inform the other ministers.

This evening the Governors come to Akabane to the quarters of the Minister of Prussia and tell him the same story.

January 3, 1861

Conference with the Governors regarding the Prussian Treaty which today was concluded definitively. Hori, Oribe no Kami,[171] died on December 31. It is rumored that he cut his own stomach, though this is being denied by the government.

January 7, 1861

The Governor,[172] Oguri, Bungo no Kami, comes to see Mr. Harris. He says that the general outlook is somewhat improved and the government has discovered some six hundred conspirators, and has arrested only a few of them, because arresting them all would cause too much confusion. (Timidity, or is the rank of the conspirators too influential?)

They ask permission to billet a few *yakunin* in the minister's own house which is denied. Mr. Harris wants everybody within the compound of the legation to pay him the usual respects when he leaves or enters, to give a bow of the head, and this the new *yakunin* of the Daimyo seem to fail to do.

The Governor says that he can answer for all the officers of the government, but that it is difficult to compel the followers of the Daimyo to do it. In time perhaps! He says that there is a law that officers on duty at the gates of a castle always stand erect and motionless, even upon seeing their parents and friends, and that they bow only to the Ometsuke who come to inspect the guard, and that he himself when passing the officers of the Daimyo is not saluted. (I follow the Governor when he leaves and I see all the officers of the Daimyo but two bow before him.)

The Governor also says that the rumor that the Prince of Satsuma will not come to Edo any more is false, that he was already en route for Edo but being taken ill he returned to his estate, that he will remain in his estate the next year because it is not the year when he should be in Edo, but that he will come the following year.

[The Governor also says] that the rumor that some Daimyo will no longer send rice to Edo is equally false, that the Daimyo never send rice because this is done through the intervention of merchants of Osaka, with the exception of the Prince of Sendai who has never ceased sending it.

It seems that a rich Japanese merchant has been arrested by the government and all his possessions confiscated, and that he himself will be sent to the islands [exiled] for having purchased great quantities of foodstuffs which he would not sell, in order to raise the price of these articles.

When the government is in difficulties, for example when the warehouses of the Taikun are consumed by fire, the officials exact a kind of forced levy. They tell the rich merchants, "We must have money because the Taikun needs it." The merchants are not forced to give it, but they fear that the *yakunin* will seek them out afterwards. Everyone gives according to his means. This is called *Goyokin.*

The above-mentioned merchant had given six thousand Koban of Goyokin six years ago. The Shirokiya who in fact lives in Kyoto would be fearful that the Taikun might eject him from Edo if he did not pay the Goyokin.

January 8, 1861

The Governors at Akabane propose the insertion of a clause in the treaty regarding the right of the Japanese to seize suspicious articles and to levy a fine or confiscation immediately after the consul has decided upon the matter, which [clause] is accepted.

I have translated a letter in which Count Eulenberg makes a final request to be received in audience by the Taikun.[173]

[The above lines were the final entry made by Heusken in his journal. One week later he met his death.]

The great debate on foreign and domestic policy, which grew in intensity and complexity after its inception in 1853, was accompanied by a growing turbulence in Japanese society. Few Japanese in positions of power and responsibility were satisfied with the status quo by July, 1859, when the new treaties came into force. The Tokugawa regime was committed to opening the country to foreign intercourse. Another strong faction supported a return to national isolation. A third group sought to reform the Tokugawa administration by a movement to unite the Imperial Court and the Bakufu, arguing that it was necessary for the Court and the great lords to have some share in the formulation of policy, if Japan was to be united and effective in her actions. Illustrative of the complexity of the contemporary debate was the fact that many Japanese, in and out of the government, supported the opening of the country, but only as a temporary expedient until such time as Japan became strong enough to close her doors once again. There was, as yet, no strong faction frankly advocating the overthrow of the Tokugawa regime.

The progressive impoverishment of many lower samurai in the late Tokugawa Age led to an increase in the number of *ronin* (masterless samurai who had left or been dismissed from the service of their former masters), which contributed greatly to the turbulence in Japanese society, since these men had no vested interest in the status quo. *Ronin* had troubled the authorities at other times in Tokugawa history and they were to play their part in its ultimate downfall.

Until July, 1859, foreigners were found in numbers only at Nagasaki and Hakodate at the two extremes of the empire. Harris and Heusken had been in virtual isolation at Shimoda, and Edo had witnessed only the official missions from the various foreign countries which had resulted in the treaties of 1858.

After July, 1859, however, increasing numbers of diplomats and foreign merchants found their way to Edo and Yokohama respectively. Many of the foreigners undoubtedly brought with them a certain arrogance since most of them came from the China Coast. Japanese samurai and *ronin* were noted for an arrogance of their own.

The impact of the foreign merchants on the Japanese economy was almost immediate. The lower ratio in Japan of gold to silver than that prevailing in the rest of the world enabled traders and, unhappily, some members of the various diplomatic corps, to purchase and export Japanese gold at incredible profits. Commodity prices rose rapidly in reply to the foreign demand, producing additional hardships on the Japanese people.

It is hardly surprising that there ensued, soon after the opening of the ports, isolated attacks upon foreigners who exposed themselves unnecessarily. A little more than a month after the opening of Yokohama a Russian officer and two sailors were murdered after dark in the streets of that port. There ensued other attacks which led to more energetic measures by the authorities to protect the legations. These efforts were accompanied by continued pleas that the foreigners exercise discretion in exposing themselves at night. There were, however, no reparations for these murders.

Finally, on January 15, 1861, eighteen months after the treaties came into force, undoubtedly the most popular of all members of the foreign community, Henry Heusken, was the victim of assassins.

Harris wrote at length to the State Department describing the manner in which Heusken met his death. In a dispatch dated January 22, 1861, he reported:

"It is my melancholy duty to inform you of the death of Mr. Henry C. J. Heusken, the able, efficient and faithful Interpreter of this Legation.

"On the night of the 15th instant, about 9 o'clock, Mr. Heusken was returning home from the Prussian Legation. He was attended by three mounted officers and four footmen bearing lanterns; one of the mounted officers preceded Mr. Heusken and the other two followed close behind him. While proceeding in this manner the party was suddenly attacked on both sides; the horses of the officers were struck and cut; the lanterns struck out and Mr. Heusken wounded on both sides of his body; he put his horse into a gallop and rode about two hundred yards, when he called out to the officers, that he was wounded and that he was dying, and then fell from his horse. The assassins, seven in number instantly fled, and easily escaped in the dark streets.

"Mr. Heusken was brought to this Legation about half past 9 o'clock. I immediately procured surgical aid from the Prussian and English Legations, and he received every possible assistance that skill and kindness could supply, but all was in vain, his wounds were mortal, and he died at ½ past 12 o'clock on the morning of the 16th.

"I enclose herewith No. 1, the report of Surgeon Lucius of the Prussian Legation.

"I was immediately waited on by Oguri Bungo no Kami, who expressed his horror at the tragic event, and condoled with me on my great loss. He informed me that orders had been sent in all directions to have an extra police force sent in search of the murderers; he added, that information of the murder had been sent to the Minister for Foreign Affairs.

"At 7 o'clock on the morning of the 16th, I was visited by Simme Boozen no Cami, Muragaki Awadsi no Cami and Oguri Bungo no Cami, who came to me with a message of condolence from the Minister of Foreign Affairs, with his assurance, that no exertions of the Government should be wanting to arrest and punish the perpetrators of this fearful crime, and tendering me any assistance I might desire.

"The funeral took place on the 18th instant, and the cortege was formed as follows:

1st   Simme Boozen no Cami,
      Muragaki Awadsi no Cami,
      Oguri Bungo no Cami,
      Takai Tamba no Cami,
      Takigawa Harima no Cami,
each attended by a large train of followers and guards.

2nd   The American, English, French, Dutch and Prussian flags in mourning, carried by Prussian sailors and guarded by six Prussian Marines.

3rd   The band of the Prussian Frigate *Arcona*.

4th   Guard of Dutch and Prussian Marines.

5th   The Abbe Girard, Vicar Apostolique in Japan with Surgeon Lucius.

6th   The Body with the American flag as a pall and supported by eight Dutch Marines.

7th   Mr. de Witt, Dutch Consul General and Mr. Harris as Chief Mourners.

8th   Mr. Alcock, Mr. de Bellecourt and Count d'Eulenberg, the English, French and Prussian Ministers.

9th   The Foreign Consuls.

10th   Attachés of the Foreign Legations.

11th   Officers from Dutch and Prussian men of war.

"I made use of all the means at my command to pay due honor to the remains of a most faithful officer of the United States, and I only regret that my appliances were so limited.

"Just before the procession started, Simme Boozen no Cami [Shimmi Masaoki, Buzen no Kami] desired that I would not attend the funeral, as he feared I might be attacked. I answered that I considered it as a sacred duty to attend, and that I should do so regardless of any danger, and I warned him, that if anything happened to me under such circumstances, that his Government would be held responsible. I informed my colleagues of this communication and they all resolved to accompany me.

"No difficulty occurred in going to, or in returning from the Cemetery [174] (which is about one mile from the Legation) nor did I observe any marks of ill will. A large crowd was attracted by the sound of the music, and by the unusual display, but all was quiet and orderly.

"I received the kindest assistance on this melancholy occasion from Count d'Eulenberg, the Prussian Envoy, and from all the Members of his Legation, and I am particularly obliged to Mr. Heine for taking the general management of the funeral.

"I am at a loss to assign any special motive, that could have influenced the assassins of Mr. Heusken. He was kind and amiable in his temper; he never used any violence towards the Japanese, and from speaking their language, he appeared to be a universal favorite. I have long been informed that there is a body of *bravoes* in this city, who make bloodshed their boast, and he that has taken the most lives is considered as the chief of the band. *It is possible* that some one of this gang may have desired to have the éclat of killing a foreigner, and Mr. Heusken was selected as offering the fairest opportunity for a safe exploit of this kind from his imprudence in being out at night.

"On my first arrival here, the authorities informed me that the streets were very unsafe at night; that they never went out themselves except in the case of necessity, and then they were always attended by a large train with many lanterns.

"I have constantly warned Mr. Heusken of the danger he was incurring and prayed him not to expose himself in the manner he did.

"For more than four months, he was in the habit of visiting the Prussian Legation, almost nightly, and would return home from 8 to 11 o'clock at night. I fear that it was this long continued and regular exposure of himself to danger that led to his untimely death.

"I am suffering deeply from this sudden and awful catastrophe. Mr. Heusken was associated with me over five years, and he was the companion of my long solitude at Simoda.

"Our relations were rather those of father and son, than *chef* and *employe*."

Although Heusken was the seventh foreigner to fall at the hands of assassins, it was not until he was cut down that the foreign community reacted with concerted vigor. However, Harris, despite his grief, refused to join with his colleagues in withdrawing from Edo. He contended in communications with them that, while the Japanese authorities must accept responsibility for what had occurred, they were making serious efforts to provide for the safety of foreigners in Japan and to honor the treaties. He held in his discussions with them that, as he had informed the authorities in Washington, Heusken had not exercised reasonable discretion in being out so frequently at night as to establish a pattern of behavior of which assassins might take advantage. He further held that withdrawal of the legations from Edo to Yokohama might well eventuate in war. The debate between Harris and the British representative, Rutherford Alcock, became acrimonious and the former finally declined to discuss the matter further. However, the British, French, Dutch, and Prussian representatives did withdraw from Edo to Yokohama, leaving Harris as the sole representative at the Shogun's capital. Some weeks later they returned to Edo when they realized that the Japanese felt pleasure rather than regret in their absence from the vicinity of the Shogun's palace.

Harris brought pressure upon the Japanese authorities to bring the assassins to justice. An indication of the difficulty facing them is revealed by the fact that even today the Japanese are not entirely certain who the assassins were. It was rumoured at the time that the assassins were *ronin* formerly of the Mito fief. Among the foreigners there developed a theory that they were followers of the late Hori, Oribe no Kami, a lesser official with whom Heusken had some difficulties. A recent study of this period declares that the assassins were really samurai from Satsuma.[175]

During ensuing months Harris was hard put to find the proper means by which the Japanese should render satisfaction for Heusken's murder. He knew that Heusken had been his mother's principal means of support. Finally in an interview with the Ministers of Foreign Affairs, Kuze Yamato no Kami and Ando Tsushima no Kami, on November 25, 1861, Harris' secured an agreement from the Japanese authorities to pay $10,000 to Mrs. Heusken, but made it quite clear to them that this did not discharge the responsibility of the authorities to bring the assassins to justice. As he put it: ". . . they must not consider this as a proposition from me to sell the blood of Mr. Heusken, or that the payment of any sum of money could atone for his murder."

Meanwhile Harris had on July 10, 1861, asked the American President, Abraham Lincoln, to accept his resignation and appoint his successor. He was succeeded by Robert H. Pruyn as minister resident in April, 1862, thus concluding a distinguished career in Japan, a career to which Henry Heusken had made no small contribution.

Among the Harris papers we find a letter from Heusken's mother dated at Amsterdam on April 2, 1862, in which Mrs. T. F. Heusken-Smit writes:

"I have the satisfaction of informing you of the receipt of your many favours the last of which dated Dec. 21 mentioned to me the happy success of your having obtained $10,000 from the Japanese government on my account, a great comfort in my sad circumstances, still deploring the loss of my tenderly beloved son.

"I can't, however, enough express in proper terms my gratitude for so many proofs of interest and concern in my dreadful fate, even in the most remote countries.

"But above all I feel obliged to pay you my heartfelt thanks for your having erected a monument for my dear son's memory and your cordial homage often paid to him, a fact which fills my eyes with warm tears and my heart with an acknowledgement which I am unable to express.

"May God bless you, therefore, on your further endeavours and preserve you from sad evils, from perils you experienced in Japan.

"When once I shall have the honor of seeing you personally, I shall be happy to show you my motherly gratitude.

"I have the honor to be with great esteem, Sir,
                              Your grateful servant,
                              the widowed T. F. Heusken-Smit."

Epilogue

At the time of his death Henry Heusken was nearing his 29th birthday. Born on January 20, 1832, he died on January 16, 1861. Approximately four years and five months of his brief life were spent in Japan, where he became perhaps the first of a new generation of "old Japan hands." It seems quite clear that he rapidly acquired a considerable sophistication in things Japanese, including some command of the language. He moved much more easily in Japanese surroundings than did his superior, Townsend Harris, who felt some constraint as the official representative of the United States.

From references to him in various travel accounts and memoirs from this period, one gathers that Heusken was probably the most popular member of the foreign community. He was also highly valued for his services as an interpreter, assisting in this capacity the British, French, and Prussian representatives in Japan.

There is no evidence to support the view that personal hostility to Heusken motivated his assassins. A theory was advanced soon after his death that Heusken had offended an official of the Tokugawa government—Hori, Oribe no Kami, who had recently committed ceremonial suicide—and that the assassins were followers of Hori seeking revenge for fancied insults to their late master. This interpretation gained no support and is not currently accepted by scholars.

Heusken's assassination was just one of a series of attacks upon foreigners in a climate of growing hostility to the arrogant and intemperate behavior of many of them.

The tragic irony of Heusken's manner of passing was that, of all foreigners in Japan at that time, he was certainly one of those most sympathetic to the Japanese.

Reference has been made to the criticisms to which Townsend Harris was subjected for his refusal to withdraw from Yedo in protest after the death of Heusken. Harris was also criticized for placing on Heusken's grave a simple headstone bearing only his name and the dates of his birth and death. The British had earlier chosen to inscribe on the tombstone over the grave of the Japanese interpreter employed by Sir Rutherford Alcock the manner in which he had been murdered by Japanese assassins. This Harris refused to do.

Today the simple grave of Henry Heusken lies untended in the weed-filled cemetery section of Korinji Temple in the Azabu district of modern Tokyo.

Notes

1. The steam frigate *San Jacinto,* under the command of Captain Henry Haywood Bell, was also the flagship of Commodore James Armstrong, Commander of the United States East Indian squadron. It left New York for the Far Eastern station on October 25, 1855, with the special assignment of transporting Townsend Harris and Henry Heusken together with considerable baggage to Siam, and after the completion of the Harris mission to Siam, onward to Japan, where Harris was assigned as the first American Consul-General with Heusken as his secretary and interpreter. Henry Heusken was a passenger on the ship from New York, but Harris elected to travel by other means as far as the island of Penang, where he joined the *San Jacinto* on March 22, 1856. Also aboard the *San Jacinto* as a member of Commodore Armstrong's staff was William Maxwell Wood, Surgeon of the Fleet. Wood has left a long account of the voyage of the ship beginning on October 25, 1855, and ending with his departure from the ship with Commodore Armstrong on January 28, 1858, when the Commodore was relieved as Commander of the East Indian squadron by Josiah Tattnall. This account was published by Harper and Brothers in New York in 1859 as *Fankwei; or The San Jacinto in the Seas of India, China, and Japan.* This book, which is now quite rare, enabled contemporary Americans to learn of many of the adventures that befell Harris and Heusken at a time when they were still engaged in their labors in Japan. This work will be cited hereafter as Wood, *Fankwei.*
2. The opening words of a patriotic song in the Netherlands.
3. Wood, *Fankwei,* pp. 27-44.

4. Wood, *Fankwei*, p. 52. Here Wood also notes with distress the problem of dealing with the numerous beggars in Funchal.

5. Bartolome Estaban Murillo [1617-1682], a Spanish painter.

6. Here we encounter the first of many instances in which Heusken sets down under a single date his description of what must have transpired over several days. Since the *San Jacinto* sailed late in the afternoon of November 17, his narrative may well cover his adventures during several days ashore.

7. We have been unable to identify these personalities. It may be that the Baptiste whom Heusken has in mind is Jean Baptiste Marie Franceschi-DeLonne, who won distinction as a cavalry general under Napoleon.

8. A legendary Roman hero who stoically held his hand in a flame and thereby won his release from captivity by Lars Porsena.

9. The blight to which Heusken refers wiped out the vineyards of Madeira. Soon, however, the natives discovered methods for controlling the disease, and the vineyards flourished again.

10. Wood, *Fankwei*, pp. 44-52.

11. Sir Hudson Lowe was the English governor of St. Helena under whom Napoleon suffered his imprisonment and exile and with whom he frequently quarreled. In this entry Heusken gives expression to the continental legend of a noble Napoleon abused by the iniquitous English that was not dispelled until after the failure of the Second Empire of Louis Napoleon, who had come to power in France partly as a result of that legend.

12. Bonny was a small coastal district in Nigeria. King Pepple had been deposed for good and sufficient reasons in 1854 by the English Consul, John Beecroft.

13. Heusken was now approaching the ripe age of twenty-four.

14. This exchange of epithets by the two Negroes is recorded by Heusken in Dutch.

15. Heusken's adventures during a period of approximately two weeks are recorded under this single date.

16. Wood, *Fankwei*, pp. 69-95. In his description of the visit at Capetown, Wood also mentions the hospitality shown him by the Cloete family.

17. Again Heusken records the events of several days' duration under a single date.

18. Wood, *Fankwei*, pp. 95-104. Wood's account of the visit of the *San Jacinto* to Île de France reveals that he, too, visited the re-

puted tombs of Paul and Virginia. Curiously, though he was a medical man, Wood makes no mention of the epidemic to which Heusken refers.

19. The novel, *Paul et Virginie,* was published in 1788. It is an argument for a return to the natural life that Bernardin de St. Pierre, under the influence of Rousseau, strongly supported.

20. The main boulevard in Marseilles.

21. A town near Marseilles whose women have a reputation for great beauty.

22. Wood, *Fankwei,* pp. 104-120. Heusken's experiences in Ceylon are recorded under the date of the arrival of the *San Jacinto.*

23. The Netherlands remained in control of Ceylon until it was captured by the British after Napoleon had added the Netherlands to his empire. As part of the struggle against Napoleon the British captured the entire Far Eastern empire of the Dutch. At this time the Dutch flag flew in only one part of the world, the tiny trading post in the harbor of Nagasaki, Japan, where the Dutch enjoyed sanctuary from the British fleet. In the decisions of the Congress of Vienna, the Dutch empire was restored to the once more independent Netherlands, with the exception of Capetown and Ceylon which remained under British control.

24. Famous French restaurateurs of the nineteenth century. The Very Brothers in Paris are associated with the recovery of the French cuisine from the depths to which it had sunk during the French Revolution.

25. Wood, *Fankwei,* pp. 122-141. Again Heusken uses only the arrival date at Penang for his entry.

26. This name is frequently spelled Kedah today.

27. Harris had been at Penang since January 19 patiently awaiting the arrival of the *San Jacinto;* Mario E. Cosenza, ed., *The Complete Journal of Townsend Harris* (New York, 1930), p. 75. Harris notes that the *San Jacinto* arrived off Penang on March 21, the date that Heusken employs for this record, but that she did not enter the harbor until the following day, March 22. Hereafter, this work will be cited as *The Harris Journal.*

28. Barend Cornelis Koekkoek [1803-1862], a Dutch painter.

29. Whampoa and Company was a Chinese trading firm in Singapore; Wood, *Fankwei,* pp. 144-145.

30. *The Harris Journal,* p. 79. Harris records the arrival of the *San Jacinto* at the bar of the Menam River on April 13; Wood,

Fankwei, pp. 149-260; Heusken again uses the single date, April 7, for his impressions of the mission to Siam that lasted approximately a month and a half.

31. The Pondoppo is a multipurpose building in Java. It is normally part of a princely residence and is considered to be part of the male section of the house. It is usually open on three sides and is of two levels.

32. This costume had been given to Don Gabriel by Sir James Brook, the English Rajah of Sarawak.

33. *The Harris Journal,* p. 130. According to Harris, this audience occurred on May 1, 1856.

34. *The Harris Journal,* p. 135. According to Harris, this occurred on May 2, 1856.

35. A grisette is a young French woman of the working class, characterized by a free and lively manner.

36. *The Harris Journal,* p. 118, footnote No. 141. The priest was Mgr. Jean Baptiste Pallegoix.

37. Usually spelled arrack, this beverage is a liqueur with a rum base and flavored with fruits and plants of the Far East.

38. Ida Laura Pfeiffer [1797-1858]. She was an Austrian who traveled widely and wrote accounts of her adventures. Her works were translated into English.

39. As rendered in the Treaty of Amity and Commerce with Siam, his name was Prince Krom Hluang Wongsa Dhiraj Snidh.

40. *The Harris Journal,* pp. 137-138. This occurred on May 9, 1856.

41. Taglioni, Cerito, and Grisi were famous ballerinas of the first half of the nineteenth century.

42. Though Heusken alleges that this person is of Portuguese ancestry, he records his complaint in Spanish.

43. *The Harris Journal,* p. 156. The Treaty was signed on May 29, 1856.

44. *Ibid.,* p. 156. Mr. Mattoon's commission was signed on May 30, 1856.

45. This entry for June 12 covers developments through the remainder of the month.

46. Heusken has left the name of the vessel blank, perhaps having forgotten it, since the events described in this entry obviously occurred over a considerable period of time after June 12. The vessel may have been the American steamer *Lily.* See Note No. 49

below. *The Harris Journal*, p. 168. Heusken left Hong Kong for Canton on June 23.

47. The Chu-kiang, or Pearl River.

48. The so-called Tartar cities were those sections of strategically located Chinese cities where Manchu troops were quartered together with their families. Virtually the entire Manchu nation was dispersed throughout China and Manchuria in such quarters.

49. This entry is probably reconstructed from notes Heusken kept during his visit to Macao. We learn from *The Harris Journal* that Heusken actually reached Macao on June 28 and that he and Harris returned to Hong Kong on the American steamer *Lily* on the evening of July 2.

50. Luiz Vaz de Camoens [1524-1580]. The *Lusiad*, which celebrates the exploits of Vasco da Gama and the period of Portuguese greatness, was composed by Camoens during a period when he served at Macao as a minor Portuguese official.

51. Heusken copied the Portuguese inscription into his journal.

52. Mr. O. H. Perry, U.S. Consul at Canton.

53. Heusken had remained in Canton from July 15th until August 3rd, when he returned to Hong Kong to await the arrival of the *San Jacinto* from Whampoa.

54. Neither Captain Buys nor his ship can be identified.

55. *The Harris Journal*, pp. 182-184; also Wood, *Fankwei*, p. 295.

56. The *San Jacinto* left Hong Kong on August 12, 1856.

57. According to Townsend Harris, the events here described occurred on August 15, 1856.

58. The second interpreter may have been Hori Tatsunosuke, who is known to have been at Shimoda earlier.

59. This audience occurred on August 25, 1856.

60. The earthquake and tidal wave to which the Japanese here refer had occurred in December, 1854.

61. Heusken has erred here. The Japanese contended that the Perry treaty provided that Consuls would be sent to Japan if *both* nations wished it.

62. This occurred on September 1, 1856.

63. This temple, which Harris used as his consulate, was located on the "bay" of Shimoda but was about five miles from the town of Shimoda in the village of Kakizaki.

64. *The Harris Journal*, p. 225. The correct date for the departure of the *San Jacinto* was September 4, 1856.

65. Guy de Lusignan was given the island of Cyprus as a kingdom by Richard I in 1192 during the Third Crusade.
66. *The Harris Journal*, pp. 237-238. Harris reports this typhoon for the night of September 22-23.
67. Heusken, apparently working from notes, erred again. This letter was written on October 25, 1856. See *The Harris Journal*, p. 247, footnote No. 313.
68. *The Harris Journal*, p. 238. Harris reports the arrival of the *Medusa (Diana)* on October 1, 1856.
69. The *Medusa* left Shimoda on October 3, 1856.
70. The *General Pierce* arrived in Shimoda on October 5 and departed on October 9; *The Harris Journal*, p. 240, footnote No. 305. An error occurs at this point where Heusken is thought to have reported in his journal that "the *General Pierce* arrived with a cargo of ammunition (sic), which the Japanese did not permit to be landed because it was found to be too old." The editor of *The Harris Journal* cited as authority an entry in G. Wagener, *Aus dem Tagebuche Hendrik Heusken* in the Tokyo *Deutsche Gesellschaft für Natür—und Völkerkunde Ostasiens, Mittheilungen*, June, 1883, Vol. 3, p. 376. It is clearly stated in the Heusken Journal that the cargo was rifles, not ammunition.
71. The *Olivuzza* arrived in Shimoda on Saturday, November 8, 1856.
72. Captain of the Second Rank, W. Rimski-Korsakoff.
73. *The Harris Journal*, p. 290. According to Harris, the *Olivuzza* left Shimoda on December 14, 1856.
74. *The Harris Journal*, p. 306. Harris recorded this invitation in his entry for Saturday, February 21, 1857. In view of the reluctance of Harris to transact business of any kind on Sunday, it is unlikely that any official contacts were made on this date, Sunday, February 22. The twenty-one gun salute took place on Monday, February 23.
75. *Ibid.*, p. 306. This visit occurred on Tuesday, February 24, 1857.
76. First known as Moriyama Yenosuke, the chief interpreter later took the name of Moriyama Takichiro.
77. The two Governors should not be confused with the great feudal lords. Inoue and Okada were merely minor landholders, or *hatamoto*, and were rather low in the Tokugawa bureaucracy.
78. Heusken vastly overrates the importance of the Governors of Shimoda, or Shimoda Bugyō as they are properly styled.
79. The *kabaya* is a loose tunic worn by the Malays and others in the

Far East. The reference here is to the Japanese *kimono,* which somewhat resembles the *kabaya.*

80. Heusken probably renders the term *bugyō* as he hears it. Inoue and Okada hold rank as Shimoda *Bugyō* and are officials of the Shogun rather than the Emperor, except in the sense that since the Shogun receives his commission from the Emperor and is, therefore, technically an imperial official, all officials under him are also imperial officials. Only in time did the foreigners learn that the Shogun (Taikun) was not in fact the Emperor of Japan.

81. *Metsuke,* whose responsibility it was to ferret out instances of maladministration on the part of members of the Tokugawa bureaucracy and to keep the feudal lords of Japan under a constant state of surveillance.

82. The treaty negotiated by Commodore Perry was the Treaty of Kanagawa.

83. *The Harris Journal,* pp. 324-327. See these pages for the various proposals concerning the reminting of American coins.

84. Reference here is to the *Rōjū,* or Great Council, which varied in number from time to time.

85. *The Harris Journal,* p. 331. The *Messenger Bird* anchored in Shimoda harbor on March 9, 1857.

86. Moriyama was undoubtedly returning to Nagasaki to assist in the negotiations that led to the Dutch Supplementary Treaty of 1857.

87. The Dutch had been compelled to abandon Hirado and take up new trading quarters at Nagasaki.

88. This agreement is usually referred to as the Shimoda Convention of 1857 and is merely an elaboration and elucidation of the Treaty of Kanagawa.

89. *The Harris Journal,* p. 369; *Ibid.,* p. 373. Here a slip of the pen occurs as Harris indicates that Dewa no Kami replaces Shinano no Kami as Shimoda Bugyō. The official replaced was Bingo no Kami.

90. Harris, who had held out for 5 per cent for some time, yielded on this point.

91. E. E. Rice, whose behavior at Hakodate was the subject of a long, critical dispatch by Harris to the State Department at a later date.

92. *The Harris Journal,* p. 381. According to the Harris record, this occurred on July 23, 1857.

93. Heusken has slightly paraphrased a portion of the fable, "The Fox and the Crow," by La Fontaine.

94. See *The Harris Journal,* p. 385. Here Harris states that Shinano no

Kami returned to Shimoda from Edo on August 14. Heusken appears to be correct, however, in assigning his return to August 24. Japanese sources support Heusken in this matter. See Dai Nihon Komonjo, Bakumatsu Gaikoku Kankei Monjo, Vol. XVI, Document 197. In this document Shinano no Kami reports to the Roju in Edo that he arrived in Shimoda on August 24.

95. Bingo no Kami had been demoted to a lower official position.

96. The Bon Festival was celebrated on the thirteenth, fourteenth, and fifteenth days of the seventh month of the old lunar calendar.

97. Kannon or in Chinese, *Kwanyin,* the Goddess of Mercy.

98. *Seishi,* or *Daiseishi,* a Buddhist saint belonging to the retinue of Amida (*Amitabha*).

99. Patmos is an island in the Dodecanese group where St. John the Divine is believed to have suffered his exile and to have written the book of Revelation.

100. On November 16, 1856, the *Portsmouth* had engaged the Barrier Forts at Canton and silenced them.

101. The name should be spelled Macomb. The first lieutenant's father, General Alexander Macomb, distinguished himself at Plattsburg and elsewhere during the War of 1812.

102. *The Harris Journal,* pp. 394-395. Harris dates this conference one day earlier, September 22, 1857.

103. *Ibid.,* pp. 405-406. Harris reports these developments for October 28, 1857, one week later than does Heusken.

104. Strictly speaking, Mt. Amagi is a number of volcanic peaks, the highest of which is Manzaburo at 4,611 feet.

105. Peak in the Himalaya mountain system at one time thought to be the highest peak.

106. This reference may be to Shuzenji Temple in the town of that name. Certain events in the life of Minamoto Yoritomo, founder of the Kamakura Shogunate, are associated with this place.

107. The Mishima Shrine was rebuilt in 1869. It is a Shinto temple to Ōyamatsumi, the god of mountains.

108. This reference is to Shizuoka, where Tokugawa Ieyasu built a great fortified castle.

109. The Hayakawa or Haya River.

110. A novice.

111. Bikuni, a nun.

112. The *Soembing* had been given to the Tokugawa government by the King of the Netherlands in 1855.

113. *The Harris Journal,* pp. 429-430.

114. This is the Heigenji Temple dedicated to Kōbō-Daishi, and popularly called the Kawasaki Daishi.

115. The Rokugō River.

116. The identity of this interpreter remains unknown.

117. *The Harris Journal,* p. 439. Harris states that these sections were 120 yards in length.

118. Heusken was quite correct in his estimate at this time, but in the ensuing four years there developed sentiments of a different kind that were to cost him his life.

119. An ethnological epithet for Caucasians. Japhet was one of the sons of Noah.

120. Tsutsui, Hizen no Kami.

121. On the evening of the fifth or the morning of the sixth of December, the Dutch population exchanges presents and "surprises," usually sent anonymously. This custom, still practiced in the Netherlands, of celebrating the Feast of St. Nicholas, Bishop of Elmira, is a custom continuing from the times when the country was occupied by the Spaniards, i.e., around 1500 A.D.

122. *The Harris Journal,* p. 478. Harris writes: "A good deal of negotiation had been used by the Japanese to get me to eat a dinner at the Palace, alone or with Mr. Heusken only. This I declined doing. I offered to partake to it provided one of the Royal Family or the Prime Minister would eat with me. I was told that their customs forbade either from doing so. I replied that the customs of my country forbade anyone to eat in a house where the host or his representative did not sit down to table with him. At last the matter was arranged by ordering the dinner to be sent to my lodgings."

123. The identity of these persons is obscured by Heusken's transliteration. The Japanese Methuselah is Takenouchi, who according to legend lived to be 350 years of age.

124. Udono, Mimbu-Shoyu.

125. A wild duck said to have a truly superior flavor.

126. *The Harris Journal,* p. 497. Harris reveals that from January 8th, Heusken was ill "with a bilious attack."

127. Harris makes no mention of these requests in his journal.

128. *The Harris Journal,* pp. 500-503.

129. *Ibid.,* pp. 505-513.

130. *Ronin,* usually samurai who have left or who have been dismissed from the service of their feudal masters.

131. *The Harris Journal,* pp. 513-516.

132. *Ibid.,* pp. 517-520.

133. *Ibid.,* pp. 520-522.

134. Nihombashi—the bridge in Edo from which distances were computed.

135. Kawasaki lies about six miles from Kanagawa and eight miles from Tokyo (Edo).

136. *The Harris Journal,* pp. 522-523.

137. *Ibid.,* pp. 523-527; Heusken writing in French renders business as "affaires" and trade as "pour le commerce."

138. Hyogo has disappeared from modern maps. It is now included within the city of Kobe.

139. *The Harris Journal,* pp. 527-530. Harris records this conference for Wednesday, February 3, 1858. In this instance, however, Heusken appears to give the correct date. Both Harris and Heusken note in their journals that the Japanese Commissioners request the postponement of the meeting until February 3 because of a festival.

140. Heusken appears to have been careless here. He refers to a concession *from* the United States, when he clearly means a concession *to* the United States.

141. In Kyoto about 30 miles from Osaka.

142. *The Harris Journal,* p. 525. Harris made this point on February 6.

143. Reference here is to the *eta* class, or pariahs of old Japan.

144. Minamoto Iesada or Tokugawa Iesada.

145. *The Harris Journal,* p. 533, Note 607. Professor Cosenza has erred in his reading of Wagener, *op. cit.,* p. 386, Note 1. Both Heusken and Wagener have the date as February 9, 1858.

146. Here Heusken uses the word *naibun,* the Japanese word for secrecy.

147. An Ephesian who, to achieve renown, set fire to the temple of Diana at Ephesus.

148. It seems clear that Shinano no Kami was attempting to give Harris and Heusken an inkling of the force of tradition in Japanese life, probably with the hope that this would cause Harris to moderate his demands in the negotiations.

149. *The Harris Journal,* p. 537. Harris tells us that the treaty had been submitted to the Daimyo in attendance at the Shogun's palace on February 11.

150. *Ibid.*, p. 543. Harris states that four of the eighteen great Daimyo favored the treaty.

151. Known in history as Toyotomi Hideyoshi, or more frequently as simply Hideyoshi.

152. If Heusken has understood Moriyama correctly, Moriyama has confused Hideyori, the son, with Hideyoshi, the father. Hideyoshi had invaded Korea in an attempt to conquer China.

153. Tokugawa Ieyasu had seized political power in an epic struggle that reached its climax in the Battle of Sekigahara in the autumn of 1600. The Prince of Mikawa (Tokugawa Ieyasu) became the first of a new dynasty of Shoguns in 1603.

154. After his death.

155. *The Harris Journal*, p. 549. The statement on this matter by Harris is somewhat clearer.

156. Cadet branches of the Tokugawa family were established by the seventh, eighth, and ninth sons of Tokugawa Ieyasu at Owari, Kii, and Mito. When a ruling Shogun was without heir, the succession fell to one of these cadet branches.

157. The authorities were concerned about the possibility of hostile Daimyo procuring arms and munitions abroad. In its final form the treaty stated in this regard: "Munitions of war shall only be sold to the Japanese government and foreigners."

158. This is the onset of an illness that nearly costs Townsend Harris his life. This date also marks the end of *The Complete Journal of Townsend Harris* as published by Professor Cosenza.

159. February 18, 1858 was the fifth day of the first month in the lunar calendar.

160. The *Kanko Maru*.

161. The texts are in Dutch and English.

162. The practice of smoking a mixture of opium and tobacco for medicinal purposes seems to have originated with the Dutch in the Far East.

163. This curious paragraph proved virtually untranslatable, due in part to the illegibility of the writing. We have hazarded this translation after considerable effort and can only speculate on the thought that Heusken was attempting to convey.

164. April 18 would be two months from the fifth day of the first month of the Japanese year and the date on which the Japanese had agreed to sign the treaty. The authorities were apparently hopeful that an additional month would be sufficient time for them to

persuade the Imperial Court to sanction the signature of the treaty.

165. Udono Minaboro.

166. Laurence Oliphant, *Narrative of the Earl of Elgin's Missions to China and Japan* (New York, 1860), p. 451. Oliphant describes this exhibition in the following fashion: "A sheet of paper torn into slips supplied all the materials. By tearing these again into small oblong pieces, and twisting them in the centre, they were made roughly to represent the body and two wings. Two of these impromptu butterflies were then puffed into the air, and kept in suspense there by the action of the fan beneath them."

167. Oliphant, *op. cit.,* pp. 443-445. Oliphant's description of the temple is in considerable detail.

168. Oliphant, *op. cit.,* pp. 407-416. Oliphant describes the beauties of the teahouse and garden at great length.

169. Heusken, like so many foreigners, was confused by the temple of Inari, the Goddess of Rice. The fox, whose image is always found in her temples, is her messenger and servant. It is said that the more ignorant worshipers sometimes mistake the fox for the goddess herself.

170. E. M. Dorr.

171. *Kami* in this case refers to a government office. Hori holds the post of Oribe no Kami in the Tokugawa government.

172. Gaikoku Bugyō, or Governor of Foreign Affairs.

173. With these words we come to the end of Heusken's account of his life and work in Japan.

174. Heusken was buried in the cemetery at Kōrinji Temple in Edo (Tokyo).

175. *Ishin Shi* (History of the Restoration), Vol. II, pp. 966-974.

Index